'HOLY, HOLIER, HOLIEST'

STUDIA TRADITIONIS THEOLOGIAE

Explorations in Early and Medieval Theology

4

Series Editor: Thomas O'Loughlin,
Professor of Historical Theology
in the University of Nottingham

'HOLY, HOLIER, HOLIEST'

The Sacred Topography of The Early Medieval Irish Church

David H. Jenkins

BREPOLS

© 2010, Brepols Publishers n.v., Turnhout, Belgium

D/2010/0095/4
ISBN 978-2-503-53316-2

CONTENTS

ACKNOWLEDGEMENTS

Growing up in Belfast in the 1960s and 1970s was at times something of a mixed blessing. The 'Troubles' provided a constantly disquieting and on occasion truly frightening backdrop to what was in many ways a great place to grow up. However for one thing I shall be ever grateful. The benefits of a first class school education which instilled in me, among other things, a love for Irish history and an understanding that it was also my history. It was here in the History Department of the Belfast Royal Academy that I was first introduced to the characters, events, and places which were eventually to people my academic study. In particular I remember with great affection the late Winston Breen, a scholar of Trinity College Dublin and a wonderful teacher of history.

This book has its genesis in a PhD thesis in the Theology and Religious Studies Department of the University of Wales, Lampeter. This was and remains an exciting and vibrant faculty in which to study the early medieval history of these islands. The original thesis was supervised by Dr Jonathan Wooding to whom I owe a significant debt of gratitude for his patience, good humour, and unfailing belief in the task. I want also to record my thanks for the warm hospitality offered to me by Jonathan and his lovely wife Dr Karen Jankulak on my many trips to Lampeter. I am also grateful to Professor Tom O'Loughlin for his assistance in preparing this book for publication and in particular for his erudition and wit in sorting out my wayward footnotes.

Finally, but most importantly, I want to thank Sarah and our children Joe, Niamh, and Ben for all their love and support. They have endured more than their fair share of site visits and have had to put up with their father's scholarly preoccupations for too many years. Despite this I hope they will grow up to share my love of Ireland and its history.

I dedicate this book to my late father, Joseph, a true son of Ulster.

INTRODUCTION

The *Exordium magnum* of Abbot Conrad of Eberbach, written *c.*AD1200, tells of a monk who in a vision imagines that the monastery of Cîteaux is not to be found on earth but in heaven.[1] However, during the course of the vision he visits the monastery on earth only to discover the monks in choir surrounded by light and accompanied above in heaven by angels. The Cistercian Abbey is thus depicted as what Cassidy-Welch refers to as an 'earthly manifestation of heavenly space'.[2] Such an understanding is, of course, not restricted to the Cistercians. All monastic endeavour is to some extent aimed at the re-creation of heavenly space here on earth. 'Monastic' space was ordered, and indeed continues to be ordered, to reflect this religious ideal. This book will seek to address what the 'template' might have been in the context of early medieval Ireland religious settlement.

The study of the enclosure and spatial ordering of 'monastic' settlement within the early medieval Irish church was initially the preserve of antiquarians and subsequently of archaeologists. The resulting discourse has been conducted within a broadly survey-based, material focused, framework. Consequently the emphasis within the critical literature on the subject has been on the phenomenology of settlement. Historians and theologians have had to struggle to some extent for their 'place at the table'. In more recent times there have been laudable attempts to redress the imbalance and to begin to move the focus of the academic debate away from the praxis of enclosure and its

---

[1] See McGuire (1992).
[2] Cassidy-Welch (2001), 47.

physicality to its motivation and/or inspiration. This, however, has to date been a task undertaken more by a minority of theologically sensitive historians than by historically literate theologians. In order to be able to interpret effectively the physical environment of religious settlement we also need to understand the motivation of those who helped to create it.[3] This book will contribute to the theological side of the debate, focusing upon the possible determinative factors in the creation of the Irish religious landscape. In particular it will consider the potential influence of scriptural paradigms of holy space upon the built ecclesial environment.

The bringing of a theological perspective is, as I have acknowledged, not a totally novel approach. Charles Doherty in his 1985 article, 'The Monastic Town in Early Medieval Ireland',[4] began to explore some of the biblical resonances found within Irish hagiography and in canonical works such as *Collectio canonum Hibernensis*.[5] Rather more directed questions were then asked by Aidan MacDonald in his 2001 article, 'Aspects of the Monastic Landscape in Adomnán's *Life of Columba*', in which he focused upon the potential of the *Hibernensis* as a tool for interpreting the sacred topography of Iona. In particular MacDonald drew attention to the analogy between Adomnán's depiction of the landscape of Iona; the topographical *schema* found within the *Hibernensis*; and the layout of the Temple as described by Ezekiel.[6] The importance of the *Hibernensis* for any discussion of Irish ecclesiology in the early medieval period had already been highlighted by, among others, Richard Sharpe,[7] Colman Etchingham,[8] and, in a more secular context, Catherine Swift.[9] However, there has not been to date a systematic consideration of the role of the Temple as a possible paradigm for the layout of early Irish religious settlement though this model has been pursued in other contexts. MacDonald's tentative observations on this possibility have remained unaddressed. It is hoped that the establishing of a scriptural hermeneutic for the decoding of the morphology of Insular religious settlement will bring fresh insight.

[3] O'Sullivan, D. (2001), 34.
[4] Doherty (1985).
[5] Referred to hereafter as *Hibernensis*.
[6] MacDonald (2001), 29–30.
[7] Sharpe (1984), 236.
[8] Etchingham (1994), 38.
[9] Swift (1998), 105-106.

The title of this book was suggested by the depiction of the threefold division of the enclosure encountered within the *Hibernensis* which reflects the tripartite division of the Tabernacle of Moses and of the Jerusalem Temple.[10] It is this sacred topographical model which forms the focus of our discussion. Far from corroborating the traditional scholarly acceptance of ecclesial abnormality (the familiar 'Celtic Church' delusion) and/or a monastic subjugation of all other forms of religiously inspired communal living, I shall argue that the enclosure and layout of religious settlement within the early Irish church reflects a generic conception of the nature of holy space. I have chosen to refer to this conception as a scriptural 'canon of planning'. The contention that the topography of early medieval religious settlement in Ireland was not ordered according to some form of essentially Insular and vernacular plan is therefore central to our thesis. Instead what we see reflected in the extant settlement archaeology, and find described in the literature, is a biblically inspired understanding of holy space. It will be argued that it was the coming together of this 'understanding', this scriptural 'canon of planning', with a number of other factors which formed the early Irish religious landscape.

Our discussion will begin by charting the development of the scholarship concerned with the phenomenon of religiously motivated enclosure. We shall discuss the historiography with reference to a wide range of site types and locations. We will begin with the early antiquarian survey-based explorations, and reflect upon the increasingly sophisticated archaeological investigation of a number of key sites from the 1920s to the present day. This overview will provide a sense of the shifting emphasis in site interpretation as our modern taxonomy of settlement has become more sophisticated and as the developing archaeological hermeneutic struggled to encompass both the severely ascetic and more mainstream manifestations of Irish ecclesial community. Included

---

[10] *Hibernensis* 44, 4.

The English translations of the Latin text are by the author unless stated otherwise.

De numero terminorum sancti loci.

Eadem Sinodus [i.e. Sinodus Hibernensis]: Quatuor terminos circa locum posuit: primum, in quem laici et mulieres intrant; alterum, in quem clerici tantum veniunt. Primus vocatur sanctus, secundus sanctior, tertius sanctissimus. Nota nomen quarto defecisse.

Concerning the number of boundaries of a sacred place.

Likewise the synod [i.e. the Irish synod] has placed four boundaries around a place: the first, in which the laity and women may enter; the other into which only clerics may enter. The first is called sacred, the second holier, the third holiest.

The name of the fourth part was not known.

will be an assessment of the revisionist critique led by scholars such as Sharpe and Etchingham which has subverted the established 'monastic hegemony' model of Irish ecclesiology. This discussion will be set alongside evidence of the increasing appreciation by a growing body of scholars of the textual witness and of the insights that a number of seminal canonical and hagiographical texts can bring to the discussion of religious topography. Finally, the chapter will seek to challenge further the aforementioned misconception of Irish ecclesiology as at best idiosyncratic and at worst heterodox by locating the praxis of Irish enclosure and zoning within a broader Anglo-Saxon and northern European setting. This putative pan-northern European ecclesial context will be explored in particular in relation to the work on Anglo-Saxon religious settlement by John Blair and Sarah Foot.[11]

In order to set an evidential context within which we might begin to think theologically about *why* and not simply *how* enclosure was practised the extant archaeological and literary 'data' for enclosure within the early Irish church will be explored in some detail in chapter two. The focus here, however, will not be solely upon the phenomenon of enclosure but also upon the internal spatial organisation of the enclosed space. A number of sites are chosen as representative of a typological cross-section and assessed in order to give both an appreciation of the diversity of settlement type under discussion as well as an introduction to the topographical motifs and architectural elements which recur across a wide range of site location and scale. This will necessarily include a consideration of the key diagnostic elements for religious settlement: an oratory, a cross-slab or free-standing cross, and a saint's or founder's tomb. These are commonly to be found within what I shall refer to as the 'sacred core' of settlement. This 'sacred core' will be defined by the presence of *at least* one of these elements but more usually two or more.[12] We shall also discuss the accompanying

---

[11] Blair (2005); Foot (2006).

[12] Content to use the epithet 'monastic' in reference to the island sites she explored, Françoise Henry initially defined a monastic site 'by the presence of one, at least,' of these 'features' (Henry (1957), 45). She also expected to find the 'oratory and its annexes' in close proximity on a raised terrace or within a separate internal enclosure wherever possible (Henry (1957), 154–155). At a later date, Michael Herity, again at ease in referring to these sites as 'monasteries', took a more explicitly essentialist approach to diagnosis. For Herity the presence of *all three* key elements, namely a cross-slab, a saint's tomb, and an oratory, at the focal point of the monastic settlement was to be expected (Herity (1977), 15, 17; (1984), 47). For our purposes a 'sacred core' will be indicated by the presence of one or more of these elements.

textual witness to both the enclosure and internal zoning of religious settlement in order to explore the ritualized and sacramental nature of the praxis of enclosure and the consequent sanctification of the area enclosed. At the heart of this debate is the need to achieve a proper understanding of the nature of the enclosure form known as the *termon*; both in terms of the extent and type of the area to be enclosed and in terms of the degree of sanctity to be accorded to its various component parts. Of especial interest is the relationship of the 'sacred core' to other parts of the *termon* named in the sources; the *platea* and the *suburbana*. Although the spatial relationship between these areas is far from certain we shall seek to define these zones and allocate to them some of the other topographical elements such as domestic buildings and agricultural lands commonly found within and around religious settlements.

It will become clear that the topographical paradigm suggested by the textual and material evidence for a 'canon of planning' is scripturally based. It will be argued that it is centred especially upon the sacred geography of the Jerusalem Temple. Chapter three will explore this possibility by examining the notion of 'sacred' or 'holy' space found within the Bible and in particular the part of the Temple in determining the biblical model of what might be meant by 'holy' space. It will be argued that the influence of the layout of the Temple upon scriptural notions of religious space is far-reaching, from the depiction of the Garden of Eden in the Book of Genesis to the New Jerusalem of the Book of Revelation, from its place as the *locus* of God's revelation to his chosen people to its developing role as a metaphor for personal piety and communal belief. We shall also consider the function of Temple imagery in patristic and early Irish exegesis and in particular within a number of key Irish texts including the *Hibernensis* and both Adomnán's *De locis sanctis* and his *Vita S. Columbae* in order to establish its seminal role in providing not only a hermeneutic framework for the theological depiction of settlement patterns but also serving as an inspiration in creating the religious landscape in the first place. A key priority will be establishing a continuum between the Temple motif encountered within scripture and the theological inspiration for the layout of religious settlement in early medieval Ireland.

There needs, however, to be recognition that the morphology of early medieval Irish religious settlement reflects formative influences other than that of the topography of the Temple. In order to untangle the relative impacts of all of these contributing, and to some extent competing factors, we need to understand first the form and mode of transmission of any scriptural 'canon of planning'. We shall employ the earliest known, and also contemporary, monastic plan, the early ninth century Carolingian/Benedictine *Plan of St Gall*, as a measure against which the Irish experience might be set. I am inclined to resist the possibility of the existence of a comparable Irish vernacular 'blue-print' for religious settlement layout. Instead it will posited that the religious landscape of the early Irish church assumed the form it did primarily as a response to the biblical portrayal of the relative quality and differentiation of the holy space of the Temple and not through adherence to a uniquely Irish *schema*. In terms of how this scriptural understanding of holy space might have reached Irish shores we will examine some of the more credible theories regarding transmission.

We shall then consider the nature and extent of the interaction between this 'canon of planning' and some of the other factors which have helped to shape the religious landscape. Among the issues to be explored will be the affect of the markedly eremitic inheritance of Irish monasticism's Middle Eastern and Gallic antecedents upon the morphology of settlement. Part of this debate will centre upon the value of the Jerusalem Temple as an exemplar for a largely rural and eremitic Irish church. We shall also explore the extent to which the form and spatial organisation of religious settlements were dictated either by the ongoing influence of Ireland's pre-Christian architectural legacy and/or by the newly emerging architectural demands of the Christian liturgy. It will be argued that the continuing adherence to vernacular building forms inherited from Ireland's pre-Christian past, such as the corbelled cell structure and the ubiquitous circular footprint of domestic dwelling, alongside the continued use of native building materials such as wood and dry-stone construction were also determinative influences upon the shape and appearance of Irish Christian topography.

In sum, this book will show that what we witness in the extant archaeology of the Irish church in the early medieval period is an encapsulation in wood and dry-stone of a biblically based understanding of how sacred topography should be ordered; an 'understanding' based upon the scriptural depiction of the sacred topography of the Jerusalem Temple. The impetus for this was not a desire to replicate the Temple structure in the architecturally alien context of early historic Ireland but rather to reflect an ideal; a desire to mirror the divinely ordered spatial arrangements of the Temple and to express them within a native Irish setting. That the built religious environment is singular in form and appearance is explained by the convergence of this biblical model with a distinctive native architectural culture. This fusion of styles, however, should not be allowed to obscure the basic spatial orthodoxy of the layout of early historic Irish religious settlement or to undermine the place of the early Irish church within the mainstream of the western church.

There remains a number of issues which need to be addressed at this stage. The debate surrounding early Irish ecclesiology has given rise to a view of the early Irish church as being in some way heterodox. The early dominance of the paradigm of monastic hegemony also served to set unhelpful parameters to the field of study from the outset; a fact we find reflected clearly both in the early historiography of the subject and in the initial exploration of potential settlement sites. The traditional expectation that the literary or material settlement evidence was primarily monastic in genesis and form ensured that its interpretation was confined within an unhelpfully narrow and predominantly monastic taxonomy. There is, however, now a discomfort with the traditionally accepted notion of early Irish ecclesiological peculiarity. Sharing that unease I believe firmly that what might hold true for Irish 'monasticism' in the period might also be normative for the rest of the early medieval western church. So the aim of this study is not to discover a uniquely Irish understanding of religious settlement, which subsequently manifested itself in an exclusively native Irish format, but rather to establish a generic understanding of how religious space might be enclosed and ordered using the textual and material evidence from early historic Ireland.

Secondly, the progression from a 'monastic hegemony' model toward something more sophisticated and more historically realistic has greatly enhanced our understanding of the ecclesiology of the early Irish church and also opened up the possibility of a much more diverse and complex spectrum of site types. The exposure of the traditional monastic hegemony model to a strongly revisionist critique has made any discussion of Irish 'monasticism' and 'monasteries' in this period insecure and as a result the term 'monastic' can no longer be used with impunity. While it is clearly reasonable to continue to view settlements such as Iona and Clonmacnoise as 'monastic' it has become more problematic to label many of the smaller, more eremitic, settlements as such. It is not the primary concern of this study to rehearse in detail the intricacies of this debate and so we shall follow the convention of using the generic term 'religious settlement' rather than 'monastery' or 'hermitage' or 'church' in order to ensure that our discussion embraces the gamut of early Irish religious settlement. This convention should not be interpreted as implying that none of the settlements under discussion merited the title 'monastery'. Equally the use of adjectives such as 'holy', 'religious', 'sacred' or even 'monastic' to describe the nature of the area enclosed should not be understood as being indicative of any attempt to differentiate between quality or type of space. The intention is that the terms should be regarded as synonymous.

Two further issues relate to geography and chronology. The first concerns the extent of the area under discussion in this book. It has long been accepted that to talk of the Irish church in this period is to talk also of the area of the Irish diaspora which includes sites such Iona, Lindisfarne, and Whithorn. This convention has been followed here and therefore references to the Irish church or to Ireland should be seen to include these geographically non-Irish settlements unless specifically stated otherwise. Finally, for ease of reference we have resorted to labelling the church of this period using a variety of epithets including 'early medieval', 'early historic', or 'early Irish'. The period under discussion is in effect that stretching from the sixth to the ninth century and it is hoped that in this context it will be acceptable to use these descriptors interchangeably without too much confusion or apology.

I. THE RELIGIOUS TOPOGRAPHY OF THE EARLY MEDIEVAL IRISH CHURCH: AN HISTORIOGRAPHICAL PERSPECTIVE

It was Bede, in his *Historia ecclesiastica*, who first commented on the *ordo inusitatus* of the early Irish church. In his discussion of the Columban churches and in particular the abbacy of Iona he observed that everyone throughout the *provincia* including bishops was subject to the authority of the abbot.[1] The initial historiographical forays into this field strongly reflected this monastic hermeneutic.[2] Writing in the middle of the nineteenth century William Reeves, in his 1857 edition of Adomnán's *Vita S. Columbae*, depicted a church which was primarily abbatial and monastic in governance and form rather than episcopal and diocesan as was normative elsewhere in western Christendom. This monochrome model was then developed further by J. H. Todd in the 1860s who first suggested a chronology for this ecclesiological irregularity. He argued that an initially episcopally-led Irish church, founded by Patrick, had metamorphosed into a predominantly monastic one by perhaps as early as the sixth century.[3] Uncertainties of dating aside, it was upon this developmental framework, embodying a transition from episcopal to abbatial leadership, that the subsequent scholarly discourse has been predicated.

---

[1] *HE*, 3, 4.

[2] For the detailed historiography of this debate see Etchingham's overview (1999, 12–46).

[3] Todd (1864); for a counter chronology see Zimmer (1902).

We have already noted the tensions between the monastic and non-monastic models of Irish ecclesiology. This dissonance set the agenda for the ensuing discussion. Nowhere is this tension brought into sharper relief than by the debate surrounding the Hiberno-Latin term *paruchia*, placed centre stage by J. F. Kenney in 1929. This debate was exiguous in the extreme and its finer detail need not concern us here. At its heart was the attempt to clarify, through determining whether *paruchia* referred to a monastic or an episcopal entity, whether the early Irish church was primarily abbatial and monastic or episcopal and diocesan in its impetus and organisation. The debate did also concern itself with the demarcation of religious space in its broadest terms, but only for ecclesiological and not theological reasons. The extent to which the *paruchia* denoted a non-territorial entity as opposed to a discrete geographical area was of interest for its organisational consequences, but not for its spiritual ones. Nevertheless, these questions began to expose the fault-lines within the traditional hermeneutic. The uniformly monastic character and neat developmental chronology of the Irish Insular church could no longer be taken as certain and Bury and Kenney among others were led to question 'whether the Irish Church in the sixth century was as exclusively monastic as it is sometimes represented',[4] warning that 'it is not until the middle and second half of the seventh century, perhaps three hundred years after the introduction of Christianity, that our sources begin to give us a serviceable picture of the Irish ecclesiastical system'.[5] Nevertheless, the 'orthodox' episcopal to monastic developmental model of Insular Irish ecclesiology inherited through scholars such as D. A. Binchy[6] remained largely intact right up until its seminal modern re-statement by Kathleen Hughes in the 1960s and provided the historiographical background noise for the archaeological exploration of early medieval Irish Christianity.

The first major figure in this field was the antiquarian George Petrie, described by C. A. R. Radford as 'the first serious student of Irish ecclesiastical architecture'.[7] His 1845 publication, *Ecclesiastical Architecture of Ireland*, remains a significant contribution to the study of these sites. It is important to note, however, that the extent of the on-site analysis was often limited by factors such as difficulty of access, the lack of shelter at many sites and the frequently inhospitable weather. Petrie's work on the

---

[4] Bury (1905), 375.
[5] Kenney (1929), 291.
[6] Binchy (1962a), 169.
[7] Radford (1977), 1.

ecclesiastical settlement on High Island off the coast of Co. Galway, which he regarded as 'one of the most interesting and best preserved in Ireland or perhaps in Europe . . .', was carried out on the basis of only one visit to the island.[8] R. A. S. Macalister's 1896 article on High Island for the Royal Society of Antiquaries of Ireland was, by his own admission, based on a very short 1895 sojourn of only a few hours on the island. Other notable nineteenth-century contributors to the work included the artist W. F. Wakeman, the geologist George Kinahan and several employees of the Ordnance survey most notably John O'Donovan and, towards the end of the century, the antiquarian Lord Dunraven. The emphasis of these visits was on survey rather than excavation and as a result the work of these early pioneers remains valuable primarily as observation of, and witness to, the topography of these sites. Without excavation or other forms of subterranean investigation much of this survey work simply provides a snapshot of a site at a given moment but tells us little about its origins and chronological development.

Excavation has not, however, always provided greater insight. H. C. Lawlor's excavation of the complex site at Nendrum in Co. Down in Northern Ireland in 1922–1924 provided the first large-scale archaeological excavation of an ecclesiastical site. This was until comparatively recently the only major Irish monastic site to have been subjected to a detailed excavation and the results published.[9] Unfortunately the techniques adopted were rudimentary, and the results have proved almost impossible to interpret.[10] A further 1954 excavation (carried out by Charles Thomas) has done little to clarify the extent of subsequent restoration. Whilst Nendrum is clearly the site of a major early medieval settlement, Lawlor's contention that there were two major phases in the development of the site, namely a prehistoric secular phase followed by an early Christian presence, is unsupported by any substantive evidence and the most probable context is a sustained early medieval ecclesiastical occupation.[11] The work at Nendrum does,

[8] Marshall and Rourke (2001), 14.

[9] Lawlor (1925); cf. Edwards (1990), 101.

[10] Nendrum has now been the subject of a much more structured investigation by Thomas McErlean and Norman Crothers. The focus of their interest was the discovery of an early medieval tidal mill at the site but their study re-examines the broader history and archaeology of the site. Of particular importance is the new dating evidence provided by the use of dendrochronology on the wooden remains of the two mills. This evidence places the monastic settlement firmly within an early seventh century milieu (McErlean and Crothers (2007), 2–3, 306).

[11] Edwards (1990), 107.

however, highlight the difficulty in establishing a plausible developmental model for a site and especially in securing reliable dating parameters. Although Charles Thomas felt able to confidently assert that the trivallate boundary of the ecclesiastical settlement at Nendrum was clearly a much older stone cashel the excavation had yielded no substantive archaeological evidence to support this.[12]

I.A. *Enclosure as an Expression of an Ascetic Ideal*

The 1950s witnessed a number of significant developments in our understanding of early Irish religious settlement and of the extent of the praxis of enclosure in particular. These included the first serious attempt to both establish a taxonomy for a number of these western sites and, more significantly, to establish a spatial relationship between their extant structural elements. Although best remembered for her work on early medieval Irish art, Françoise Henry also took a keen interest in the ecclesiastical remains of the small church sites she visited, mainly on the Iveragh peninsula. In her impressive 1957 survey, 'Early Monasteries, Beehive Huts, and Dry-stone Houses in the Neighbourhood of Cahirciveen and Waterville (Co. Kerry)', she made two key observations which were to set the agenda for their subsequent study. First, starting from the then orthodox premise that Irish Christianity was essentially monastic in character, and thus interpreting the majority of sites that could boast evidence of habitation as monastic,[13] she argued that Irish monasticism was primarily eremitical and attracted to remote locations. She coined the phrase 'eremitic monastery' to describe this peculiarly Irish blend of coenobitic settlement and anchorite spirituality. Secondly, Henry noted a consistency of internal planning within enclosures on these remote western settlements,[14] and posited that these settlements were defined by the presence of *at least one* of a number of key elements, including an oratory of the Gallarus type, a stone cross, an inscribed cross-slab (referred to by Henry as a 'cross-bearing slab') and a shrine (referred to by Henry as a 'monumental tomb made of stone slabs').[15] She further observed

[12] Thomas (1971), 33.
[13] Henry (1957), 45 n. 1.
[14] Henry (1957), 154–158.
[15] Henry (1957), 45–46.

that these recurring elements, a cross-slab, a saint's tomb and a rectangular oratory, were usually positioned in close proximity to each other and that they were usually separated from the other elements within the enclosure by being situated on a raised terrace or enclosed by a wall or fence of slabs.[16]

This insight into the spatial relationships between the elements of monastic settlement has not been universally accepted and many scholars remain sceptical about the reality of such an implicit 'canon of planning' for monastic layout in this period.[17] Liam de Paor, and Kathleen Hughes and Ann Hamlin, have subsequently argued that the layout of early Irish monasteries did not adhere to a set *schema*. On the contrary, Hughes and Hamlin maintained that sites such as Nendrum, Killabuonia and Inishmurray rather illustrate the 'irregular' nature of early Irish monastic planning although they did acknowledge the possibility of zoning.[18] Others, however, have been convinced by the integrity of Henry's argument. In more recent times, and in a similar south-west Irish context, Tomás Ó Carragáin has noted a consistency of layout including key settlement elements and significant enclosing features over the majority of the sixty-six substantial ecclesiastical sites examined on the Iveragh and Dingle peninsulas.[19] The ecclesiastical situation in Dingle and Iveragh he interprets as probably reflecting the broad pattern of development throughout the rest of Ireland, at least in the hundred years from AD750 to AD850.[20] Whatever the truth of this suggestion there remains no doubt that Henry's observation of a consistency of layout at the heart of many of these western island sites centred on enclosure and the presence of cross-slab, saint's tomb and rectangular oratory and the establishing of a spatial relationship between the structural elements of these sites was a seminal moment in their study.

---

[16] Henry (1957), 154–155.

Henry suggested that the order in which these elements came together was determined in most cases by the primary presence of an oratory (Henry (1957), 155–156). This, of course, runs counter to the model posited by Thomas Fanning following his excavation of the site at Reask (Fanning (1981), 150) and to Charles Thomas's suggestion that the cemetery was the primary element in early church settlement (Thomas (1971), 49–51). These issues will be discussed further below.

[17] MacDonald (1984), 297.

[18] M. and L. de Paor (1958), 64; Hughes and Hamlin (1977), 73.

[19] Ó Carragáin (2003), 129.

[20] Ó Carragáin (2003), 147.

One obvious key to better site interpretation would be a clearer understanding of the origin, form and evolution of the various elements identified by Henry. A major contribution to this task came from the architect Harold Leask.[21] Following in a tradition of architectural historians, stretching from Petrie and Dunraven in the nineteenth century to A. C. Champneys in the early twentieth century, Leask provided a detailed and informed account of the ecclesiastical architecture of early medieval Ireland. Despite the need for some revision, Leask's work remains to be superseded and is still a standard reference work for scholars of the period.[22] His observation that the internal measurements of small single-cell oblong churches, such as Gallarus, the proportion of length to width being 1.5 to 1,[23] was indicative of an early dating has been influential.[24] In particular, his dating of the Gallarus oratory to the mid seventh century[25] provided a potential dating parameter for other similar structures. However, from our perspective his comments about enclosure are especially pertinent. Noting the ubiquity of Irish enclosure, described by him as 'as necessary a monastery as to a farmhouse of the times', he acknowledged the debt of Irish coenobiticism to its Syrian and Egyptian antecedents and affirmed the faith impetus behind the practice of enclosure.[26] He went on at greater length to discuss the possible pre-Christian origins of enclosure but argued that the majority of what he called 'monastic cashels' were probably 'monkish erections'; an argument he accompanied with a brief survey of relevant sites.[27] Perhaps what is most significant is that for Leask, as for Henry, enclosure and monastic settlement were synonymous.

Alongside Henry's survey work and Leask's architectural insights, the 1950s also saw the development of a more professional and rigorous approach to the exploration of the extant archaeology. The pioneering work in this field is undoubtedly that of Michael O'Kelly whose 1950s excavation of Church Island, a small tidal islet off the coast of Co. Kerry, has been acclaimed as a 'key event in the historiography of

---

[21] Leask (1955).

[22] Edwards (1990), 101.

[23] Leask (1955), 49–51.

[24] O'Kelly (1958), 119–120.

For a *contra* view see Harbison (1970).

[25] Leask (1955), 2.

[26] Leask (1955), 11.

[27] Leask (1955), 11–15.

medieval architectural history in Ireland'.[28] Described by Philip Rahtz as a 'classic example' of the undocumented monastic settlement[29] this site does indeed appear to boast all the key diagnostic elements for an 'eremitic monastery'. Certainly O'Kelly was strongly of the opinion, both before and after excavation, that this was a small monastic site.[30] However, although all of the major elements of a monastic layout were present, and despite the fact that the site largely fitted the eremitic monastic profile, there was no substantive evidence of specifically monastic activity as opposed to a more broadly ecclesiastical or even secular Christian usage. Further, the presence of a female among the phase one burials discovered on the site needed to be explained.[31] In response Nancy Edwards has suggested that the site may have become the focus for a community cemetery.[32] Charles Thomas's initial view that Church Island was simply an example of an unenclosed developed cemetery mellowed somewhat to allow the possibility that the site began as an eremitical settlement with the cemetery representing a later addition.[33] More recently, it has been suggested that Church Island may well have been a 'proprietary church' or the domain of a 'hereditary church family' rather than a monastic or eremitic settlement.[34] As to dating it has been suggested that the site might have been occupied as early as the seventh century but although we can be fairly confident of the chronological sequence of the development of the site we cannot be certain of the dating spectrum.[35]

[28] O'Keeffe (1998), 112.

[29] Rahtz (1973), 126.

[30] O'Kelly (1958), 57, 115.

[31] O'Kelly (1958), 61.

[32] O'Kelly (1958), 117–118; Edwards (1990), 117.

[33] Thomas (1971), 69–70; (1995), 68.

[34] Ó Corráin (1981), 339; Hurley (1982), 324.

[35] One potential dating marker was the ogham-inscribed cross-slab bearing a cross in the shape of a *flabellum* discovered in the south west sector of the enclosure but not *in situ,* having been clearly broken from its base which has not been found (O'Kelly (1958), 77–79). The *flabellum* design of the ogham-inscribed cross-slab was dated to AD650–750 by O'Kelly (O'Kelly (1958), 128; O'Sullivan, A. and Sheehan (1996), 258), with the ogham inscription probably being a later addition (O'Kelly (1973), 11).

Although O'Kelly's tentative dating of the Gallarus-style stone oratory on Church Island to the mid eighth century (O'Kelly (1958), 128) followed hard on the heels of Leask's dating for Gallarus Charles Thomas has suggested that O'Kelly has been over-cautious in his dating and that the timber oratory might be as early as the seventh century (Thomas (1967), 171). This possibility has subsequently been acknowledged by the excavator (O'Kelly (1973), 11).

What is most striking about Church Island within the context of our discussion of enclosure is the fact that the enclosing stone wall most unusually was constructed last.[36] O'Kelly was clear that the reason for building the wall could not have been defensive as it was unlikely to have exceeded 1.5m in height and contained within it a number of unguarded open gaps.[37] What he felt was more likely was that the wall was unusually constructed at a later stage of site development in order to provide shelter from the elements although he did allow that it was quite possible that the wall represented an attempt to mark out the area of the monastery as holy ground.[38] He acknowledged this latter possibility again several years after the excavation but did not develop this theme further.[39] The reason for this break with what he regarded as the usual construction sequence may remain elusive but we do need to consider what impact the irregular sequence at Church Island might have upon our understanding of the motivation and praxis of enclosure in an Irish context. Church Island may simply be the exception that proves the rule or it may be that enclosure as a theological signature was predated by other key elements of religious settlement not just here but elsewhere. Equally, the later addition of an enclosing feature may signify in a very marked manner an architectural or even theological significance. Certainly the unusual building sequence found on Church Island and the lack of evidence for specifically monastic activity challenged the orthodoxy of the day and began to raise questions about the nature of these sites.

If Church Island raised some perturbing questions about 'monastic' typology and layout the exploration of the nearby settlement on Skellig Michael seemed to reaffirm the traditional monastic hermeneutic.[40] Surveyed by Liam de Paor in the mid-1950s the island has since been the subject of a much more thorough and ongoing excavation by Walter Horn, Jenny White Marshall and Grellan Rourke, but even

---

[36] O'Kelly's excavation had revealed two major stages of early medieval occupation: in Phase 1 the earliest buildings had been a small wooden rectilinear structure on the same alignment as a number of burials and a circular wooden hut. In Phase 2 these structures were replaced by a rectangular stone oratory and a circular stone house (Edwards (1990), 116). A rectangular stone house was then built on the north east edge of the island. Finally the stone cashel was constructed (O' Kelly (1958), 58; (1973), 9).

[37] O'Kelly (1958), 126.

[38] O'Kelly (1958), 127.

[39] O'Kelly (1973), 9.

[40] The founding of the ecclesiastical settlement is attributed to the sixth century Saint Fionan although the exact identity of this saint is unclear (Smith (1756), 113).

from the most cursory of examinations it was clear that the site represented the paradigm of the Henrician 'eremitic monastery'. Of interest to us is the material evidence for the enclosure and internal subdivision of the enclosed space not only on the main ecclesiastical settlement on the broad north-eastern summit but also on the hermitage site on the South Peak.[41] De Paor limited his exploration to the main settlement site where he observed 'a system of walled enclosures with stone huts and oratories'[42] but Horn, Marshall and Rourke extended the investigation to the South Peak hermitage. Although the precarious position of both the main monastery and the exposed hermitage arguably made the building of enclosing walls an engineering necessity in order to provide firm foundation for the rest of the settlement the question remains whether the enclosure of the hermitage was also of theological significance given the technical difficulty of the task and the considerable personal risk to the builders.[43] The further subdivision of such a small area as the hermitage enclosure in order to create a separate enclosed space for the reliquary shrine can only increase this possibility. The excavators certainly recognized the possibility of a 'symbolic significance' to the spatial separation of the reliquary shrine on the South Peak from the rest of the hermitage but made little other comment.[44]

In terms of dating parameters the excavators were clear that the establishment of the monastery and hermitage on Skellig Michael was inspired by the ascetic example of Egyptian monasticism and was an expression of enthusiasm for the Culdee revival; viewed by the excavators as a direct spiritual response to the overweening power of the monastic *paruchiae*. If this supposition is correct then a dating horizon of the late eighth and early ninth century would suggest itself for the enclosure and ordering of the hermitage.[45] However, it is difficult to date the history of enclosure on the site or even to establish a chronological relationship between the enclosing walls on the main site and the buildings they enclose.[46] All we can probably say with confidence

---

[41] de Paor (1955), 177 fig. 3; Fanning (1981), 150; Horn, Marshall and Rourke (1990), 50.

[42] de Paor (1955), 180.

Although de Paor did not extend his survey to the South Peak he did note the presence of structures on it (de Paor (1955), 186; Horn, Marshall and Rourke (1990), 18).

[43] Horn, Marshall and Rourke (1990), 73.

[44] Horn, Marshall and Rourke (1990), 50.

[45] Horn, Marshall and Rourke (1990), 71, 76–79.

[46] Herity (1983), 34–35.

is that there is material evidence that enclosure and zoning was practised in the ninth century (and probably much earlier) on a very remote site where there can have been little or no defensive benefit provided by enclosure in addition to what nature had already provided.

Skellig Michael is undoubtedly an iconic western island site and, as such, its monastic credentials are beyond reproach. However, O'Kelly's findings on Church Island had challenged the monastic orthodoxy and opened up the possibility of a non-monastic or even secular origin for these remote island settlements. Further, the previously accepted chronological sequence of such sites, and the place of enclosure within it, was brought into question by the constructional sequence there. To complicate matters further, analogous difficulties of interpretation were to surface during the excavation of the small mainland site at Reask. Here, once again, the site appeared to fit the putative 'eremitic monastery' profile although there was little on the site to indicate a monastic past and even the small finds offered very little of an ecclesiastical nature and again the excavator, Tom Fanning, like O'Kelly before him, found himself caught between the archaeology and the historiography. So while he was cautious about placing a mainland site like Reask in the same category of settlement as the island sites such as Church Island and Skellig Michael, Fanning's acceptance of the orthodox developmental model of Irish ecclesiology as moving from episcopal to monastic between the sixth and late seventh century led him to suggest that Reask might represent the very earliest phase of monastic activity in Ireland dating from as early as the sixth and seventh centuries.[47] Interestingly, like Church Island, Reask has now been interpreted by some as a possible 'proprietary church'.[48]

Our interest in Reask is aroused primarily by the unusual history and pattern of enclosure on the site. The actual building sequence here is less certain than that for Church Island although it too appears to have had two major phases, the first dating from the fifth to seventh centuries and the second extending from as early as the seventh or eighth centuries to the twelfth. The link between the settlement area and the cemetery are unclear but it would appear that in phase one the initial settlement area was focused on the central area and was enclosed by a cashel-type wall.[49] The second major phase of building on the site began with the erection of a small stone oratory over some of the early

[47] Fanning (1981), 159–160.
[48] Mytum (1992), 63.
[49] Fanning (1981), 157–158.

lintel graves. An internal dividing wall was built at the same time as the oratory along with the paving leading to the oratory.[50] As O'Kelly suggested for Church Island, these acts of enclosure were interpreted by Fanning as an attempt to separate off an especially significant space within the enclosure but there was no discussion of any theological justification for such a planning motif.[51] Fanning also observed that the position of the oratory in the eastern part of the enclosure was typical of similar sites throughout Kerry. Again there was little discussion of this phenomenon although it was noted that this position was related to the area chosen as the focus for the primary cemetery and thus it was the burials rather than the oratory which provided the original focal attraction.[52] However, the layout does fit with the planning canon outlined by Henry in her survey of eremitic sites, if not her suggested developmental chronology,[53] and gave archaeological substance to the suggestion that there was a regularity of layout on these small monastic settlement sites.

In many respects these early investigations of Irish religious settlement raised more questions than they answered. The 'eremitic monastery' model proposed by Henry was predicated upon a prior assumption that the vast majority of the sites surveyed were monastic in character. The function and purpose of sites such as Reask and Church Island remain unclear but there is little substantive evidence to support the supposed monastic nature of these settlements. The prevailing monastic hermeneutic for the interpretation of these settlements and the modelling of Skellig Michael as the archetypical remote western ascetic site may prove to have been unhelpful. Others have since suggested that some of these churches might have been proprietary or parochial rather than monastic in origin.[54] The literary and archaeological evidence would indicate that Skellig Michael was in fact an *atypically* large coenobitic settlement with a strong eremitic

---

[50] Fanning (1981), 78–79, 150, 158.

[51] O'Kelly (1973), 9; Fanning (1981), 150, 155.

[52] Fanning (1981), 150.

McCormick has commented that the graves on a number of sites, including those at Reask, might have been separated from the rest of the enclosure because, at least initially, the dead were regarded as 'unclean' (McCormick (1997), 64–65). This runs counter to an understanding that the tomb of the saint provided a sacred 'attraction' for the planners of these sites. I believe it is more credible that graves were subject to segregation because they were regarded as sacred rather than as unclean.

[53] See above n. 16.

[54] Ó Carragáin (2003), 130; Ó Corráin (1981), 339; Mytum (1992), 63.

impulse, the very paradigm of the 'eremitic monastery', whose very uniqueness may have been allowed to distort scholarly perspective in relation to other less impressive sites. Its neighbours boast extant remains of a much less extensive nature and their genesis and development is much less clear. It may be that we have to reject a rigorous taxonomy for these sites and settle instead upon a possible functional diversity.

Henry's broad typological sweep turned the south-western tip of Ireland into something of an ideological 'battlefield' between opposing models of early Irish ecclesiology.[55] The first serious challenge to the Henrician orthodoxy came from Charles Thomas, in his 1971 book, *The Early Christian Archaeology of North Britain*. In this survey of the archaeology of northern Britain, Thomas sought to counter the Henrician self-confessed 'strange picture',[56] by placing religious settlement in a broader context through examination of a range of sites of varying size across a wide geographical area. Cautious about the overuse of the epithet 'monastic' he endeavoured to apply a more nuanced taxonomy to religious settlement drawing a distinction between what he termed 'full monasteries', 'eremitic monasteries', and 'developed cemeteries'.[57] In his discussion he made a number of observations about enclosure, its form and motivation. With regard to form he argued speculatively and somewhat controversially that the monastic enclosure on the larger sites such as Iona, Clonmacnoise and Glendalough might be rectilinear[58] although he acknowledged that the ideal was the 'sacral circle' even if rarely attained on the ground.[59] Further, he suggested that 'reoccupations' of pre-Christian forts and earthworks such as on Inishmurray and at Nendrum might have determined the shape of enclosure in these cases.[60] As to purpose he would appear to have viewed the widespread enclosure of monastic space by a *vallum monasterii* as the creation of a spiritual and legal barrier within which the abbot's diktat could reign supreme.[61]

Most significantly Thomas questioned the developmental chronology and accepted taxonomy of a number of smaller 'eremitic' sites

[55] Ó Carragáin (2003), 129.
[56] Henry (1957), 157.
[57] Thomas (1971), 38, 44, 67–68.
[58] Thomas (1971), 29–31.
[59] Thomas (1971), 38–39.
[60] Thomas (1971), 33.
[61] Thomas (1971), 29, 33.

noting that the history of enclosure within any given settlement remained elusive because it was rarely possible to connect the enclosing structure with a particular building phase.[62] He also argued that enclosure was not an exclusive signature of monastic settlement but was rather a motif of what he regarded as the primary field monument of Insular Christianity, the cemetery (dating from as early as the late fifth and early sixth centuries). The cemetery was 'developed' by the addition of chapels and habitation buildings,[63] in much the same way as the Mediterranean martyrial relic-tombs had developed into the *cella memoriae* of the fourth and fifth centuries and then into more substantial memorial architecture such as churches and basilicas.[64] Thus sites such as Church Island and Ardwall Isle, which had been regarded as 'eremitic monasteries', were more properly to be labelled 'developed cemeteries'[65] although he admitted that it was often impossible to differentiate a 'developed cemetery' from a small 'eremitic monastery'.[66]

Thomas's work in a non-Irish context also highlights the unreliability of some of the supposedly monastic terminology of enclosure. In particular his analysis of the usage of the term *llan* or *lan* suggests that it has been so widely employed to describe a variety of religious settlement types from a simple cleared space to a developed enclosed cemetery that it has largely been devalued as an indicator of any form of early monastic influence.[67] Ann Preston-Jones, working in a Cornish context, has also traced the term's semantic development. She has been more confident in her reliance upon the diagnostic potential of the term arguing that *llan*, which was an undoubtedly early element, metamorphosed from initially simply denoting an enclosure to later accrue the meaning 'monastery' or 'cemetery'.[68] However, Preston-Jones fails to provide a monastic typology against which such a proposition might be tested. Further, staying within a western British context, serious questions have been raised more recently about the

---

[62] Thomas (1967), 143.

[63] Thomas (1971), 49–51.

[64] Thomas (1971), 138–140.

[65] Thomas (1971), 69–73.

[66] Thomas (1971), 68.

[67] Thomas (1971), 87.

Thomas also inferred that the same was almost certainly true of the Irish equivalent *cell* or *cill* (Thomas (1971), 87–88).

[68] Preston-Jones (1992), 108–109, 115–116.

validity of the 'developed cemetery' model proposed by Thomas.[69] David Petts has argued that there is no convincing material evidence for such a developmental sequence in western Britain before c.AD800.[70] Further, both John Reuben Davies and Oliver Padel have suggested that the usage of the term *llan* may in fact have continued until a relatively late.[71] This would clearly impact upon its reliability as an indicator of antiquity, monastic or otherwise. Indeed, such etymological ambiguity was not restricted to Cornwall. Deirdre Flanagan states, in relation to her work on Irish place-names, that it is impossible to establish any substantive correlation between types of ecclesiastical foundation on the ground and the generic words used to describe them.[72] Richard Sharpe similarly highlighted the difficulties posed by over-reliance upon the supposedly monastic tenor of the nomenclature used to describe differing types of ecclesiastic foundation.[73] David Dumville has argued that in Insular Latin usage monastic terminology was employed in a non-forensic sense to apply to a whole range of ecclesiastical buildings and settlements and following in the footsteps of Colmán Etchingham dismisses scornfully 'those who have continued to speak simplistically of Irish monasteries and monasticism'.[74]

The indiscriminate use of monastic terminology by the documentary sources is also noted by Vincent Hurley in his important study of religious settlement in south-west Ireland, 'The Early Church in the South-West of Ireland: Settlement and Organisation'.[75] Acknowledging the paucity of textual evidence for the area and the potentially distorting focus to date on western sites[76] he questioned the variety of site types listed as monasteries and, like Thomas, sought to provide a more developed taxonomy for the classification of south-western ecclesiastical settlements.[77] He further suggested that the prevalence of

[69] Turner (2003), 171–174

[70] Petts (2002).

Evidence from western *Irish* sites would suggest that the model also does not travel well. Ó Carragáin has argued that many ecclesiastical sites there started life as small settlements rather than burial grounds that were later enclosed as churchyards (Ó Carragáin (2003), 129–130).

[71] Davies, J. R. (1998), 45–46; Padel (1985), 144.

[72] Flanagan (1984).

[73] Sharpe (1992), 91, 101–102.

[74] Dumville (1997b), 106–107; (1997a), 460; Etchingham (1996), 136–137.

[75] Hurley (1982).

[76] Hurley (1982), 301.

[77] Hurley (1982), 299.

ecclesiastical sites of whatever category was much greater than previously thought; their presence being indicated by either the documentary sources or more reliably by extant material remains such as oratories, cross-slabs, decorated stones, slab-shrines, *leachts*, and, of course, enclosures.[78] The use of an enclosure footprint to indicate church settlement was for Hurley a recent but significant development. His description of these enclosing features as comprising usually an earthen bank with accompanying ditch or a stone wall is fairly standard but he does note the great variation in diameter and location. He also draws our attention to the praxis of internal enclosure particularly on the larger sites, such as that at Templebryan, Co. Cork, and to an example of trivallate enclosure with multiple internal zones at Kilmacoo.[79] In his detailed discussion of these sites Hurley affirms the priority of the circle as the form of enclosure and places the enclosing of space within a ritual context by reference to the numerous textual allusions to the process of enclosure and within a planning context by reference to the *schema* of the late eighth to early ninth century Irish text, the *Book of Mulling*.[80] The function of enclosure was not simply defensive (although he did recognize defence as a purpose) but also symbolic, demarcating the area of the *termon*, from the Latin word *terminus* denoting the area surrounding a church or religious settlement, which he interprets from a legal rather than a spiritual perspective as an area of ecclesiastical sanctuary.

I.B. *Monastic Hegemony: A Revisionist Critique*

The archaeological ambiguity of sites such as Church Island and Reask and the refined settlement taxonomy offered by Thomas and Hurley posed a challenge to the hegemony of a monastic context for Irish enclosure; a challenge which formed part of a wider historiographical reaction against the simplex modelling of the episcopal-abbatial paradigm for early Irish church ecclesiology. We have already observed the considerable scholarly disagreement, particularly with reference

---

[78] Hurley (1982), 304, 306, 311.

[79] Hurley (1982), 314; see also 326.

[80] Hurley (1982), 320.

Michael Herity also clearly regards the diagram in the colophon of the *Book of Mulling* as explicit textual evidence of the existence of planning conventions regarding the siting of High Crosses (Herity (1983), 42).

to Ireland, about the evolution/revolution nature of the impact of emergent monasticism upon the existing ecclesiastical scene and the extent to which it replaced the pre-existing diocesan administration. Kathleen Hughes, drawing on the reservations of earlier scholars, had already conceded that the monastic hegemony of the Irish church may not have been as total or as rapid as first thought.[81] She advocated a more sophisticated process and chronology of change whilst still adhering to what has been rather critically referred to by Etchingham as 'a confidently formulated periodisation'.[82]

The final assault on the bastions of orthodoxy when it arrived came primarily from two scholars, first Richard Sharpe and then Colmán Etchingham. Sharpe's insights in particular have profound consequences for our deliberations and form part of the same discourse initiated by Hurley's discussion of the various grades of church existing within the hierarchy of the *paruchia*.[83] Once again the flashpoint was the discussion around the monastic versus diocesan origins of the concept of *paruchia*. In his 1984 paper, 'Some Problems Concerning the Organisation of the Church in Early Medieval Ireland', Sharpe refuted the widely accepted developmental framework for the early medieval Irish church, rejecting both the early existence and putative eventual demise of dioceses and the subsequent prevalence of the 'monastic *paruchia*' as an ecclesiological norm.[84] Instead, controversially, he stated that there was 'no sign that the growth of the church or its organisation were the subject of any form of control'.[85] Resisting the temptation to view early Irish ecclesial organisation as uniform, thus denying it the sort of plurality which clearly marked post-conquest monasticism in Britain and Ireland, Sharpe advocated an organic organisational model characterized by diversity and continuity rather than by change and confrontation.[86] This unstructured growth allowed for the co-existence of episcopal territorial jurisdiction alongside a burgeoning monastic

---

[81] Hughes (1966), 79–81.

[82] Etchingham (1999), 6.

[83] Hurley (1982), 323.

[84] Etchingham has noted that the word *paruchia* occurs seven times in the *Hibernensis*, twice in the 'First Synod of Patrick' and once in the 'Second Synod of Patrick'. Of these ten occurrences half understand the term *paruchia* to have clear episcopal and territorial connotations (Etchingham (1999), 106–107). It is probably fair to argue that current academic opinion is equally evenly divided between the 'territorial' and the 'cultic' camps.

[85] Sharpe (1984), 241.

[86] Sharpe (1984), 265–267; Etchingham (1999), 25.

presence.[87] Sharpe saw no monastic nuance in the use of the term *paruchia* in the Patrician hagiography arguing that the key element in the *paruchia* relationship as evidenced by the Patrician material was 'the proprietary control of a mother-church over its dependencies' such as that pioneered and exercised by Armagh and Kildare.[88] This 'proprietary *paruchia*' model stood in sharp contrast to the monastic relationship as represented by the confederations based around the great monasteries such as Iona and Durrow which were more properly to be labelled *familia*. Sharpe's questioning of the exclusively monastic nature of the forensic language surrounding Irish ecclesiology in this period found some tangential support from other scholars including Máire Herbert. In her work on the monastic *familia* of Colum Cille she warned of the dangers of arguing from the particular to the universal stating that the Iona organisational model could not be extrapolated to any broader generalisation.[89]

Key to Sharpe's critique of the '*monastic paruchia*' model was the question of pastoral care. Did the 'monastic *paruchia*' model make ecclesiological sense? Could a primarily monastic church truly be church? Could it effectively deliver pastoral and spiritual care at a proto-parochial level; an absolute necessity if it was to survive and grow. A church that could not deliver effective pastoral care would founder and the monastery, most of whose monks were not priests, could not possibly deliver widespread pastoral care to scattered congregations. In Sharpe's alternative model pastoral responsibility remained with the bishop and other secular clergy, who may well have lived among the monastic community which would have been governed by an official who was not necessarily an abbot or a bishop.[90] To support his argument for ongoing episcopal pastoral responsibility Sharpe turned to the eighth-century text *Ríagal Phátraic* with its emphasis on the bishop's wide-ranging role including the selection of ordinands, the sacraments of ordination and confirmation, the consecration of churches, and the maintenance of good church order.[91] At the local level the pastoral care would have had to be delivered by secular clergy from numerous smaller churches having some form of relationship to their larger counterparts. Sharpe went on to argue that, although the

---

[87] Sharpe (1984), 261, 263.
[88] Sharpe (1984), 244–247.
[89] Herbert (1988), 34.
[90] Sharpe (1984), 263–265.
[91] Sharpe (1984), 252–253.

nature of the relationship between these different grades of church remained elusive,[92] there was clearly in place in early medieval Ireland a hierarchy for the provision of pastoral care based on the mother church. These churches were themselves often the property of greater churches such as Armagh or Durrow, and disseminated through smaller local churches with perhaps only a single priest, providing 'what in its time was one of the most comprehensive pastoral organizations in northern Europe'.[93]

To some extent this ecclesial mixed economy reflects the situation described by Huw Pryce for Wales in the same period who writes:

'The cumulative impression conveyed by the evidence, then, is that a key component of the ecclesiastical structure in Wales from the sixth century onwards were communities to which a monastic vocabulary was applied, but which also contained ordinary clergy who could have performed pastoral work'.[94] Indeed, Sharpe also suggested that a diversity of provision was not simply an Irish or even English phenomenon but a characteristic of the north-western European church;[95] a suggestion developed further by Blair in relation to Anglo-Saxon ecclesiastical settlement.[96]

Sharpe's reliance upon the density of small church sites in the Dingle peninsula as evidence for this extensive pastoral coverage has been challenged by Ó Carragáin who has suggested that many of these churches may well have been proprietary churches, privately owned and not primarily concerned with pastoralia.[97] It is also possible that, like Iona, Dingle represents an atypical ecclesial situation. Nevertheless, the ecclesiological model outlined by Sharpe would suggest that despite the predominance of monastic language the key structural element of the early Irish medieval church, at least in its later stages, was more properly akin to that of the cathedral priory than to the monastic cloister, and that parallels should be sought not with the Desert Fathers but in Gaul and Anglo-Saxon England.[98]

---

[92] Sharpe (1992), 95.

[93] Sharpe (1992), 102, 105–109; see also Hurley (1982), 323–324.

[94] Pryce (1992), 54.

[95] Sharpe (1992), 101.

[96] Blair (2005), 3, 73–74.

[97] Sharpe (1992), 90, 108–109; Ó Carragáin (2003), 130.

[98] Sharpe (1992), 101–102.

Sharpe was, of course, not alone in questioning the validity of the monastic paradigm.[99] Colmán Etchingham, in a 1994 article, 'Bishops in the Early Irish Church: A Reassessment', affirmed much of what Sharpe had attested especially in relation to the episcopal ministry and pastoral care. Like Sharpe, Etchingham employed the evidence of *Ríagal Phátraic* to highlight the ongoing importance of the pastoral role of the bishop[100] but he also focused upon the textual evidence of the eighth century *Collectio canonum Hibernensis* to illustrate the continuing significance of the episcopal liturgical, pastoral, judicial and teaching role within the church.[101] Etchingham, however, arguably displays a somewhat clearer conception of the ecclesiological distinction between 'monastic' and 'non-monastic' religious settlement.[102] This is reflected in the dissonance between the two scholars over Sharpe's apparent dichotomy between the 'proprietary *paruchia*' and the *familia*. Etchingham rather saw the terms *paruchia* and *familia* as reflecting different aspects of the same essentially non-monastic ecclesiological system with the latter term referring to clerical personnel as opposed to jurisdiction.[103] In his view the *Hibernensis* provided contemporary eighth century evidence that the territorially defined *paruchia* was still functioning and of significance at the time of composition.[104] Further there was sufficient annalistic evidence to support the reality of territorially defined episcopal jurisdiction as late as the tenth century.[105]

However, both Etchingham and Sharpe agreed that the early Irish church did not know only one system of church government nor did it undergo a neat paradigm shift from diocesan to abbatial rule. This truth had been hinted at from as early as the work of Todd and Bury but it was only now that the complexity of Insular ecclesiology was properly acknowledged. Even then it was not yet fully understood, although if David Dumville is indeed correct in his somewhat acerbic

---

[99] Sharpe's critique has itself come in for criticism not least because the 'new orthodoxy' for which he is responsible might suggest that there was no early medieval church organisation in Ireland at all (Ó Cróinín (1995), 150).

[100] Etchingham (1994), 45–47.

[101] For example see Etchingham (1999), 39 and 39 nn.13 and 14.

[102] Etchingham (1994), 35–62.

[103] Etchingham (1999), 168.

[104] Etchingham (1999), 114.

[105] Etchingham (1999), 459.

analysis that *paruchia* was simply the Hiberno-Latin spelling of the late Latin term *parrochia*, and not a concept in its own right, then a significant degree of academic energy has been wasted in a vain quest.[106]

Yet, as Donnchadh Ó Corráin acknowledged in the aftermath of the Sharpe-Etchingham critique, the model of change put forward by Kathleen Hughes had been effectively demolished to be replaced by something much more complex.[107] Historiography was now requiring a more sophisticated hermeneutic within which the material evidence of early Irish religious settlement might be understood. As we noted, the initial archaeological exploration of some of the more remote ascetically-inspired settlement sites in the west of Ireland had also suggested a diversity of function and context. This challenged an understanding of enclosure as a specifically monastic marker and suggested that enclosure was more properly understood as a characteristic of all types of religious settlement, monastic and non-monastic.

The excavation of the settlement remains on High Island was to raise the further possibility that the praxis of enclosure actually had its genesis in pre-Christian culture. High Island, off the coast of Co. Galway, was excavated by Jenny White Marshall and Grellan Rourke sporadically over a twenty year period throughout the 1980s and 1990s. As with Church Island and Reask the dating of the monastic settlement remains uncertain. Its foundation has traditionally been attributed to the seventh-century saint Féchin of Fore who founded several monasteries including the Fore in Westmeath and Cong in Mayo.[108] The site has the profile of an eremitic settlement with all the key elements being present and the excavators did not seriously question its monastic credentials;[109] once again affirming the spiritual debt of this form of ascetic monasticism to Egyptian monasticism, much as they had done for Skellig Michael.[110] High Island boasts a monastic enclosure wall of exceptional width, noted by several early commentators including John O'Donovan and W. F. Wakeman.[111] The site also provides evidence of the internal enclosure of space with a secondary enclosure wall surrounding the oratory; a feature found on a number of sites including Gallarus and Reask although again this is an unusually

---

[106] Dumville (1997a), 461.

[107] Ó Corráin (1994), 28.

[108] Herity (1990), 179; Marshall and Rourke (2001), 8–9.

[109] Marshall and Rourke (2001), 5.

[110] Marshall and Rourke (2001), 1–2; Horn, Marshall and Rourke (1990), 76.

[111] O'Donovan (1839), 75–87; Wakeman (1863).

substantial example.[112] The excavators' generic discussion explicitly set Irish monastic enclosure in its vernacular context arguing that the sub-circular form of enclosure derived from the Irish ring-fort or *cashel* or *ráth* in much the same way as the shape of the buildings depicted within the Benedictine *Plan of St Gall* developed from a Roman villa culture.[113] In the case of High Island they have suggested that the size of the enclosure might be indicative of a secular and pre-Christian origin; perhaps a gift given by powerful landowners to the monks. This sequence, they argued, would parallel that put forward for other putative pre-Christian sites such as Nendrum, Inishmurray, Illauntannig, and even Iona.[114] They then went on to argue that High Island and Illauntannig in particular, rather than being cashels, might belong to a group of larger stone forts whose distinguishing features including wall chambers are found on both sites; a possibility we shall return to later.[115]

Once again, as we have noted, dating evidence was largely circum-stantial and although the longest term occupation seems to have been that of the monks there is no hard archaeological evidence for a seventh-century foundation date for the monastic settlement. Most of the church complex that is still visible belongs to the period from the late tenth century to the twelfth century, the last phase of monastic occupation.[116] Generally the extant remains on High Island would appear to have come from the same dating horizon as those found on similar sites elsewhere off the west coast of Ireland and to have been similar in evolution and topography. The term 'monastery' cannot be used with confidence about any of these sites but it would seem rea-sonable to assume that High Island was indeed a coenobitic settlement for at least part of its history. The High Island excavation is significant for our discussion. It helped to establish the broader context of enclo-sure but it was unable to resolve with any precision the dating issues which remain an ongoing concern for anyone trying to resolve the evolution of the enclosure.

A first success in the quest to secure a firm chronology for smallwest-ern settlement sites came with the excavation carried out by Marshall

---

[112] Fanning (1981), 78–79, 150; Cuppage (1986), 286, 339; Marshall and Rourke (2001), 71.

[113] Marshall and Rourke (2001), 45.

[114] Marshall and Rourke (2001), 175–176.

[115] Marshall and Rourke (2001), 180–181.

[116] Marshall and Rourke (2001), 217, 222.

and Walsh in the early 1990s on Illaunloughan, another island site off
Kerry. During the course of four seasons Jenny Marshall and Claire
Walsh excavated this small island settlement in the hope that substantive
dating evidence might be found.[117] Vincent Hurley's suggestion that
such sites might have formed the basis of a community church[118] is
negated in this case by the presence of exclusively male burials, eliminat-
ing the ambiguity found on Church Island.[119] The initial working
hypothesis for the excavators was that this was a small eremitic settlement similar to that found on neighbouring islands.[120] However,
although it is likely that many of these western island sites started off as
simple hermitages and were then enlarged to accommodate a small community[121] the evidence would suggest that Illaunloughan was founded
not by one or two men but by as many as five or six.[122] This caused its
excavators to upgrade their initial description of the site as 'a small
eremitical settlement' to that of a 'small monastery'.[123] This rather sup-
poses the existence of a precise and reliable monastic taxonomy which
would allow the allocation of a site to a particular 'class' of monastic settlement. What might distinguish a 'small eremitical settlement' from a
'small monastery' is unclear but the key factor for the excavators appears
to have been the potential size of the community.[124]

What nevertheless remains of interest here is the evidence for a possible early dating for enclosure. Once again it is clear that this site
underwent a series of transitions over a prolonged period with Period
I stretching from the mid seventh to the mid eighth centuries and

---

[117] As with the sites of Church Island and Reask there is little historical reference to
the island although Lochán may be a saint's name (there is a reference to a Lochán in
the entry for 31st December in the *Martyrology of Oengus*, written *c*.AD830). The visible remains consisted of a small rectilinear dry-stone oratory, a circular dry-stone cell at
the south-western end of the island, a stone-lined well, and a gable-shrine located on a
mound demarcated by orthostats. There were fifty upright slabs, most of which are
probably related to Illaunloughan's more recent role as a *ceallúnach* (Marshall and
Walsh (1998), 103; O'Sullivan, A. and Sheehan (1996), 307–308).
For a general description see also Henry (1957), 96–98.

[118] Hurley (1982), 299.

[119] Marshall and Walsh (1998), 103, 105; Marshall and Walsh (2005), 125.
The presence of a child in the reliquary cist of the shrine is highly unusual but may
be explained by close kinship (Marshall and Walsh (2005), 85).

[120] Marshall and Walsh (1998), 103.

[121] Herity (1989), 48.

[122] Marshall and Walsh (2005), 125.

[123] Marshall and Walsh (1998), 103; Marshall and Walsh (2005), 125.

[124] Marshall and Walsh (2005), 8–10.

Period 2 from the eighth to the ninth century. During this first period a number of sod structures were built consisting of three domestic huts and an oratory.[125] Two of these huts were conjoined, in a similar pattern to that found at Reask, and were built up against an outer wall and were therefore later. Although it has been claimed that there is no present trace of an enclosure wall[126] this outer wall may well be the remains of an enclosing wall, similar to that found on Church Island and other typologically similar sites but, unlike the wall on Church Island which was added later, the wall on Illaunloughan appears to have been a primary feature.[127] In addition there is once again material evidence of an attempt to subdivide the enclosed space in order to focus attention on the shrine. The presence of paving leading to the shrine and the division by orthostats between external and internal areas of the shrine mound is resonant of the site at Reask, among others.[128]

Having established a developmental sequence the excavators were then able to provide a detailed dating context. At a general level the presence of lintelled graves on the island suggested an early date for we know that lintelled graves and long-cists were in use in Britain from the fourth century and the lintel grave cemetery at Whithorn has been dated to the first half of the sixth century.[129] Similar graves on Reask have been dated to between the fifth and seventh centuries.[130] More significantly, the use of carbon dating gave us for the first time detailed and relatively accurate parameters for the development of the settlement.[131] These results encouraged the excavators to argue for a late seventh to ninth century milieu for the occupation of the settlement on

---

[125] Marshall and Walsh (2005), 11, 37.

[126] Herity (1983), 35.

[127] Marshall and Walsh (2005), 12–16.

[128] Marshall and Walsh (2005), 128.

[129] Hill (1992), 8.

[130] Fanning (1981), 79.

[131] The best dating evidence from Period 1 is the charcoal from what was labelled Hut B, metal working debris which dates from the seventh to eighth century, and the translated bones in the reliquary shrine. All fall within a range from AD660 to AD730–740 (Marshall and Walsh (2005), 11–12). Carbon dating of the bones beneath the gable-shrine has given a date of early seventh century for one individual and the middle of the eighth century for a second (Marshall and Walsh (1998), 108). C14 dating of material from animal bone found beneath the dry-stone cell in the hut area gives a date of AD775 to AD961 (Marshall and Walsh (1998), 108–110). Carbon dating of charcoal detected in the midden gives an eleventh century dating (O'Sullivan, A. and Sheehan (1996), 308).

Illaunloughan.[132] This may of course indicate a possible seventh century dating horizon for typologically similar sites such as Church Island, Reask, and High Island. Further, if enclosure was indeed a primary feature on Illaunloughan, the results would provide evidence for the relatively early praxis of enclosure.

We noted at the beginning of our discussion the difficulty in securing a reliable taxonomy for Irish religious settlement in the early medieval period. The longstanding assumption that it was primarily monastic in character has contributed to a most unhelpful hermeneutic for the study of Insular Irish ecclesiology and archaeology, the tension between the abbatial and episcopal ecclesial paradigm being reflected not just in the historiography but also in the interpretation of the material evidence. Charles Doherty's and Harold Mytum's shared observation that the archaeology of many ecclesiastical sites provides no firm indication of a specifically monastic typology[133] and Thomas's warnings with regard to enclosure did not prevent scholars continuing to regard enclosure as a specifically monastic signature.[134] We have already noted some of the difficulties with such a view. Not only has it proved difficult to distinguish between types of religious settlement it has also proved challenging to differentiate a religious settlement from a secular one.[135] That the enclosure of secular space was practised in Ireland before the arrival of Christianity is clearly evidenced by the

[132] Marshall and Walsh (2005), viii; Ó Carragáin has argued for a more cautious eighth to ninth century cultural horizon (Ó Carragáin (2003), 129).

[133] Doherty (1985), 53; Mytum (1992), 63.

[134] Radford (1977), 7; Bradley (1990), 41.

[135] The differentiation of the material remains of religious settlement from those of secular occupation has proved to be fraught with difficulty. The issues are well illustrated by the example of Tintagel in Cornwall which was excavated by C. A. R. Radford in the 1930s. It was initially thought that the numerous rectilinear huts scattered over the headland site were of Dark-Age provenance. Early examinations of the site and the discovery of a number of these small rectangular slate-walled rooms or cells led several eminent archaeologists, most notably Radford and later Thomas, to believe that it was the site of a major Celtic monastic settlement (Radford (1973b), 401–419; Thomas (1971), 25–26). However, the absence of a monastic cemetery has been acknowledged as significant and more recent field archaeology has established that the cells are most probably medieval and built for a non-religious purpose (Thomas (1986), 73; Burrow (1973), 99–103; Dark (1985), 1–18). The current prevailing view is that these extant remains are medieval and secular rather than 'Celtic' and monastic (Padel (1981), 28–29). Of developing interest is the cliff-top site at the parish church of St Matheriana half a mile south of the castle where there is evidence of significant Christian funerary activity (Turner (2003), 176). Thomas has described the site as the 'sacred' equivalent of its castle counterpart (Thomas (1993), 99).

presence of substantial pre-Christian stone forts dotted over the land-scape. The later adoption of these vernacular building structures for religious use on sites such as High Island presents the archaeologist with particular challenges.[136] This has resulted in a scholarly preoccu-pation with the morphology and typology of religious settlement rather than seeking to establish what that topography might tell us about the motivation of the founder; a concentration on the 'what' rather than on the 'why'. As we have seen from our survey of the schol-arship so far, the focus of attention, at least with regard to the smaller western sites, has been on the form and categorisation of religious set-tlement and not upon its spiritual and/or theological genesis. How-ever, it was the attempt to understand better the topography of the larger settlement sites including two of the most enigmatic of these, Iona and Lindisfarne, which was to provoke reflection upon the motivation for enclosure.

I.c. *Enclosure as an Expression of Power and Influence*

The ecclesiastical status of the island settlement sites might be a mat-ter of some debate but the monastic credentials of the larger mainland sites such as Clonmacnoise, Kells, Glendalough, and Armagh would seem at first sight to be more secure. The annalistic and hagiographi-cal literature provides clear evidence of substantial ecclesial centres based around a worshipping coenobitic community of monks and her-mits providing sanctuary, hospitality, education, even rudimentary healthcare fitting comfortably into Thomas's description of a monastery as a 'permanent, fixed, enclosed community under an abbot, obedient to a Rule, and with such outward manifestations as education, deliberate missionary work, dependent hermitages, and eventually daughter-houses'.[137] However, the archaeological explo-ration of such sites has necessarily been rather limited as several of these large ecclesiastical settlements, such as Armagh, eventually formed the nucleus for later urban development which has made exca-vation difficult. As a result the work on sites has been piecemeal and conducted within the necessary constraints imposed by contemporary habitation; an obstacle not encountered among the much more prolific

---

[136] Marshall and Rourke (2000), 180–181.
[137] Thomas (1971), 21–22.

and remote sites in the west of Ireland. Yet paradoxically it is precisely the relationship between these sites and urban genesis which has provided the stimulus for academic attention.

The kindling for this lively debate was provided by three articles written by Charles Doherty in the early to mid 1980s in which he likened these larger eastern settlements to 'monastic towns'.[138] He was not the first to use this phrase. Hurley had described the larger monasteries such as Clonmacnoise, Clonard, and Durrow as the 'equivalent of towns'.[139] Ó Corráin had used it to describe major eighth and ninth century churches and Hughes had talked about the 'monastic city' as early at the mid 1960s but Doherty was the first to develop an ecclesiological model around the concept.[140] The notion has not been without its detractors such as Brian Graham, Mary Valante, and Catherine Swift.[141] These critics were uneasy about ascribing urban or even proto-urban characteristics to early medieval ecclesiastical settlement. Binchy had observed as early as the late 1950s that the concept of the town was alien to the Celtic mindset being rather a Scandinavian import.[142] The intricacies of the arguments surrounding the possibility of early medieval proto-urbanisation need only concern us here in as far as they impact upon our discussion of settlement layout. Drawing upon the archaeological evidence and putative dating parameters from a relatively limited number of small excavated sites, including Reask and Church Island, Doherty argued that settlements adhered to a fairly sophisticated standard plan prevalent throughout Irish churches from the seventh and eighth centuries onwards. Again this assertion did not pass unchallenged. In particular Catherine Swift questioned Doherty's assertion that the seventh and eighth centuries saw the imposition of a standard layout upon ecclesiastical sites arguing that the dating evidence from sites such as Reask, Church Island, and Iona was far from definitive. Whilst acknowledging a consistency of planning over a large number of sites she also rejected Doherty's belief that this period witnessed the widespread emergence of stone churches, *valla monasterii*, and even 'streets' as being 'exaggerated'.[143]

[138] Doherty (1980); (1982); (1985).
[139] Hurley (1982), 324.
[140] Ó Corráin (1972), 87; Hughes (1966), 148 n. 4, 149.
[141] Graham (1987); Valante (1998); Swift (1998).
[142] Binchy (1962b), 122.
[143] Doherty (1985), 54; Swift (1998), 115.

Whatever the vagaries of Doherty's dating analysis what is seminal for this study is his discussion of the literary depiction of enclosure found in a number of key texts and his attempt to provide a detailed conceptual framework for monastic planning. Drawing upon anthropological and sociological insights Doherty sought to set the praxis of enclosure within both its pagan and Christian contexts. Employing the literary evidence from a number of key sources within a seventh to eighth century dating horizon (including Cogitosus's mid seventh century *Vita S. Brigidae*, the mid to late seventh century *Liber Angeli*, and the early eighth century *Hibernensis*) he sought to determine the organisation of the enclosed space, the *termon*, and to establish a scriptural parallel with the ordering of the Levitical cities of the Old Testament and in particular with the layout of the city of the Levites described by Ezekiel in ch. 48. Suggesting a philosophical continuum from the pre-Christian celestial city through to biblical notions of the Levitical 'city of refuge' and the theological concept of the 'city of God' he advocated a fusion of scriptural, theological and native ideas as being the genesis of the idealized form reflected in the *Hibernensis* and embodied in the monastic layout. In particular, the forensic terminology of enclosure found in the textual evidence was used to examine the relationship between the different areas of enclosed space, the *sanctus*, *sanctior*, and *sanctissimus*, and to establish a *schema* of layout for monastic settlement.[144]

Doherty's hermeneutic drew heavily upon both the biblical notion of the *civitas refugii* and the Irish vernacular legal concept of sanctuary,[145] which could perhaps open Doherty, and indeed Hughes before him,[146] to a charge of interpreting enclosure and zoning primarily in the context of sanctuary rather than sanctity. However, Doherty also acknowledged the canonical regularising of enclosure and zoning as a response to the spoliation of ritual space.[147] The unseemly wrangle over the remains of Patrick depicted in Muirchú's *Vita S. Patricii*[148] and the strange tale of the desecration of the grave of a certain Báitán

---

[144] Doherty (1985), 45–60; Doherty (1982), 301–302.
[145] Doherty (1985), 57.
[146] Hughes (1966), 148–149.
[147] Doherty (1985), 54.
[148] Muirchú, *Vita S. Patricii*, 120–122.
Bieler's edition of Muirchú's *Vita S. Patricii* provides two parallel numbering systems for the text's subdivisions. Therefore, for clarity, I have cited Muirchú's *Vita* by the page number of the Latin text of Bieler's edition.

by a woman and her sheep in the burial place of the monastery at Derry, recounted in Adomnán's *Vita S. Columbae*,[149] were interpreted by Doherty as indicating an increasing lack of respect for the dead. This led him to assert that the detailed burial regulations and strict rules controlling movement within the *termon* detailed by the *Hibernensis* were primarily a response to this contemporary issue.[150] More significantly his use of the biblical model of the Levitical cities to illustrate the subdivision of the *termon* into *suburbana* drew attention to the complex spatial relationship that existed within the enclosure. There is no doubt that his discussion of this internal organisation was seminal in pointing the way to a greater understanding of the morphology and ethos of enclosure and zoning.

One weakness in Doherty's argument which made him vulnerable to his critics was the limited nature of his material evidence base. Much of his organisational *schema* was predicated upon textual evidence and his only substantive archaeological evidence for enclosure and zoning came from the very small western ascetic sites of Reask and Church Island.[151] Yet the 'monastic town' model of enclosure and layout was presented as essentially a phenomenon of large eastern settlement sites such as the key exemplars cited, Kildare and Clonmacnoise which were much less well excavated. John Bradley, an ardent supporter of Doherty's advocacy of the 'monastic town', deployed what limited archaeological evidence we have from the major settlement sites, in suggesting that the evidence from a number of such sites indicated the existence of an ideal monastic town plan in the minds of those responsible for their layout.[152] In his 1990 article, 'The Role of Town Plan Analysis in the Study of the Medieval Irish Town', he cited as three examples of the 'monastic town', Armagh, Kells, and Kildare. These he saw as displaying key topographical characteristics including the presence of a sub-circular enclosing feature, the subdivision of the outer enclosure, and an inner sanctum containing the principal religious buildings in a consistency of layout similar to that found on the smaller and more remote western sites.[153] Further, Bradley argued that this regular settlement complexity which reached its apogee in the

---

[149] *VC*, 1, 20.
[150] *Hibernensis*, 44, 5 and 44, 8.
[151] Doherty (1985), 54.
[152] Bradley (1998), 50.
[153] Bradley (1990), 41, 46.

eleventh and twelfth centuries may have had its genesis as far back as the seventh century.[154]

Bradley's use of archaeology to support a 'monastic town' model provoked similar opposition to Doherty's use of textual evidence for the same purpose. Again Catherine Swift dismisses Bradley's attempts to redress the imbalance between the literary and archaeological evidence by arguing that his 'archaeological' case study of Clonmacnoise remained heavily dependent upon documentary evidence which more properly referred to the eleventh and twelfth centuries rather than to any earlier period.[155] Turning her attention from the archaeology to the textual evidence, especially the *Hibernensis*, she criticized his use of seventh and eighth century texts to support what was fundamentally a tenth century model.[156] Finally, although, as we have already noted, she acknowledged a consistency of planning for these major ecclesiastical settlements, Swift rejected any significant difference in organisation between an ecclesiastical and secular site of similar standing; the sacral core of the former being paralleled by the domestic quarters of the most important inhabitant of the latter.[157]

The contribution of Doherty and Bradley to our understanding of the praxis of enclosure should, however, not be dismissed lightly but rather placed within the context of a developing understanding of the anatomy of the larger eastern settlement sites. Michael Herity, in a series of articles in the late 1970s and early to mid 1980s, identified not only a regularity of planning in the placing of the key sacral elements at the east end of the enclosure on western hermitage sites but he linked this to a similar development on the larger eastern mainland monastic sites, such as Clonmacnoise, where these key sacral elements also formed the spiritual and liturgical core of the enclosure.[158] Aerial and cartographic analysis by Leo Swan of several Irish mainland monastic sites including Armagh, Kells, Kildare, and Tuam, also strongly suggested that these sites followed a set pattern of layout similar to that found in the west[159] although Swan hesitated to use the

---

[154] Bradley (1998), 50; (1990), 40–41.

[155] Swift (1998), 105.

[156] Swift (1998), 118.

[157] Swift (1998), 106, 118.
See also Etchingham (2007), 1023–1024.

[158] Herity (1977), 15; (1984), 59–61.

[159] Swan (1985), 77–102.

label 'monastic' to describe the larger enclosed settlements preferring to regard them as 'villages' with churches and cemeteries.[160] Ann Hamlin in 1985 felt confident enough to assert that 'monastic settlement' was indeed an appropriate descriptor for such sites and that enclosure would have been normative for an eighth century settlement of this type.[161] She went on to describe in some detail the anatomy of the enclosed space and its subdivision into various zones including the *termon* and the *suburbana*.[162] She finished, however, with the telling admission that her reconstruction of a large monastery in the eighth century remained heavily dependant upon literary rather than material evidence. Hamlin also warned of the daunting task that awaited anyone who attempted to reconstruct the topography of religious settlement from the material remains alone given the early likely dependence upon wood as a building material and the prevalence of later accretions.[163] These admissions would seem to prefigure Swift's challenge to Bradley's 'archaeological' evidence for the 'monastic town' *schema*.

Yet despite Hamlin's caveats, and Swift's subsequent comments, more reliable archaeological evidence for large scale enclosure was beginning to emerge. We have already noted the problematic quality of the work carried out on the trivallate enclosure at Nendrum by Lawlor in the 1920s but excavation of several other large settlement sites had since taken place or was underway, most notably at Armagh, Whithorn, and Clonmacnoise. This evidence coupled with the growing body of survey evidence gave substance to Doherty and Bradley's 'canon of planning' if not to their advocacy of proto-urbanisation. There was now at least some archaeological evidence that suggested both large-scale enclosure and a sophisticated subdivision of space on a significant number of major sites which resonated with the textual depiction of the division of the enclosed space into *termon* and *suburbana*.[164] In the case of Armagh although the findings were not published fully

---

[160] Swan (1983), 276–277; Hamlin (1985), 282.

[161] Hamlin (1985), 280–282.

[162] Hamlin (1985), 297.

[163] Hamlin (1985), 297–299.

[164] Interestingly but rather speculatively it has been suggested that this tripartite division at Armagh was designed to facilitate a processional route from the inner enclosure outwards whereby relics could be carried on special occasions and the great feasts of the Church (Aitchinson (1994), 266–267). This has resonances with O'Reilly's observations about Adomnán's eyewitness account of the ending of a drought on Iona by the processing of Columba's relics through the fields (O'Reilly (1997), 90–94).

until the 1980s work actually began there in the 1960s; largely concentrated around the Scotch Street area of the city[165] and on Cathedral Hill.[166] Based on these findings, a tripartite topography for the settlement was suggested by Bradley, which clearly reflected the settlement morphology evidenced by the *Hibernensis* and cited by Doherty.[167] This was centred around an inner enclosure situated on the highest ground within an enclosed area known as 'the Rath'. Here were built the *damhliac mór* and two other churches known as *damhliac an tsabhaill* and *damhliac na toe* along with the *Céli Dé* priory (pre-AD919) and various other ecclesiastical buildings including at least one round tower. Located at the bottom of the hill and contained within a defensive outer enclosure was found a second annular zone. This outer ring was then divided into three distinct sections known as *trians*. In these outer areas were dwellings and a number of service industries needed to maintain the settlement. Beyond this boundary was the area now known as Scotch Street; a linear development based around the burial-ground of *fertae martyrum*.[168] Further, despite Swift's subsequent questioning of Bradley's dating parameters, Swan argued that the discovery of seventh-century material and artefacts within a possible enclosing feature indicated a potential early first millennium AD dating for an enclosed settlement at Armagh.[169]

The evidence for enclosure and zoning from Armagh might seem fairly straightforward and to sit convincingly within an emerging pattern for early historic Irish religious topography. Certainly Bradley was clear that the layout found at Armagh and other such sites paralleled that found on the smaller remote monasteries of the west coast of Ireland.[170] However, some of the evidence for large scale enclosure could be rather more enigmatic. Although multiple zoning was also uncovered by Peter Hill at Whithorn[171] it was on a potentially much larger scale.

[165] Lynn (1988), 69–84.
[166] Gaskell Brown and Harper, (1984).
[167] Bradley (1990), 42–43.
[168] Bradley (1998), 44.
[169] Swan (1985), 84.
[170] Bradley (1990), 46.
[171] Despite the 'mythic quality' of much of the literary evidence concerning Ninian (Hill (1991), 27) Whithorn was almost certainly part of the Irish Christian colonisation of Galwegian sites such as Ardwall Isle (Thomas (1967), 177, 183) although the present layout of the site is largely the result of the Northumbrian occupation of the site which began in AD731 with the arrival of the first Anglian bishop in the region, Pecthelm and ended by the mid ninth century (*HE*, 5, 23; Hill (1991), 33).

The original 1984-1991 excavations revealed the possibility of concentric enclosure lines, dating from Hill's Period 1/4, and therefore possibly pre-English and Insular in inspiration, which were interpreted as defining an inner precinct and an outer zone where craft activity took place.[172] From map evidence and a more recent walk-over survey there can also be discerned a previously unrecorded further outer boundary[173] but the additional and potentially much wider enclosure initially noted by Hill during the original excavations would appear to belong to a class of much larger enclosure for which parallels are hard to find.[174] Suggestions that work carried out at Clonmacnoise by a team headed by Heather King[175] might indicate enclosure on an equally grand scale need to be treated with some caution.[176] John Bradley and Harold Mytum have rightly drawn our attention to the presence of settlement complexity at Clonmacnoise over an extended area but there remains no substantive evidence of concentric rings of activity demarcated by boundary features as suggested for Nendrum. Attempts by Mytum and Michael Herity to construct universally applicable spatial models for large monasteries from the material evidence available at Clonmacnoise are of interest if in need of further work.[177] We shall examine these models and the other material and hagiographical evidence concerning Clonmacnoise in greater detail in the next chapter.

Setting aside their controversial espousal of an incipient urbanisation within early medieval ecclesiastical settlement, Doherty and Bradley's exploration of the internal complexity of large scale religious settlement offered a more evolved hermeneutic for understanding the conceptual framework within which enclosure and zoning arose. Nor was the 'monastic town' model without its supporters. Thomas Charles-Edwards was content both to use the term *civitas* to refer to major early Irish ecclesiastical settlement and to affirm their urban characteristics. Further, he interpreted the religiously inspired zoning of enclosed space not only as a response to the need to define areas of sanctuary but also as a reflection of the zoning of space around secular settlement. This pre-Christian praxis was then combined with the

---

[172] Hill (1997), 31–33.

[173] Lowe (2001), 5, 7.

[174] Hill (1997), 6 fig. 1.4; Lowe (2001), 5, 7–8.

[175] See King (1998) and (2003).

[176] Murphy (2003), 22–23.

[177] Bradley (1998), 45–47; Mytum (2003), 39, 53–57; Herity (1983), 50; Herity (1984), 59–61.

scriptural notion of the *civitas refugii* to give a foundation for ecclesiastical sanctuary. In order to secure the effective provision and protection of this form of sanctuary rules were required, such as those contained within the *Hibernensis*, to protect the holy ground from trespass and violation. As a result the layout of major ecclesiastical settlement was inevitably complex.[178] Yet even if one did not accept the 'monastic town' premiss, at the very least the model reflected a wider concern to marry the textual evidence with the extant topography and emerging archaeology of large scale religious settlement. This concern clearly influenced the work of a number of scholars who have turned their attention respectively to two of the most enigmatic of ecclesiastical settlement sites, Iona and Lindisfarne.

I.D. *Enclosure as an Expression of Sacred Identity*

In the popular imagination the settlements on Iona and Lindisfarne undoubtedly represent the embodiment of whatever we might mean when we talk of 'Celtic Christianity' and yet both are relatively uncharted territory archaeologically.[179] Iona's ongoing ritual role has meant that numerous accretions have been made to the site over the centuries. Constant rebuilding particularly during the Benedictine period has resulted in the destruction of much of the evidence of the early medieval settlement. Consequently most of the recovered material is late medieval.[180] The situation is exacerbated by the piecemeal nature of much of the archaeological exploration[181] and the fact that excavation is all but impossible underneath the present abbey.[182] On Lindisfarne the pre-conquest monastery was succeeded in the eleventh century (from when it became known as Holy Island) by a Benedictine cell of Durham cathedral. The site now consists of mainly post-conquest Benedictine remains with only a few carved stones visibly remaining of the original early church and monastery although there are extant remains of both phases outside the precinct of the later monastery. It is not the intention to rehearse here the morphology of each site in detail but it can be usefully observed that the history of

---

[178] Charles-Edwards (2000), 119–120.
[179] O'Sullivan, D. (1989), 128.
[180] O'Sullivan, D. (1989), 219–220.
[181] O'Sullivan, D. (1989), 216.
[182] McCormick (1997), 45.

enclosure on both sites is unclear and that, despite the clear textual evidence attesting to the praxis of enclosure on Iona in particular, the material evidence for its presence on either site is not substantive.[183]

Alongside the archaeological explorations of such sites there has been an attempt to decode the material remains of settlement using the literary evidence. Lisa Bitel, working within a fairly traditional hermeneutic, employed the extant hagiographical material to explore the ritual marking out and layout of monastic settlement in Ireland. For her the layout of the monastic architecture was dictated by the monks' desire to organize their settlements around the display of the founding saint's relics. She acknowledged the praxis of internal division, especially of the 'sacred core' from the rest of the settlement site; a process driven by the need to maintain a close physical but exclusive contact with the saint's remains.[184] Like Charles Thomas and Vincent Hurley before her she too viewed the curvilinear enclosure as the shape of choice for religious settlement and, like them, Bitel based this conclusion partly upon the textual evidence of the *Book of Mulling*.[185] We can note at this stage that even if we were to accept the argument that the *Book of Mulling* drawing does indeed depict an early medieval Irish monastic layout the potentially late dating would suggest that it was a product of, or a representation of, a physical reality rather than a planning blueprint. It is unlikely to have served as any form of inspiration.

---

[183] However, on Iona the one important early medieval feature that is still partly visible is indeed the *vallum*, the boundary bank surrounding the monastery enclosure (Thomas (1957), 10–14; Thomas (1971), 27–31), which was mentioned by Adomnán in his *Vita S. Columbae* (*VC*, 2, 29). In the case of Iona this *vallum* is apparently rectilinear (McCormick (1993), 78–108), enclosing an area of some twenty acres or more (Sharpe (1995), 66). This shape is unusual for an early medieval Irish monastic enclosure and attempts to find parallels in Ireland have failed despite Thomas's assertion to the contrary (Thomas (1971), 30–31). The most likely explanation is that the Columban monks utilized an already existing bank or ditch to form the western part of the monastic *vallum* (McCormick (1997), 49). The discovery of two deep ditches lying about 100m apart may suggest that the monastery was within a double enclosure (Barber (1981); Reece (1981)). This would of course parallel Irish sites such as Nendrum, Co. Down with its triple enclosure (Lawlor (1925)). Nevertheless, the evidence for a major banked boundary enclosure at Iona remains elusive (McCormick (1997), 51).

The physical evidence for enclosure on Lindisfarne also remains weak (O'Sullivan, D. (1989), 136). O'Sullivan has suggested two possible boundary patterns in the street layout of the modern village of Holy Island (O'Sullivan, D. (2001), 40).

[184] Bitel (1990), 57–82.

[185] Bitel (1990), 59; Thomas (1971), 38–40; Hurley (1982), 320.

In the case of Iona, given the relative paucity of material evidence, Aidan MacDonald in a series of three articles[186] has engaged the text of Adomnán's *Vita S. Columbae* as a prism through which we might be able to reconstruct and to interpret the anatomy of the Columban settlement on Iona using Adomnán's often incidental topographical and architectural references. Whilst recognising the limitations of what could be achieved[187] he also commented upon the potential enclosure and layout of the site with reference to a number of other key texts including Adomnán's *De locis sanctis* and the *Hibernensis*. Drawing on this evidence MacDonald depicted an Ionan layout which was defined by multiple enclosures and the segregation of space. The reference points for his discussion of the enclosure were Adomnán's two allusions in the *Vita* to the presence of an enclosing feature, first at Clonmacnoise and then at Iona.[188] Like Thomas before him, he was explicit that the primary purpose of enclosure was spiritual and legal rather than defensive and he suggested that, rather than constructing walls or banks and ditches, enclosure might be accomplished by the use of more temporary means such as wooden fences and hedges.[189] This would tie in to some extent with the material evidence from the site where the evidence for a major banked boundary enclosure at Iona remains ambiguous.[190] What *is* clear is that for MacDonald the ideal of enclosure was as important as its monumentality. This represented an advance on preceding scholastic approaches to enclosure which had tended to focus upon its structural form rather than its conceptual significance.

MacDonald also discusses the interior layout of the enclosed space. In particular he tentatively begins to explore the connections between the layout of Iona as described by Adomnán and the 'canon of planning' contained within the *Hibernensis* with its depiction of zoning and entry prohibitions and its reliance upon scriptural models of spatial planning.[191] Some of his most interesting insights concerning the spatial relationships within the enclosure are reserved for the area(s) known as the *platea* or *plateola*. Both terms occur in both the *Vita*[192]

[186] MacDonald (1984); (1997); (2001).
[187] MacDonald (1984), 299–300.
[188] *VC*, 1, 3; 2, 29.
[189] MacDonald (1997), 42.
[190] McCormick (1997), 49–50.
[191] MacDonald (1984), 294–296.
[192] *VC*, 1, 50; 3, 6.

and *De locis sanctis*;[193] used variously to denote a 'street' or an 'open area' or 'courtyard' but MacDonald argues that the monastic *platea* was more properly an open space or courtyard contained within the enclosure *around* which some or indeed all of the principal monastic buildings would have been arranged.[194] This, he suggests, might indicate that the *platea* would have been rectilinear rather than circular, inspired possibly by the Temple of Ezekiel and the heavenly city of Revelation. This leads him to question two common assumptions about ecclesiastical enclosure and layout; first that the layout within the *vallum* was haphazard, and secondly that enclosure, particularly in the sixth and seventh centuries, was always curvilinear.[195] Nevertheless, he remained unwilling to commit to the notion for any significant standardisation of layout in the pre-twelfth century period in Ireland while being suspicious of Thomas's advocacy of the relatively late widespread rectilinear enclosure of large sites.[196]

What is of particular interest, however, is MacDonald's suggestion that for Adomnán the whole of Iona was sacred space with the monastery and the island often being referred to as if they were synonymous This is reflected in the description of Columba's island monastery as '*insulanum monasterium*'.[197] Indeed he further suggests that in the *Vita* the Ionan landscape is viewed as a homology for the biblical terrain evidenced by the account of Columba's blessing of the community from the summit of the small hill overlooking the monastery, by Adomnán's allusion to Jacob's pillow (Genesis 28:10-19) in the story of Columba's pillow-stone,and by clearly recalling various scriptural accounts of mountain theophanies.[198] Support for a biblical context for Adomnán's reading of the Iona's topography is forthcoming from other scholars including Jennifer O'Reilly and Thomas O'Loughlin. For O'Reilly the description of the holy city in *De locis sanctis* can be seen to resonate with, or indeed pre-figure, the description of Iona found in the *Vita S. Columbae*. Jerusalem was not simply the birthplace of the church, the gate of heaven,[199] the centre of the world,[200] but was for Adomnán an archetype for his own monastic settlement,

---

[193] *DLS*, 1, 1, 9; 1, 6, 3.
[194] MacDonald (1984), 296.
[195] MacDonald (1984), 297.
[196] MacDonald (1997), 29; (1984), 297.
[197] *VC*, 2, 39; MacDonald (2001), 23–24.
[198] *VC*, 3, 23; MacDonald (2001), 24–25, 28–29.
[199] Genesis 28:17.
[200] Ezekiel 5:5.

a holy land on the very edges of Christendom.[201] O'Loughlin has further argued that the geographical organisation of both the *Vita* and his earlier work *De locis sanctis* mirrors the three stage missionary impulse depicted in Luke-Acts (Acts 1:8).[202] This is significant for Adomnán because it helps to place the conversion of Ireland and the Iona mission within a scriptural framework with Iona depicted as the *ultimum terrae*, the very end of the earth.[203] Such an understanding perceived Columba's mission as the fulfilling of scripture and placed Iona at the eschatological edge of the church's mission. We encounter a similar interpretation of the significance of the geographical location of the Irish church within Patrick's *Confessio* in which he too seeks to preach the gospel to the ends of the earth in order to usher in the Last Judgement.[204]

Having drawn our attention to the biblical resonances which reflect the sanctity of the island as a whole it is MacDonald's depiction of the gradation of holiness within the landscape that is especially pertinent. Once again employing Adomnán as a guide he depicts a tripartite division of sacred space on the island with the boundaries being marked by the foreshore of the island, the monastic enclosure, the *vallum*, and the enclosure containing the church and cemetery.[205] The textual evidence from the *Vita* to support this zoning is rehearsed elsewhere in the present study and does not need repeating in detail here. MacDonald revisits the connection between the Ionan sacred topography and the *schema* outlined within the *Hibernensis* and makes the further suggestion that the ultimate exemplar for the 'canon of planning' of both the *Hibernensis* and the *Vita* is the post-exilic ideal temple of Ezekiel with its tripartite division of the sanctuary as a whole into an outer and inner court and a temple which is then itself further subdivided into three, the *Ulam*, *Hekal* and *Debir*. He also draws our attention to other possible threefold spatial divisions within Ezekiel's scheme that might be pertinent.[206] The topographical resonance between the biblical and Irish evidence is clearly of interest and raises an intriguing possibility which will be explored in detail later.

---

[201] O'Reilly (1997), 86.
[202] O'Loughlin (1996), 114–115.
[203] O'Loughlin (1996), 116.
[204] Patrick, *Confessio*, 38–40.
See de Paor (1993), 96, 102–105; O'Loughlin (1997c), 14.
[205] MacDonald (2001), 15–19.
[206] MacDonald (2001), 29–30; 30 n. 39.

Following on from the work of Jennifer O'Reilly in relation to Iona, Deirdre O'Sullivan also adopts a scriptural hermeneutic in her discussion of Lindisfarne. She argues that the location of the settlement on Lindisfarne, despite its many echoes of Iona, is not simply a 'sentimental memorialisation of Iona' but also a 'potential embodiment of Mount Nebo, overlooking the plains of Jordan'.[207] Paralleling MacDonald's interpretation of the sanctity of the Ionan landscape O'Sullivan also appears to view the whole of the island of Lindisfarne as holy ground; island and monastery as one, although again the suggested presence of a *vallum* would indicate a desire to divide the landscape into zones.[208] Further, as O'Sullivan points out, we have in the case of Lindisfarne evidence of the opportunity for significant spatial isolation outside of any enclosing feature.[209] St Cuthbert's Isle is clearly a hermitage site rather than a monastic one[210] and may well be the place referred to by Bede in his *Vita S. Cuthberti* as being where Cuthbert lived in solitude before retiring to Farne Island.[211] Farne is, of course, also mentioned by Bede in both the *Vita S. Cuthberti* and in the *Historia ecclesiastica* where it was depicted as a place of solitude and retreat for both Aidan and Cuthbert.[212]

As with Iona, we have on Lindisfarne an example of a large scale settlement where the interpretation of the site has been predicated upon the assumption that enclosure took place. Yet evidence for this remains archaeologically elusive. O'Sullivan, relying upon the probability of a recurring Insular monastic typology, has argued that we should expect to find evidence for enclosure on the island on account of its Ionan antecedents and that therefore in this case it is the lack of evidence for enclosure that is noteworthy.[213] It has been assumed that the monastery of Aidan at Lindisfarne was modelled on that of the

---

[207] O'Sullivan, D. (2001), 36–37.

[208] O'Sullivan, D. (2001), 37–38.

[209] O'Sullivan, D. (1989), 136.

[210] Thomas (1971), 85, 87.

[211] *VCB*, 17.

[212] *VCB*, 17; *HE*, 3, 16; 4, 27.

[213] O'Sullivan, D. (1989), 136–138.
Our primary literary source for evidence that Lindisfarne was an island monastery is Bede who gives an account of the founding of the monastery by Aidan in AD634–635. Described by Bede as a monk of Iona and the first bishop of Lindisfarne, Aidan was sent to the area at the request of Oswald to convert his people to Christianity (*HE*, 3, 3). Aidan's mission was highly successful and Lindisfarne became a focal point for a flourishing Christian community (Herbert (1988), 44).

mother-house of Iona[214] although O'Sullivan acknowledges there is no substantive evidence to support this.[215] Also while listing the various textual references to the usual elements of religious settlement within the monastic space such as the watchtower,[216] a guesthouse,[217] a dormitory[218] and the construction of two churches including one built of oak by Finan, Aidan's immediate successor,[219] she accepts that attempts to reconstruct the possible contour of the *vallum monasterii* using natural features and present street layout are highly speculative and will remain so until a proper excavation has taken place.[220] Nevertheless, O'Sullivan remains confident that enclosure was practised on Lindisfarne and that its outline can potentially be traced through the street patterns of the village.[221] For O'Sullivan the praxis of enclosure on Iona and on Lindisfarne was not dictated solely or even primarily by the need to delineate space but rather by the dictates of ceremonial need. The boundary did not only define sacred space it was part of it. To illustrate the point she argued that Aitchison's observations about the circumambulatory layout of the tripartite ecclesiastical enclosure at Armagh potentially representing a processional way[222] might also be relevant for the layout not only on Iona but also for that discerned by her on Lindisfarne. She further proposed that it was the ceremonial need, the procession, which might define the boundary rather than the other way round. O'Reilly has also drawn our attention to the significance of ceremonial procession within the monastic community's life on Iona.[223] This suggestion clearly resonates to an extent with the textual evidence for the ritual marking out of sacred space but as O'Sullivan readily admits is without any corroborative historical evidence.[224]

Of course, one might expect the early medieval monastery on Lindisfarne to reflect not just an Ionan influence on its topography through Aidan but also to provide a bridge with the Anglo-Saxon world of Cuthbert. Thomas suspected that although the footprint of

---

[214] Thomas (1971), 38.

[215] O'Sullivan, D. (1989), 128.

[216] *VCB*, 40.

[217] *VCA*, 4, 16.

[218] *VCB*, 16.

[219] *HE*, 3, 17; 3, 25.

[220] O'Sullivan, D. (1989), 139–140.

[221] O'Sullivan, D. (2001), 40.

[222] Aitchison (1994), 267 fig. 59.4.

[223] *VC*, 2, 44; O'Reilly (1997), 93–94.

[224] O'Sullivan, D. (2001), 38–40.

the early monastery had been obliterated by the medieval foundation the first monastery on Lindisfarne was dependant upon the Ionan example for the choice of location and physical layout.[225] Following a similar line of enquiry O'Sullivan suggests that a nucleus of possibly Anglo-Saxon settlement can be detected within the area of the eleventh century priory and the raised rocky feature known as the Heugh.[226] Whether or not Lindisfarne might provide an archaeological bridge between the 'Celtic' and 'Anglo-Saxon' monastic worlds remains to be proved but the relationship between the early Irish enclosure of sacred space and that found in Anglo-Saxon England and further afield in Merovingian and Carolingian Gaul has attracted the attention of scholars.[227]

I.E. *Enclosure in a Non-Irish Context*

We have already noted that the historiography of Irish religious settlement has long been predicated upon two longstanding assumptions. First, that it was primarily monastic in character and, secondly, that it was in some way atypical in form and motivation in relation to religious settlement elsewhere within Christendom. This notion of monastic hegemony and its supposed vernacular peculiarity has contributed to a most unhelpful hermeneutic for the study of Insular Irish ecclesiology and archaeology, the tension between the abbatial and episcopal ecclesial paradigm being reflected not just in the historiography but also in the interpretation of the material evidence. We shall suggest, however, that far from being essentially 'irregular' early medieval Irish monasticism can be placed firmly within a western European milieu encompassing Anglo-Saxon England and Merovingian/Carolingian Gaul. From this one then may infer that the formative influences upon the layout of early Irish monastic settlement were not purely native but reflect a much wider understanding of the ordering of religious topography.

Many of the questions facing scholars of early Irish monasticism are equally pertinent for those studying its Anglo-Saxon counterpart.

---

[225] Thomas (1971), 37–38.

[226] O'Sullivan, D. (1989), 141. She also noted a more dispersed monastic settlement pattern than might have been expected.

[227] Gittos (2002), 205.

Foremost among these is the extent to which monasticism laid hold upon the English church in the early medieval period. David Dumville has maintained that nothing of any value can be said about church organisation in either Britain or Ireland in this period[228] but it is probable that the church in Britain in the immediate sub-Roman period was a continuation of its Roman forebear and therefore primarily diocesan based on proto-urban centres. Charles Thomas has argued that the fifth century church in northern Britain was a diocesan one with Ninian at Whithorn and Kentigern at Strathclyde.[229] It was a continuation of episcopal jurisdiction in Wales during this period that led Wendy Davies to make a distinction between the Welsh and Irish experience.[230] In the 800s Asser, the Welsh biographer of King Alfred, refers to his own church of St David as consisting of a *monasterium* and a *parochia*; which can be translated as a 'monastery and the jurisdiction of St David'. Asser also makes reference to the expulsion of bishops 'who were in charge of it'.[231] This would strongly suggest the existence of a pastoral unit led by bishops based within a monastery.

With respect to early English religious settlement the traditional hermeneutic certainly included a strong monastic element. Rosemary Cramp has drawn our attention to the monastic characteristics of a number of sites including Jarrow, Monkwearmouth, and Hartlepool.[232] Yet in recent years there has been something of a reaction against the confident assertion of monastic antecedents for a range of Anglian settlements. For example, Chris Loveluck's review of the excavation of Flixborough where the number of radical changes in the settlement pattern would mitigate against the use of any generic descriptor such as 'monastic' to denote the character of the site provides some substance for that caution.[233] However, two recent publications have been much more confident about asserting the reality of a monastic presence in an early English context. John Blair in his 2005 publication, *The Church in Anglo-Saxon Society*, has expressed some impatience with the reticence of modern archaeology to affirm the monastic credentials of significant sites such as Flixborough and Brandon[234] and

---

[228] Dumville (1984), 23.

[229] Thomas (1971), 14.

[230] Davies, W. (1992).

[231] Asser, *De Rebus Gestis Ælfredi*, 79.

[232] Cramp (1973).

[233] Loveluck (2001), 115, 120.

[234] Blair (2005), 211.

has asserted that monastic settlement after AD650 was normative for English ecclesiology; a view endorsed by Sarah Foot.[235] Ironically, Blair suggests that in many respects English church organisation resembled the unreconstructed model originally suggested for Irish church organisation in the same period.[236]

As with Ireland, what constituted a 'monastery' in Anglo-Saxon England is a challenging question. Sharpe's warning that the words used to denote churches do not necessarily indicate their function is apposite here.[237] Despite the picture of monastic uniformity painted initially by Bede in his *Historia ecclesiastica*,[238] and later retrospectively by the monastic reformers of the tenth century,[239] Blair argues for a much more diverse reality.[240] Echoing to an extent the Hiberno-Latin usage of the word *monasterium* in an Irish context, he deliberately interprets the Old English equivalent term *mynster* to denote a wide spectrum of settlement type ranging from the traditional form of monastery found at Jarrow-Wearmouth and the Frankish style double house at Whitby (both institutions of which Bede approved) to the aristocratic monasteries decried by Bede in his *Epistola ad Ecgbertum Episcopum*,[241] and to the double house at Coldingham of which Bede most certainly did not approve.[242] Within this inclusive discourse, Blair advocates an organic, eclectic model albeit with some native aspects[243] which he places firmly within a north-western European context;[244] a possibility hinted at by Sharpe in his discussion of pastoral care in early medieval Ireland.[245] In the Anglo-Saxon setting the dominant structural form is what Blair refers to as the 'monastic centre' which he describes as a 'complex, multi-functional ecclesiastical settlement'.[246] This model allows for the presence of the super-holy of the traditional hermeneutic alongside the more prosaic reality of everyday communal life.

[235] Foot (2006), 4.
[236] Blair (2005), 73.
[237] Sharpe (1992), 101.
[238] Foot (2006), 18, 23–24.
[239] Foot (2006), 13–14.
[240] Blair (2005), 3.
[241] Bede, *Epistola ad Ecgbertum Episcopum*, 12.
[242] *HE*, 4, 25.
[243] Blair (2005), 5.
[244] Blair (2005), 3, 73–74.
[245] Sharpe (1992), 108–109.
[246] Blair (2005), 74.

The etymological largesse of this approach does, however, seem to run counter to scholarly attempts in an Irish context to urge caution about the use of the term 'monastic'. Such a broad spectrum definition of the term 'minster' also effectively transmutes a discussion about possible monastic settlement and its form and impetus into a more generic discussion of religious settlement which is, of course, valid and of interest but needs to be admitted. This difficulty is indeed recognized and discussed by Sarah Foot in her 2006 work. Like Blair, she also acknowledges the diversity of ecclesiastical site type potentially embraced by the term *monasterium* or its Old English equivalent *mynster*.[247] Yet she is uncomfortable with the suggestion of uniform contemplative discipline implied by the term 'monastery', which she deems inappropriate in an Anglo-Saxon context. In a nicely nuanced approach to the issue she too opts to use the term 'minster' while in so doing she is clearly seeking to free it from the more forensic interpretations imputed to it by some scholars in recent years and to restore its original generic meaning as simply denoting a place of communal religious settlement.[248]

In seeking to define what a 'monastery' *was* attention inevitably focuses upon what a monastery *did* and once again a key issue was the provision of pastoral care. The dominant ecclesiological model of pastoral care within the early English church has been what has become known as the 'minster model'.[249] This strongly topographical model views the minster as the bed-rock of the later post-conquest English parochial system. It seeks to refocus our attention upon the need for ongoing pastoral provision within the church and to suggest that such work was being carried out by ordained clergy through the minster which in turn served as some form of proto-parish. However, more recently Blair and Foot have questioned both the rigidity of this model and the appropriateness of its application to a period as early as that under present discussion.[250] They argue instead in favour of a more diverse and flexible ecclesiological system in which the key structural element in this English variant of the para-monastic church remains the 'minster' but which also recognizes the ongoing pastoral role of the bishop and priest within a predominantly monastic structural setting.

[247] Foot (2006), 5–6, 19, 289.
[248] Foot (2006), 6.
[249] Blair (2005), 4; Foot (2006), 287–288.
See also Sharpe (1992), 84.
[250] Blair (2005), 3–5; Foot (2006), 6.

In the same vein Foot seeks to remind us that the modern dichotomy between 'religious' and 'secular' clergy is not appropriate for this period.[251] Rather pastoral ministry was almost certainly exercised by ordained clergy (although not exclusively) living alongside those called to a more contemplative lifestyle within the conventual setting of the minster.[252] Certainly this is a pastoral model which Bede seems to recognize although he appears to view pastoralia as the specific preserve of the ordained.[253] Such contemporary evidence must, of course, always be treated with caution but what we can be confident of is the fact that for both Blair and Foot any attempt to differentiate between types and functions of early English religious settlements on the basis of the nomenclature alone is anachronistic and unhelpful. Further, it is clear that the ecclesial reality in Anglo-Saxon England was much more diverse than originally depicted by Bede and subsequently accepted by scholars.

Another significant element within Blair's critique of early English religious settlement is his advocacy of a pan-northern European context for religious settlement. This is also initially attractive in that it would seem to resolve many of the issues around the genesis of monastic praxis in the west but is not without difficulties. Certainly from an Irish perspective the negation of the traditional nativist monastic model and the recognition of the vernacular aspects of religious settlement across Ireland, England, and Gaul are to be welcomed. Blair rejects the rigid ecclesial taxonomy imposed by the 'Celtic church' and the 'Roman church' typology of the traditional academic hermeneutic.[254] He is also cautious about the extent to which Irish ecclesial praxis can be argued

---

[251] Foot (2006), 6.

Despite Foot's confident statement, she does draw our attention to contemporary evidence of a perceived *functional* difference between ordained clergy and other religious (Foot (2006), 66–67). She further mentions that a distinction was drawn between 'canons' and 'regulars', secular and religious clergy, in the injunctions of the legatine council convened in AD786 during a visit by papal legates to England (Foot (2006), 58–59). There was also by the very early ninth century a clear differentiation made between religious who dwelt in minsters under the authority of the abbot and those secular clergy who lived in cathedral communities under the authority of the bishop (Foot (2006), 61–69). Her initial position that the term 'monastery' was an unhelpful descriptor of the type of English 'mixed' community found in this period still has force.

[252] Foot (2006), 290–291, 331–333.

[253] *HE*, 3, 26.

See Blair (2005), 164–165.

[254] Blair (2005), 5.

to have influenced its Anglo-Saxon counterpart.[255] His suggestion that the basic format of the circular or 'sub-circular' enclosure of bank and ditch cannot be viewed as a uniquely Irish signature but rather can be found throughout Western Europe in the period as well as in other parts of Britain[256] finds a resonance in Edward James's questioning of the possible Irish antecedents of the settlement layout at Solignac.[257] However, it remains unclear if Blair's alternative developmental model satisfactorily answers the conundrum as to which settlement type initially influenced the others or whether they are all dependant upon a common, probably Middle Eastern, root.

Of course a north European context for enclosure does not necessarily negate the traditional assumption that initially at least enclosure was an Insular Irish phenomenon. Blair certainly acknowledges that English ecclesiology drew on Irish, Gallic and Roman influences. In his discussion of enclosure, despite his espousal of a predominantly indigenous evolutionary model for English monasticism, he recognizes that a developmental impact of Irish praxis upon its English counterpart is likely.[258] In contrast Sarah Foot is reluctant in general to draw too close a comparison between Irish, Merovingian, and English religious settlement patterns not least because of the ever-changing and often insecure nature of the available evidence. She draws our attention to the often contradictory nature of the settlement evidence even from within a single geographical context. So, for example, she compares the textual description of the ordered layout of Jumièges to the archaeological evidence from Nivelles which reflects no discernible topographical plan as a warning against asking too much of the available evidence. She also reminds us that there is little connection to be made between the relevant monastic injunctions regarding communal living and any putative formal planning *schema* for enclosure.[259] However, elsewhere, again concurring with Blair's analysis, she willing acknowledges the influence of Irish and Merovingian monasticism upon the development of the Anglo-Saxon variety while asserting its ultimately unique English character.[260]

[255] Blair (2005), 45.

[256] Blair (2005), 198.
The seventh century monastery at Abingdon (founded AD675 by Cissa) is a good example of the presence of a circular enclosure in an English context (Horn (1973), 30).

[257] James (1982), 386.

[258] Blair (2005), 198.

[259] Foot (2006), 110.

[260] Foot (2006), 11, 11 n. 23; Blair (2005), 5.

The physical impact of the English ecclesial mixed economy upon the landscape is equally difficult to assess. The lack of archaeological evidence for English settlement in general is partly explained by the subsequent development of English sites to an extent not experienced in Ireland. Further, the textual and material evidence for English *religious* settlement is often no less ambiguous than its Irish counterpart. As in an Irish context it is frequently unclear in archaeological terms whether or not one is looking at traces of a religious settlement or rather at a high status secular site.[261] Issues surrounding the Christian and/or pre-Christian origins of sites such as Yeavering highlights effectively the variety of Christian and pre-Christian functions that can be evidenced on a single site.[262] We can be confident that the choice of site location was paramount and both the English and the Irish were attracted by physical isolation.[263] Sites such as that chosen by Cedd at Lastingham[264] and by Ecgberht for the minster of Æthelwulf[265] illustrate clearly the desire for wild and remote places.[266] Also like the Irish, the English seem to have been adept at recycling non-Christian secular and religious sites alongside the creation of new settlements. This may partly be the result of Gregory's famous letter of AD601 to Mellitus giving the papal imprimatur to this practice despite the Pope's initial desire to see such sites destroyed[267] and it is likely that a variety of prehistoric, Roman and Anglo-Saxon pagan sites were taken over for use as Christian settlements.[268] Blair has suggested it is even possible that English founders may have appropriated, sometimes violently, British Christian sites such as that at Whithorn which experienced an early eighth century Anglian takeover of a sixth to seventh century 'Celtic' settlement.[269] Another key issue for Foot was the

---

[261] Anglo-Saxon monasteries were of course not limited to England. We have literary traces of Anglo-Saxon monastic communities in Ireland including a community at Mag nEó na Sacsan (Mayo of the Saxons) formed in the aftermath of the synod of Whitby (Orschel (2001)) and at Rath Melsigi (see *HE*, 3, 27; probably Clonmelsh, Co. Carlow) where the Northumbrian Willibrord received his priestly training and was ordained in AD690.

[262] Blair (2005), 54–57.

[263] Blair (2005), 191–195; Foot (2006), 97–101.

[264] *HE*, 3, 23.

[265] Æthelwulf, *De abbatibus*, 6.

[266] Blair (2005) 191–193; Foot (2006), 99–101.

[267] *HE*, 1, 30.

[268] Blair (2005), 183–184; Foot (2006), 47.

[269] Blair (2005), 187.

extent to which the choice of terrain for a particular site might significantly affect its potential spatial organisation, especially in the case of
larger settlements.[270] We shall discuss the potential impact of the landscape upon the ordering of religious topography further in the next
chapter.

On the issue of enclosure in particular the difficulty in assessing the
Anglo-Saxon context again lies in the paucity of the evidence for the
practice of enclosure in comparison with Ireland. As Blair points out,
this is perhaps not surprising given that secular enclosure, even on
larger sites, was rare in Anglo-Saxon England in the sixth and early seventh century.[271] As a result Anglo-Saxon ecclesiastical enclosure would
appear to have been less developed than that found in Ireland where
the concept of defined sacred space is both textually and archaeologically prior. Gittos notes that the significant change in the Anglo-Saxon
perception of sacred space indicated by the development of an Anglo-
Saxon consecration rite for burial grounds was relatively late (ninth/
tenth century) compared to the highly developed Irish understanding
of sacred space which appears to have developed independently of other
models several centuries earlier.[272] Nevertheless, Blair has argued that
enclosure was as fundamental to Anglo-Saxon monasticism as it was to
its Irish counterpart[273] citing some of the limited literary evidence
attesting to English enclosure including the surrounding of Wilfrid's
minster at Oundle by a 'great thorn hedge' and Bede's disparaging reference, already noted elsewhere, to the decadent lifestyle of the 'aristocratic' monasteries, carried on *intra septa*, 'inside the monastic precincts'.[274]

Sarah Foot, citing much of the same evidence,[275] equally confidently affirms the prevalence of the practice of enclosure at 'all minsters',[276] further suggesting that it was usually curvilinear in form.[277]
She also argues for the internal subdivision of the enclosure into zones
of differing activity in much the same way as one would encounter in
an Irish context. These divisions served not only to separate various

---

[270] Foot (2006), 47.

[271] Blair (2005), 196 n. 66.

[272] Gittos (2002), 201, 206.

[273] Blair (2005), 196.

[274] Eddius Stephanus, *Vita S. Wilfridi*, 67; Bede, *Epistola ad Ecgbertum Episcopum*, 12.
See Blair (2005), 196.

[275] Foot (2006), 99–105.

[276] Foot (2006), 97.

[277] Foot (2006), 101.

functions but to keep the laity at bay and, in double-houses, to separate the sexes.[278] Again, as in Ireland, the focal point of the enclosed space was the church with the ancillary or support activities such as hospitality appearing to have been exiled to the perimeter of the community settlement perhaps so as not to disturb the monastic routine.[279] Blair also calls upon the hagiography for evidence of the ritual/liturgical marking out of the monastic space. This includes the anonymous *Vita S. Cuthberti* and the *Vita S. Guthlaci*, both of which portray their eponymous heroes as casting out demons from their solitary abodes,[280] and Bede's account of Cedd's founding of the monastery at Lastingham in the early 650s which includes a description of Cedd cleansing the site by prayer and fasting for the whole of Lent, a practice Bede ascribes to his Irish training.[281] Blair further points out that in an Anglo-Saxon context enclosing features were often conceived in the landscape rather than imposed upon it.[282] This would appear to accord with the material evidence from Whithorn and Hoddom where topography has been used to demarcate some of the boundaries.[283]

The fact that Blair and Foot have relied so heavily upon textual evidence in their work highlights effectively the limited and indeterminate nature of much of the material evidence for enclosure in an Anglo-Saxon context. Indeed we might justifiably ask to what extent we would be able to say much of significance about English religious settlement in this period without the various literary depictions to help us decode the sparse archaeology. This raises the further possibility that we are in danger of over-relying upon the often equally fragile textual material to impose a topographical *schema* upon what few archaeological remains we do have. As Lowe points out few Anglo-Saxon *valla* have been detected never mind excavated.[284] However, preliminary investigations would indicate the presence of *valla* at several

---

[278] Foot (2006), 106.

[279] Foot (2006), 108–110.

[280] *VCA*, 3, 1; Felix, *Vita S. Guthlaci*, 25–36.
See Blair (2005), 184.

[281] *HE*, 3, 23.
See Blair (2005), 191.

[282] Blair (2005), 196; see also Lowe (2001), 7; Gittos (2002), 207.

[283] Lowe (2001), 5, 7.

[284] Lowe (2001), 4.

sites including Glastonbury,[285] Whitby,[286] Jarrow,[287] Hartlepool,[288] and two Scottish Anglian sites, Hoddom[289] and Whithorn.[290] To this list might be added Flixborough[291] and Coldingham.[292] It is also possible that multivallation, or at least zoning, occurred at some of these sites including Whithorn and Hoddom[293] and possibly Coldingham.[294] In his discussion of Whithorn Lowe has focused on the possibility of multivallate enclosure on the site noting its relative rarity both in an Anglian context and on the scale putatively recorded at Whithorn.[295] The presence of multivallation at Whithorn and also possibly at Hoddom[296] would suggest, of course, that the *zoning* or subdivision of internal monastic space was known within Anglo-Saxon religious settlement despite Blair's assertion that 'English monastic sites seem not to display the clear-cut zoning of Irish ones'.[297] Describing the complex site at Whitby as 'rambling', he did nevertheless acknowledge the presence of a settlement nucleus based around the church; a pattern repeated on other sites.[298] Hill also attested to a regularly planned settlement pattern (centred upon axially aligned churches) at the core of the Northumbrian site at Whithorn which appeared to include zoning,[299] and Blair himself has drawn our attention to the presence of a church and mortuary chapel on the outer limits of the Whithorn settlement which he admits as being indicative of both regular planning and zoning of the enclosed space.[300] More recently Lowe has affirmed the presence of zoning within the enclosure of the Anglian settlement at Hoddom.[301]

[285] Cramp (1976).
[286] Peers and Radford (1943), 29; Rahtz (1976), 462.
[287] Radford (1954).
[288] Daniels (1988), 161–162.
[289] Lowe (2006), 32–38.
[290] Hill (1997), 31–33; see also 33 fig. 2.6.
[291] Loveluck (2001), 85.
[292] Stronach (2005), 415–419.
[293] Lowe (2001), 7–8.
[294] Stronach (2005), 419.
[295] Lowe (2001), 7.
[296] Lowe (2001), 5.
[297] Blair (2005), 222.
[298] Blair (2005), 199.
[299] Hill (1997), 40–48, 134–182.
[300] Blair (2005), 202.
[301] Lowe (2006), 187–190.

All of this emerging physical evidence may well allow us to be more confident about the early English context although as Cramp rightly points out even late seventh century Jarrow and Wearmouth, both under the control of the same abbot, Benedict Biscop, were sufficiently different in layout and design to suggest that planning uniformity was still to be achieved; a reality perhaps also indicated by the silence of the various monastic rules on the subject.[302] However, as we have just observed, a number of Anglian sites have since been excavated to varying degrees including, more recently, the sites at Whithorn[303] and Hoddom,[304] and although the results from the latter two sites have still to be fully assimilated it would appear that certainly by the eighth century an Anglian layout pattern was emerging, centred around the presence of axially aligned churches. This *schema* is a well attested feature of other Northumbrian monasteries and is found not only at Whithorn as noted above and potentially at Hoddom, but also at Hexham, Lindisfarne, and at Jarrow.[305] At Hoddom, as in an Irish context, the layout included the siting of a number of ancillary buildings such as sleeping quarters, kitchens and infirmary on the periphery of the settlement. In addition the guest-house, again reflecting Irish praxis, would appear to have been placed near the entrance to the enclosure.[306] The putative presence of the axially aligned churches at Hoddom along with a curvilinear enclosure, the peripheral service buildings and the internal zoning of the site have been interpreted by Christopher Lowe as being indicative of monastic settlement[307] although his explanation for

[302] Cramp (1973), 123.

None of these foundations would have ascribed to a particular monastic observance for England in this period knew no normative monastic rule. The various rules which pertained in Anglo-Saxon England prior to the Benedictine hegemony imposed by Edgar in the tenth century (Foot (1990), 49, 51), such as the highly composite rule used by Benedict Biscop at Wearmouth-Jarrow (Foot (2006), 56), were not a response to, or prescribed by, any centralized norm (Blair (2005), 80–81). However, although the route by which the Benedictine Rule came to England is far from settled its influence upon monastic life in England by the seventh century was considerable (Foot (2006), 50–56). At both Wearmouth-Jarrow and Melrose the Rule of St Benedict appears to have existed alongside more vernacular creations and to have been revered and followed (Foot (2006), 55–57). We are also told in the anonymous *Vita S. Cuthberti* that the monks of Lindisfarne followed Cuthbert's own rule alongside the Rule of St Benedict (*VCA*, 3, 1; see Foot (2006), 56).

[303] Hill (1997).

[304] Lowe (2006).

[305] Lowe (2006), 194–195.

[306] Lowe (1999), 50.

[307] Lowe (2006), 195.

the motivation behind the praxis of subdivision is somewhat disappointingly pragmatic and markedly un-theological.[308]

It is interesting in the light of earlier discussion to note that the existence of multivallate enclosure on Anglian sites such as Whithorn and Hoddom has been interpreted by some as resonant of Irish sites such as Nendrum and Kilmacoo.[309] Further, despite Helen Gittos's warning against the danger of interpreting the monastic topography of sites such as Whithorn through an Irish prism,[310] Blair has highlighted two possible sources of inspiration for English monastic layout, both with potentially Irish resonances.[311] The first is the square based on the heavenly Jerusalem of Revelation ch. 21 with its lavish description of walls and gates. He is clearly comfortable with the notion of the 'monastic town' as a physical expression of a seventh century sacred ideal, drawing comparison with Cogitosus's depiction of Kildare.[312] Blair suggests that while mid seventh century England could not boast any settlement that could be labelled a city or even a town it was within these reclaimed ruins that the English discovered this 'symbolic Christian urbanism'.[313] We have already noted the potential significance of the 'holy city' motif for the Irish church and certainly the adoption of Roman fort sites such as that at Reculver, given by Ecgbert of Kent to the Christian priest Bassa in AD669, or Bradwell-on-Sea, given by Sigeberht of Essex to Cedd, may reflect this ideal but attempts to suggest that the re-use of these Romano-British ruins might have been inspired by the biblical ideal of the heavenly Jerusalem as the paradigm of the holy city need to be approached with caution. Gittos's advice against over-reliance on an Irish monastic paradigm as an interpretative tool would also suggest that comparison with Cogitosus's description of Brigid's Kildare may be unhelpful.[314] Further, there remains much more work to be done on the possibility of widespread rectilinear planning on non-Roman sites.[315]

The second archetype is the circle, redolent of the archetypical early medieval Irish monastic site. However, Blair is almost certainly

[308] Lowe (2006), 190.

[309] Lawlor (1925); Hurley (1982), 314.
See Lowe (2001), 7.

[310] Gittos (2002), 207.

[311] Blair (2005) 196–198

[312] Cogitosus, *Vita S. Brigidae*, 32; Blair (2005), 246–248, 262.

[313] Blair (2005), 249.

[314] Blair (2005), 198; Gittos (2002), 207.

[315] Blair (2005), 188, 196.

correct when he asserts that the division of sacred space into concentric circles as inspired by Ezekiel's vision of the Temple, and described in the eighth century Irish collection of laws, the *Hibernensis*, had limited impact on England and that there is very little evidence, before the tenth century, for defined territorial circuits on the Irish pattern.[316] The circular multivallate layout detected at Whithorn and Hoddom may simply reflect Irish custom in an area which was almost certainly part of the Irish Christian colonisation of Galwegian sites[317] and should not be extrapolated to suggest an Anglian 'canon of planning'. What might be asserted with greater confidence is that both Anglian and Irish religious settlement planning, to what ever degree it might have existed, reflects an attempt to express materially an idealized notion of religious space.

I.F. *Conclusion*

This survey has illustrated that until very recently the focus for scholarly endeavour in this field has indeed been the reconstruction of the morphology of settlement rather than the discernment of its motivation, with a concentration upon the archaeology. With regard to the former there would now appear to be a general academic consensus, with a few notable exceptions, that the topography of religious settlement reflected a consistency of layout at least in Ireland. Whether or not we can label that settlement type as 'monastic' with impunity is still a vexed issue but it is clear that religiously inspired settlement across a wide geographical and historical spectrum manifested a topographical regularity. Further, in terms of the textual evidence we have drawn attention to an increasing recognition of its potential as an interpretative tool in understanding the extant archaeology. This shift has been determined partly by a more theologically aware approach on the part of historians such as Doherty and MacDonald who have sought to marry the material and literary evidence for religious settlement and to place it in a theological context which might have been understood by those who created it.

We shall return to an analysis of the motivation and causal factors behind early medieval Irish religious topography at a later stage in our

---

[316] Blair (2005), 222.
[317] Thomas (1967), 177–183.

discussion. It is probably sufficient at this point simply to note the self-evident nature of Lisa Bitel's comment that 'no plan of St Gall exists for early Ireland'[318] and to make clear that the 'canon of planning' which I am seeking to advance, perhaps only one among several possible determinative influences upon the sacred topography of the early Irish church, is not dependant upon the existence of such a document or blueprint. Our next task now will be to examine the archaeological and textual material to verify the evidential base for the thesis that early medieval Irish religious settlement adhered to a regularity of layout. We will look in detail at what might helpfully be referred to as the 'anatomy' of religious settlement including a discussion of its key constituent elements. This will involve examining a number of typologically iconic sites and establishing a range of diagnostic markers to denote the presence of religious settlement. We will then seek to verify that these markers exist across a wide spectrum of sites of varying dimension and location in order to elucidate what I have chosen to call a 'canon of planning' which we will then set against the textual evidence, both canonical and hagiographical, relating to religious settlement. Whist recognising that it is seldom possible to marry convincingly the documentary and material evidence I will hope to establish that both attest to a topographical regularity that can best be explained by setting it within a theological and scriptural context which makes sense not only of the extant topography but resonates with the extant textual depiction of the form and spirituality of early medieval Irish religious settlement.

---

[318] Bitel (1990), 74.

2. 'SLAB-SHRINES AND ORATORIES' : THE ANATOMY OF RELIGIOUS SETTLEMENT WITHIN THE EARLY MEDIEVAL IRISH CHURCH

The contention of this study is that Irish religious space was ordered to a regular pattern. In order to establish the validity of this contention we need first to examine the available material and textual witness to the topography of Irish religious settlement in the early medieval period so as to confirm the likely existence of this pattern. Archaeology provides substantive evidence of the recurring presence of a number of physical diagnostic features such as enclosures, oratories, cross-slabs and founders' shrines. Archaeology also provides some insight into their spatial relationship and any possible pattern that can be discerned. A problem arises, however, with the archaeological evidence when it is used simply as evidence for spatial arrangement, without reference to relative chronology. It is also necessary to date developments precisely. So I will seek to secure some reliable dating parameters for these elements and for their sites. The literary evidence will be used not only to supply an historical context for these sites but to help us begin to explore some of the philosophical and/or theological factors which have helped to determine what these key elements were and how they relate to each other. The coming together of these two types of evidence should at least allow us to then make some observations about how and why these sites were constructed and ordered in the manner they were. However, I am very conscious of the potential shortcomings of both types of evidence, and there will be an assessment of the validity and reliability of both the archaeology and literary witness.

We shall look at four sites which I have selected as paradigmatic of the most common forms of religious settlement encountered in Ireland in this period. These will be used as exemplars against which typologically similar sites can be assessed. The four selected sites have been chosen primarily because they each contain the key diagnostic elements under discussion, and, I will argue, reflect a similar spatial organisation despite their obvious disparity in terms of size and location, and type of religious settlement. They include two island sites; Skellig Michael, an exemplar of the numerous remote island monasteries located off the western coast of Ireland, and High Island, whose likely pre-Christian antecedents place its enclosure history within a distinct subset of island and mainland settlement types. We shall also examine two mainland sites, the small south-west Irish settlement at Reask and the large midland monastic community of Clonmacnoise.

We have already referred briefly in the literature survey to the morphology of a number of sites. We shall now examine the layout of the selected sites in detail in an attempt to establish the extent of any spatial regularity across a dimensional, geographical and chronological spectrum of settlement type. Alongside this review of the archaeology of settlement we shall consider the surviving literary testament to the praxis of enclosure and zoning, much of which is implicit or indirect but nevertheless of value. In this context we also need to recognize the often idealized nature of the depiction of religious space encountered within the textual evidence, especially within hagiography. If there really was a scriptural 'canon of planning' which helped to determine early Irish religious topography we would expect to see evidence, textual and physical, that this canon could survive the impact of other potential influences, both native and non-native. This would include the ability of the canon to adapt to the demands of the varied and often irregular geography of the area occupied by the early Irish church. Therefore among the key issues to be explored is the extent to which the geography of a site impacted upon the settlement topography or, expressed in another way, we need to determine the extent to which any putative 'canon of planning' was required to accommodate the vagaries of the chosen terrain. Here the crucial issue is the balancing of factors such as the demands of the canon with the demands of the terrain. We also need to explore how the demands of an emerging Christian landscape impacted upon the pre-existent secular and pagan built environment. In other words to what extent was any embryonic Christian topographical *schema* able to absorb, or adapt to, the architecture and settlement morphology of a pre-Christian past? The expectation is that our discussion will confirm that the anatomy of early Irish settlement did indeed reflect a recognisable and consistent pattern. The task of the following chapter will then be to establish wherein the genesis of this pattern might lie.

2.A. *The Anatomy of Settlement: An Archaeological Context*

The first of our chosen sites is Skellig Michael, one of the numerous island settlements which exist along the west coast of Ireland. Situated almost 12 miles off Bolus Head on the tip of the Iveragh peninsula, Co. Kerry, this is undoubtedly the most desolate and windswept of the island sites with the extant features appearing to cling to the rock face. The site has been subjected to two main episodes of investigation.[1] The first, more survey than excavation, conducted by de Paor in the 1950s and the second a more extensive and in depth exploration in the 1980s focusing in particular on the South Peak of the island, led by Walter Horn.[2] As a result of these we have a comprehensive picture of the extant topography of the site. The main ecclesiastical settlement is on the broad north-eastern summit, over six hundred feet up, and is built on a terraced shelf contained within a series of enclosure walls. On the main terrace the remains consist of six dry-stone corbelled cells[3]

---

[1] There has also been some recent small-scale excavation for conservation purposes under the direction of Edmund Bourke but this has not yet been published (*pers comm* J Wooding).

[2] For a detailed drawing of the layout of the South Peak settlement see Horn, Marshall, and Rourke (1990), 48–49. The same work also contains a striking aerial view of the main monastic site (Horn, Marshall, and Rourke (1990), 8–9) which gives the reader some idea of the exposure endured by the residents. A sketch plan of the main site, accompanied by a number of helpful sketch drawings, can be found in de Paor (1955).

[3] The six cells on the main terrace, with the possible exception of one, are dry-stone and corbelled. The cells are all rectangular on plan and roughly externally curvilinear although two of the cells (labelled A and E, see de Paor (1955), 176 fig. 2; O'Sullivan, A. and Sheehan (1996), 278 fig. 178) are larger, squatter and more markedly rectangular on both exterior and interior plan. Cells A and E measure respectively 4.65m × 4.1m and 3.8m × 3.8m internally. A further difference is that they are constructed of smaller stones and not the massive blocks used for the other cells (O'Sullivan, A. and Sheehan (1996), 284–285).

and a small oratory of similar construction[4] as well as the mortared church of St Michael and a *leacht*-like structure known as the 'Monk's Graveyard'. On the upper terrace are situated a second smaller oratory and the remains of a *necessarium*, similar to that of Cuthbert on Farne. The third and lower terrace is also enclosed by a stone wall and may have included an area for cultivation ('The Monks Garden').[5]

Separated from the north summit by 'Christ's Saddle' is the South Peak where are situated the remains of a tiny hermitage, arguably the most precarious in western Christendom, visible only to God.[6] On the way up to the hermitage just beyond the Needle's Eye is located a small u-shaped enclosure containing the remains of a crude stone cross which has been interpreted by the excavators as a possible *locus* for prayer and meditation.[7] The hermitage is once again constructed on three terraces but this time with room for only one person.[8] Incredibly, given the size of the area concerned, here was found evidence of enclosure as well as an oratory,[9] a cross-inscribed slab (bearing a developed ring cross), a *leacht* and a reliquary shrine.[10] The most significant of the three terraces, named the Oratory Terrace by Horn, Marshall and Rourke,[11] contains the *leacht*, cross-inscribed slab and the oratory situated to the right of the enclosure. There is also evidence of paving leading from the door of the oratory to the *leacht*.[12] The eastern

---

[4] The two oratories on the main settlement site are similar in style to that found at Gallarus but more roughly built (de Paor (1955), 185). The larger of the two oratories, situated on the main terrace, is of dry-stone corbelled construction and measures 6.1m × 4.25m externally and 3.65m × 2.45m internally. It is aligned SW-NE. The walls have average basal thickness of 1.1m.

The second oratory is situated on the upper terrace some distance apart from the rest of the enclosed buildings. It is of similar construction to the larger oratory and measures 4.05m × 3.85m externally and 2.45m × 1.85m internally. It is aligned E-W (O'Sullivan, A. and Sheehan (1996), 283–284). Both oratories are rectilinear in plan (O'Sullivan, A. and Sheehan (1996), 278 fig. 178).

Underlying the walls of the larger oratory on the north side are the traces of a rectangular *leacht* measuring 0.6m high and 3.65m long (O'Sullivan, A. and Sheehan (1996), 285).

[5] O'Sullivan, A. and Sheehan (1996), 279–280; Henry (1957), 113–129.

[6] Horn, Marshall, and Rourke (1990), 84.

[7] Horn, Marshall, and Rourke (1990), 30–32.

[8] Herity (1983), 35.

[9] Measuring 2.1m wide (O'Sullivan, A. and Sheehan (1996), 288).

[10] For a detailed description of the site see Horn, Marshall, and Rourke (1990), 30–65; O'Sullivan, A. and Sheehan (1996), 287–288.

[11] Horn, Marshall, and Rourke (1990), 37.

[12] Horn, Marshall, and Rourke (1990), 40.

extension to the Oratory Terrace contains three orthostats which have been interpreted as the remains of a reliquary shrine.[13] A further almost inaccessible terrace (the Outer Terrace) is isolated from the rest of the hermitage and despite traces of wall and cell its purpose remains uncertain.[14] Again it is possible that the lowest of the three terraces (the Garden Terrace) was used for cultivation but this is speculative.[15]

Skellig Michael (referred to simply as Skellig) is named several times in the documentary sources from the eighth to the eleventh centuries and it may have had connections with the *Céli Dé* revival of the late eighth century.[16] However although we have fairly rich literary source material for the later period in the history of the settlement there is something of a documentary *lacuna* before the late eighth century. Thus the legendary attribution of the founding of the ecclesiastical settlement to the sixth century St Fionan should be treated with extreme caution.[17] The first reliable reference to a religious settlement on the Skelligs is that found in the entry for 28th April in *The Martyrology of Tallaght* which makes mention of the death of a monk referred to as 'Suibni of the Sceilg'.[18] A number of Viking raids on the island are also recorded, the earliest reliable testimony being found in the *Annals of Inishfallen* for the year AD824.[19] The *Annals of Inishfallen* also record the death of Aed Sceilic in the year AD1044.[20] We have two further annalistic references from the *Annals of the Four Masters*, an

---

[13] Horn, Marshall, and Rourke (1990), 50.

[14] Horn, Marshall, and Rourke (1990), 60.

[15] Horn, Marshall, and Rourke (1990), 36.

[16] Edwards (1990), 118.

[17] This legend is first mentioned by Charles Smith (Smith (1756), 113). See Horn, Marshall, and Rourke (1990), 10 n. 3.

[18] *The Martyrology of Tallaght* is reputed to have been compiled by the monk Máel-ruain at his monastery at Tallaght near Dublin towards the end of the eighth century (d. AD792) (Horn, Marshall, and Rourke (1990), 10). However, Ó Riain has dated both this text, and the closely related *Martyrology of Oengus*, to c. AD828–833 (Ó Riain, 1990, 38).

[19] *Annals of Inisfallen, s.a.* 824.3.

This raid is also recorded in both the *Annals of Ulster* and the *War of the Gaedhil with the Gaill* in almost identical wording under the entry for AD821–823 (see Horn, Marshall, and Rourke (1990), 79 n. 19).

All the extant manuscripts of the Irish annals are, of course, late. The earliest, the *Annals of Inisfallen*, date from no earlier than the end of the eleventh century. This is not to deny that the annals undoubtedly draw upon a much earlier textual witness which Charles-Edwards has labelled the *Chronicle of Ireland* (Charles-Edwards (2000), xix) but they should be treated with caution.

[20] *Annals of Inisfallen, s.a.* 1044.7.

entry for AD950 which refers to Skellig, and one for AD1044 which again refers to the death of Aed Sceilic, but this time referring to the settlement as Skellig Michael.[21] This change of nomenclature is potentially supported by the archaeological evidence from St Michael's Church which dates architecturally from this period and may well have been built to celebrate the new dedication.[22] Gerald of Wales, writing in the twelfth century, also makes mention of St Michael's Church on the island.[23]

In archaeological terms the dating of the buildings on the main monastic site is more challenging and again there are certainly no traces of any sixth century presence. Among the cells the design and plan of the two larger cells (A and E) would suggest that they are not contemporary with the other buildings within the enclosure. Their difference in type (externally and internally quadrangular in plan) and their perimeter position probably indicate a later development.[24] The other cells may well represent a stage of evolution from the traditional beehive hut (internally quadrangular in plan but externally curvilinear) to the more rectilinear plan of the cells on the periphery. Excavation evidence from other sites has suggested a transition from a round to a rectangular plan for domestic construction during the eighth and ninth centuries.[25] A number of factors would suggest that the South Peak hermitage is also of ninth century origin. Horn, Marshall, and Rourke have suggested that these might include the Skellig monks' espousal of the Culdee revival of the late eighth century and the impact of the Viking raids on the monastery in the early ninth century.[26] The material evidence is perhaps more compelling. The cross-slab discovered on the oratory terrace was a developed ring cross and therefore can be fairly safely dated to the ninth century. An unusual feature is its presence on an erect as opposed to a recumbent slab but this is by no means a unique occurrence.[27] Secondly, the hermitage must have post-dated the main monastic site for why else would one have constructed a hermitage on the South Peak rather than the more accessible north-east

---

[21] *Annals of the Four Masters, s.a.* 950.3 and *s.a.* 1044.3.
The *Annals of the Four Masters* is a seventeenth century composite document, based largely upon the *Annals of Ulster*.

[22] Horn, Marshall, and Rourke (1990), 10; see also O'Keefe (1998), 114.

[23] Giraldus Cambrensis, *Topographia Hiberniae*, 63.

[24] de Paor (1955), 185.

[25] Lynn (1978), 29–45.

[26] Horn, Marshall, and Rourke (1990), 76–80.

[27] Horn, Marshall, and Rourke (1990), 80–81; Lionard (1961), 126–127.

summit. The technical difficulties of building the hermitage would strongly indicate the presence of an established monastic settlement with sufficient manpower and expertise.[28]

With regard to enclosure Bitel describes the layout on Skellig Michael as being 'confined by walls that wandered seemingly aimlessly among the island's rocks', acknowledging that this was almost certainly because the terrain would allow no other option.[29] Nevertheless, despite the precipitous and challenging nature of the physical environment of Skellig Michael it would appear that a determined attempt had been undertaken to conform to construct a recognisably sub-circular enclosure. This is not to deny that landscape could and did affect settlement layout both here on Skellig Michael and elsewhere.[30] We can see similar accommodation to the strictures of the physical environment being made on other sites. For example, as we shall discuss further below, Herity has suggested that the sub-circular shape of the enclosure on High Island was prescribed by the terrace and lake to the east and south of the feature; a view endorsed by Marshall and Rourke.[31] A similar adaptation to the topographical demands of the terrain is also probable for the sites at Killabuonia and Reask[32] and in an Anglian monastic context it has been argued strongly that the shape of the enclosure at Hoddom was determined by the course of an old river terrace.[33] As we have already observed what is key here is the balance being struck between the pressure being exerted by the putative 'canon of planning' and the difficulties presented by the natural topography. The fact that on Skellig Michael, and on other sites, we see such a conscious effort to adhere to a shared topographical *schema* is arguably powerful evidence of the importance of this schema in the religious mind-set of those who built these settlements.

Again in relation to the enclosed space itself we see a conscious effort on Skellig Michael to conform to a topographical pattern discernible elsewhere. The suggestion, also made within an English context, that the natural topography of a site, rather than any idealized concept of holy space, would be the determinative factor in its internal

---

[28] Horn, Marshall, and Rourke (1990), 71–73.

[29] Bitel (1990), 59.

[30] A phenomenon acknowledged by Charles Thomas (1971), 38.

[31] Herity (1977), 14; Marshall and Rourke (2000), 46–47.

[32] Herity (1977), 14; Fanning (1981), 155.

[33] Lowe (2006), 186.

spatial organisation[34] is not borne out by the material evidence from this topographically very challenging site. Instead we encounter on Skellig Michael a recurring settlement pattern which is based around an open space to the west of the oratory; a feature found both on the smaller western sites such as Reask and on the larger eastern monastic settlement sites such as Clonmacnoise, Kells, Armagh and Glendalough.[35] Within this space, adjacent to the oratory's west end, were to be found the key sacral elements such as the oratory, a cross-slab, and a founder's tomb.[36] Admittedly on occasion the terrain and the environment could enforce a deviation from this *schema* even in an Irish setting. So for example the atypical siting of the oratory on Church Island on the west of the site was almost certainly dictated by the topography of the island. However, here the final location of choice was not a good one as the west of the oratory eventually collapsed because it was built on sand;[37] this despite clear scriptural warning as to the hazards of such a location. Another determining factor for the morphology of the Church Island site may have been the exposure to the elements whose fierceness was attested to by the excavators. This was subsequently proposed as a possible reason for the eventual construction of an enclosing wall.[38] However Church Island is the exception that proves the rule. On Skellig we encounter the more orthodox layout form with the larger of the two oratories, situated to the east of the enclosure, facing west into an open space which Herity refers to as the *plateola*; the intrusive presence of St Michael's Church being of course a much later addition.[39] To the north and south of the oratory are cross-slabs which have been interpreted by Herity as being indicative of the presence of an ancient tomb-shrine.[40] Even more strikingly, on the South Peak hermitage site one encounters a similar layout albeit on a much reduced scale. Here the oratory faces west into an open space containing fragments of a cross-slab. At the other end of this open area are the remains of a *leacht*.

[34] Foot (2006), 47.

[35] Herity (1984), 57, 60–61.

[36] Herity argues (Herity (1984), 61) that this is potentially an early phenomenon on the strength of archaeological evidence from Reask and Clonmacnoise, and the textual references in Adomnán's *Vita S. Columbae*, written of course no later than AD704, to a *plateola* at Iona and to a potentially more substantial *platea* at Coleraine (*VC*, 3, 6; 1, 50).

[37] O'Kelly (1958), 118.

[38] O'Kelly (1958), 127.

[39] Herity (1984), 58, 64.

[40] Herity (1983), 35.

At one level it could be argued that Skellig Michael is atypical of western Irish insular *or* mainland religious settlement. Its iconic status only serves to highlight the disparity between it and its neighbours. Few of the surrounding settlements with the possible exception of the mainland site at Killabuonia[41] are built on the same scale and its extreme eremitic statement marks it out from otherwise typologically similar island sites. Yet on Skellig Michael we have substantive material evidence indicating not only the presence of enclosure but also the zoning of space on both *loci* of settlement on the island reflecting practice elsewhere. So if Henry, Herity, and Fanning are all correct in their assumption that western sites adhered to a pattern of layout based around what I have labelled a 'sacred core'[42] or what Fanning refers to as a 'sanctuary',[43] consisting of some or all of the following, an oratory, a founder's tomb, and a cross-slab, then there is clear evidence to suggest that the settlements on Skellig Michael, despite the terrain, attempt to adhere to that layout not just on the larger monastic site but also on the site of the tiny South Peak hermitage. This contention is strengthened by the evidence of other planning resonances with other broadly typologically similar sites. For example to the east of the South Peak oratory is a reliquary shrine enclosed within a separate rectilinear area; a feature found on several others sites although the rectilinear (as opposed to A-shaped) shape of the shrine itself is apparently unique.[44] Further, the presence of paving leading from the oratory to the *leacht* is also paralleled elsewhere including Reask and Church Island.[45] These shared features, in addition to the topographical parallels with other sites, place Skellig Michael within a *schema* of layout which is established and distinctive.

High Island (Ardoileán), the second of our island sites, is also situated off the west coast of Ireland, one of a long line of islands stretching from Inishtrahull off the coast of Co. Donegal down to Clear Island off Cork. Situated beyond Friar's Island it is surrounded by other similar church and hermitage islands such as Inishshark, Inishbofin, Inishturk and Omey Island (more properly a tidal islet). There

---

[41] Herity (1983), 35.

[42] Henry (1957), 45–46, 154–155; Herity (1984), 57; (1977), 15, 17.

[43] Fanning (1981), 150.

[44] Horn, Marshall, and Rourke (1990), 50.
Slab-shrines will be discussed in greater detail below in relation to that found at Reask.

[45] Fanning (1981), 78–79, 150, 158; O'Kelly (1958), 75–76, see also plate XVII.

have been a number of survey based investigations of High Island but the most in-depth survey was conducted by Jenny White Marshall and Grellan Rourke over a twenty year period culminating in the publication of the results of their research in 2000.[46] The island has an area of some thirty two hectares (eighty acres) with three possible landing-places (the most frequently used two at the eastern end of the island and a third at the south-western end of the island near the settlement but virtually inaccessible in poor weather). There are stone remains of varying antiquity scattered all over the island but the main monastic settlement is situated in a hollow at the south-western end of the island beside the larger of the two permanent fresh water lakes on the island.[47]

Undoubtedly the most striking feature of the site is the significant enclosing wall whose shape, described as 'rhomboid' by Herity[48] and perhaps more accurately as 'ovoid' by Marshall and Rourke,[49] would appear to have been partly dictated by the surrounding terrain; a probability we have already noted. This wall boasts a thickness which varies from 2.5m to 3.2m[50] and has several structures attached to it or contained within it. Attached to its south-eastern entrance are three structures including a sub-rectangular *clochán*, possibly a guesthouse[51], a small chamber (described by Herity as a possible porter's lodge) and a *leacht*.[52] Also built into the enclosure wall on the north side is a small corbelled cell, similar in position to that noted on Reask by Fanning.[53] Described by Petrie as the 'Abbot's cell',[54] this tiny cell was externally circular above plinth level but rectangular in plan. It could not have

[46] Marshall and Rourke (2000), ix.
An aerial view of the entire island gives a clear picture of the scale and location of the High Island settlement (Marshall and Rourke (2000), 9). Further on in the same work there is also provided a sketch plan of the topography of the settlement itself (Marshall and Rourke (2000), 47).
[47] Marshall and Rourke (2000), 7–8.
[48] Herity (1990), 185.
[49] Marshall and Rourke (2000), 46.
[50] Marshall and Rourke (2000), 180.
[51] The guesthouse measures between 2.9m and 3.8m in width and 3.7m and 4.3m in length. This is approximately the same size as the potential guesthouse excavated by O'Kelly on Church Island (O'Kelly (1958), 124–125).
The *leacht* is 1.4 × 1.06 × 0.55m in dimension (Marshall and Rourke (2000), 49–51).
[52] Herity (1990), 187; Marshall and Rourke (2000), 49.
[53] Fanning (1981), 90–92.
[54] Petrie (1845), 420.

held more than one monk and may therefore have belonged to the abbot who would in all probability have had his own cell.[55] Intriguingly within the wall itself are two wall chambers which may well have been used for storage although their purpose remains obscure.[56]

The diameter of the enclosure is estimated to range from 24 to 37m.[57] It contains a number of buildings, including an oratory, a second cell, a *leacht* and a cross-slab. The building known as the oratory, a small single cell building aligned east-west measuring internally 3.15m × 3.50m (11sq m)), is enclosed by a second substantial enclosure wall,[58] a feature found on a number of sites including Reask and Gallarus. It is unusual however in that it is built too close to the oratory to allow for any significant burial ground within the church enclosure although at the exterior of the east end of the oratory are a number of burials of lintel-cist type. The presence of a founder's tomb-shrine at the east gable of the oratory, attested to by Petrie, is no longer visible and may have since been destroyed.[59] The oratory and its enclosure on Caher Island in Co. Mayo are very similar in layout but here there is sufficient space to allow for burials to take place.[60] The second cell, incorrectly referred to locally as the *scriptorium*, is larger than the 'Abbot's Cell' measuring 2.63m × 2.74m internally and like its smaller counterpart is externally rounded but rectangular in plan.[61] It is however too small to have served as a refectory or communal room and is more likely to have been the dwelling place for two or three monks.[62] The cross-slab situated to the south of the church enclosure bears a developed expansional cross design and is one of a group of the most distinctive and elaborate cross designs on High Island and rare on Ireland's west coast.[63]

As with so many of these island settlements dating remains a challenge.[64] A strong local tradition associates the island with St Féchín of Fore who founded several monasteries including Fore in Westmeath

[55] The 'Abbot's Cell' measures only 2.1m × 1.90m internally (Marshall and Rourke (2000), 130).

[56] The larger chamber measures roughly 6.3m long × 1.3m wide and the smaller 2.2.m long × 0.65–0.95m wide (Marshall and Rourke (2000), 56–59).

[57] Marshall and Rourke (2000), 46.

[58] Marshall and Rourke (2000), 71.

[59] Marshall and Rourke (2000), 105.

[60] Marshall and Rourke (2000), 122.

[61] Marshall and Rourke (2000), 133.

[62] Marshall and Rourke (2000), 136.

[63] Marshall and Rourke (2000), 165, 167.

[64] See Herity (1990), 179; Marshall and Rourke (2000), 8–11.

and Cong in Mayo. The *Annals of Ulster*[65] tell us that Féchín died of the yellow plague in AD664[66] and he is mentioned in two festologies under 20th January, *The Martyrology of Tallaght* and *The Martyrology of Oengus*, both dating from the late eighth or possibly early ninth century.[67] The only reference we have to Féchín visiting High Island is in a Latin Life of Saint Féchín (compiled by John Colgan in 1645 from Irish sources, translated by him into Latin, and also entered in Colgan's *Acta sanctorum* under the heading of 20th January).[68] The dating of the monastic settlement therefore remains uncertain. The longest term occupation seems to have been that of the monks but there is no hard archaeological evidence for a seventh century foundation date for the monastic settlement and most of the church complex that is still visible belongs to the period from the late tenth century to the twelfth century, the last phase of monastic occupation.[69] No structure outside the enclosure wall can be dated although the 'guesthouse' is probably at least ninth century; a dating suggested by its transitional external and internal rectangular plan with external rounded corners. As we have already noted from our discussion of Skellig Michael excavation evidence from other sites has suggested a transition from a round to a rectangular plan for domestic construction during the eighth and ninth centuries[70] and therefore this building is unlikely to have been much earlier than ninth century. It also is unlikely to be much later than the ninth century because of its relationship to the watermill (*c.*AD770-850?) which it clearly predates.[71] The cells within the main enclosure cannot be dated with any precision, although they are again transitional in design and similar in style and plan to each other and therefore probably contemporary. The cell traditionally designated as the *scriptorium* is built right up against the church enclosure wall and clearly post-dates it. Both cells are perhaps tenth to twelfth century in date.[72]

---

[65] The accuracy of the dating within the *Annals of Ulster* has long been a subject of debate; the *sub anno* references below are as found in the text.

[66] *Annals of Ulster, s.a.* 665.3.
See also *Annals of the Four Masters, s.a.* 664.1.

[67] Marshall and Rourke (2000), 9–11; see also n. 18 above.

[68] Anon., *Vita S. Fechini*, 22.
See Marshall and Rourke (2000), 11.

[69] Marshall and Rourke (2000), 217, 222.

[70] Lynn (1978), 29–45.

[71] Marshall and Rourke (2000), 52, 217–218.

[72] Marshall and Rourke (2000), 135–136, 222.

Other possible dating parameters such as the oratory and the cross-slab are also unreliable. The oratory as we now see it is a composite building of at least three different churches with the final mortared masonry church dating from as late as the eleventh or twelfth centuries although the misalignment of the axis of the church enclosure wall with the walls of the last and still visible church probably signify the priority of the enclosure wall.[73] The burials at the east end of the oratory, the earliest of which has been carbon-dated to no earlier than the late ninth century,[74] appear to have been high status burials and indeed it is likely that one of the graves is that of St Gormgal who died in AD1017; an event recorded in the *Annals of the Four Masters*[75] and in the *Annals of Ulster.*[76] There is also no trace of a monastic burial ground on High Island and most of the cross-inscribed slabs were not found *in situ*. Herity's contention that the cross-slab south of the church can be fairly reliably dated to the late seventh century[77] runs contrary to Lionard's argument that the developed expansional cross design of which this cross is an example was an Irish innovation originating at Clonmacnoise no earlier than the ninth century.[78] It is therefore unlikely to have reached High Island earlier than the tenth century.[79] The incised Latin style quadrilobal cross found in the church enclosure wall predates the wall[80] and may be as early as the eighth century.[81]

In terms of the enclosure history of the site on High Island the size of the enclosing wall is of significance. The dimensions of this wall have been noted earlier and it is clear that it was a substantial structure.[82] Hughes has made the observation that size mattered as a status symbol[83]

---

[73] Marshall and Rourke (2000), 73, 121–124.

[74] Marshall and Rourke (2000), 121.

[75] *Annals of the Four Masters, s.a.* 1017.2.

[76] *Annals of Ulster, s.a.* 1018.1.
The abbot's death is also mentioned in the *Annals of Inisfallen* for the year AD1018 (*s.a.* 1018.3) and in the *Chronicum Scotorum* for the year AD1016. His death must have been a significant event and High Island an important monastic site to warrant inclusion in the annals.

[77] Herity (1977), 13.

[78] Lionard (1961), 133–136.

[79] Marshall and Rourke (2000), 169.

[80] Marshall (1989), 153.

[81] Marshall and Rourke (2000), 163–164.

[82] Just how substantial these enclosing walls could be is evident from an aerial photograph of the cashel at Inishmurray (O'Sullivan, J. and Ó Carragáin (2008), 12).

[83] Hughes (1972), 164.

but it is also possible that these walls started life as secular defensive structures and were taken over by monastic settlements at a later date. One possible example of this practice is Iona, where McCormick has shown that the reason for the strangely rectilinear enclosure is most likely that the monastery used an already pre-existing Iron Age earth bank for the western part of the *vallum*.[84] There are several other examples of this development among the small monastic sites off the west coast of Ireland where stone has been used rather than earth bank which is the more usual method of enclosing ecclesiastical sites. Indeed these stone boundaries, both ecclesiastical and secular, are found almost exclusively on the west coast of Ireland.[85] Illauntannig, also known as St Senach's Isle, one of the Magharee Islands off the coast of Co. Kerry, contains a massive, possibly pre-Christian, stone cashel measuring between 4.5m and 5.5m in width.[86] Within this impressive structure are situated two stone oratories, three beehive huts, three burial sites, and a cross.[87] A further possible example is that of Inishmurray, an island off the coast of Co. Sligo, where the cashel is also of an unusually large size (53m in diameter) with extant walls between 2–5m in basal width and over 4m high.[88] Unfortunately, as we have already admitted with reference to Nendrum, the putative secular origin for the apparently typologically similar cashel on Inishmurray also remains insecure.[89] Nevertheless, it has been suggested that the use of stone combined with the exceptional dimensions and the presence of wall chambers and other uncommon features would strongly indicate that structures such as that on High Island were secular in origin.[90] This raises the possibility that the reason for the building of such massive walls on sea-girt islands was that these enclosure walls were originally defensive in purpose. This is of course a very different purpose from the majority of enclosing features surveyed at

[84] McCormick (1993), 78–107; (1997), 49–51.

[85] Marshall and Rourke (2000), 177.

[86] O'Kelly (1973), 13; Marshall and Rourke (2000), 180.

[87] Harbison (1992), 174.

[88] Leask (1955), 13; Edwards (1990), 118.

[89] Hamlin has argued that the 'commonly accepted 'pagan' secular origin' for both Nendrum and Inishmurray remains unsubstantiated by the archaeological evidence (Hamlin (1985), 283). For an equally cautious approach see also Harbison (1976), 65–67. The more recent exploration of Inishmurray by O'Sullivan and Ó Carragáin has also failed so far to provide any material evidence to support Thomas's initial suggestion of a pre-Christian origin for the cashel (O'Sullivan, J. and Ó Carragáin (2008), 33).

[90] Marshall and Rourke (2000), 180–181.

early Christian sites which are on the whole not substantial enough to serve any function other than a delimiting and /or apotropaic one.

As we have already noted, Marshall and Rourke have further suggested that High Island and Illauntannig were not merely cashels but represent an altogether more impressive form of enclosure known as the 'Western Stone Fort'.[91] The Western Stone Fort Project led by Claire Cotter has identified a category of walled enclosures, distinctive in location, size and design from other cashels and promontory forts. So far about 30 of these forts have been identified including Staigue, Co. Kerry and Dún Aonghasa on the Aran Islands, Co. Galway. Extensive excavation of several of these forts, including Cathair Chomáin in Co. Clare, and Leacanabuaile, Dunbeg and Loher in Co. Kerry had originally suggested a foundation date in the early Christian period but more recently discoveries at Dunbeg and Cathair Chomáin has led to a possible pre-Christian dating.[92] The revised dating indicated by these new finds has been supported by other indications of a pre-Christian origin for these forts, including wall chambers, mural steps, interior terracing and *chevaux de frise*, sharp angular stones set upright to deter attack.[93] Indeed it has been argued that architecturally these forts would appear to be similar to the Iron Age forts found along the western European seaboard.[94]

However, it is the fieldwork on the seven large stone forts on the Aran Islands, and in particular on the layout of the largest of these Dún Aonghasa on Inis Mór, with an enclosed area of 5.7 ha (14 acres), which has thrown up the most interesting of features. Here the three main enclosing walls divide the enclosed space into three distinct areas. The outer enclosure is a rough inhospitable area surrounded by *chevaux de frise* and perhaps used for cattle grazing. The middle area is of better quality and here there are traces of huts. Finally the inner space, surrounded on three sides by a huge wall, 4.9m high and 5.8m thick, is raised above the rest of the enclosure. This was perhaps a later addition and may have served as a focal point for ritual activity during the Iron Age.[95] The radio carbon dating evidence for Dún Aonghasa suggests that people had settled here by the Late Bronze Age and that

---

[91] Marshall and Rourke (2000), 180–181.

[92] Cotter (1994), 24–25.

[93] Marshall and Rourke (2000), 181.

[94] Cotter (1994), 25.

[95] The layout of the fort complex at Dún Aonghasa is described in detail, with accompanying aerial photographs, in Cotter (1994), 26–27.

the site remained inhabited right up until the sixth century AD, well into the early Christian period. Further, it is generally thought that the majority of the extant standing remains are Iron Age in origin thus potentially providing material evidence of trivallate enclosure and zoning within a pre-Christian context.[96] We shall discuss further the possible influence of pre-Christian and/or secular architectural modes upon the Christian landscape in chapter four.

Despite the divergent settlement histories of Skellig Michael and High Island and their differing topographies the two island sites attest to a common understanding of how religious space might be enclosed and subdivided and of the constituent structural elements necessary for Christian communal living. Both settlements evidence the significance of enclosure and zoning for the early church and adhere to the putative but apparently widespread pattern of religious settlement layout which focuses upon the 'sacred core' at its centre and exerts a centrifugal pressure upon the domestic and ancillary activities of the community such as habitation, hospitality and cultivation which are placed towards or on the periphery. That said, there has been a strong tendency within Irish Insular studies to view island monasticism as typologically distinct from other expressions of the coenobitic and eremitic life of the early medieval Irish church. Our next task will be to establish that far from being peculiar the layout of island-based religious settlement reflects a much wider understanding of how religious space might be enclosed and organized and exhibits similar material characteristics and spiritually motivated architectural aspirations to its mainland counterpart. Further, there is no evidence to suggest that the religious topography of early Irish religious settlements was especially in debt to the layout of somewhere like Clonmacnoise any more than it was to somewhere such as High Island or Skellig Michael. Of course issues of scale and settlement complexity are pertinent here as many of the island sites are primitive in layout and construction but this is also true of many of the mainland settlements as we shall see below in our discussion of Reask. If we are seeking to challenge the misconception that the morphology of island-based religious settlement was a western Irish eccentricity divergent from the rest of the early medieval Irish ecclesial establishment then we need also to challenge the equally unhelpful canard that the typology of mainland religious settlement in the period was reflected solely by the presence of the larger developed

---

[96] Cotter (1994), 27–28.

monastic sites such as Clonmacnoise and Armagh. In order to do this we need to establish that in many ways all of these sites, regardless of location and scale, were typologically similar in that they contained not only the same diagnostic elements but also exhibited a similar spatial organisation. We turn our attention first to the small mainland site at Reask in Co. Kerry.

The site at Reask is located about 1.25m east of the village of Bally-ferriter on the highest point of this low-lying area. There is virtually no historical evidence relating to the site[97] and prior to its excavation by Tom Fanning the only visible elements were the cross-inscribed pillar, another smaller cross-slab, and some traces of the cells.[98] We have already noted in the previous chapter some of the issues arising from the site at Reask including the difficulties in establishing a clear rela-tionship between the development of the habitation area and the cemetery and the likelihood of a two phase construction history on the site. Nevertheless a tentative developmental framework has been posited.[99] The initial settlement activity was focused on the centre of the enclosure and probably included the cell labelled G by Fanning and possibly also cell F (see Fanning (1981), 71 fig. 2).[100] This first phase would have included the primary enclosure wall and the lintel grave cemetery.[101] The enclosure wall was oval-shaped, containing an area measuring 45m × 43m in diameter. The remains indicate that origi-nally it was a substantial cashel-type wall with an average thickness of

---

[97] Fanning (1981), 70.

[98] Cuppage (1986), 337.

Fanning however provides a detailed sketch plan of the Reask site (Fanning (1981), 71 fig. 2). His excavation report also contains a series of photographs of the site and its environs which help both to locate the settlement within the Co. Kerry countryside and to give a sense of the scale of the enclosure and buildings. These plates can be found in the appendix at the end of the work.

[99] Fanning (1981), 157–158.

[100] Cuppage (1986), 338.

Cell F is situated to the south-east of the enclosure and is a small dry-stone circu-lar structure measuring 3.5m diameter internally and with an average wall thickness of 0.9m. Like cells A and B on the site it has an *annulus* similar to that found on Church Island (O'Kelly (1958), 70). The entrance on the north-eastern side faces the oratory (Cuppage (1986), 340; Fanning (1981), 96, 154).

Cell G is located in the north-eastern sector and is a sub-circular dry-stone structure with a 2.75m internal diameter and an average wall thickness of 0.9m. This structure and the enclosure wall may well have been contemporary and thus this cell may well have been the earliest (Cuppage (1986), 340–341; Fanning (1981), 97–98, 154).

[101] Fanning (1981), 157–158.

2.20m and a height of perhaps 1-1.5m[102] although it is still significantly smaller that the cashels on Illaunntanig or Inishmurray and more comparable to that found on Church Island. Its sub-ovoid shape is unusual but not unique and as we have already suggested probably determined by the terrain.[103] The lintel grave cemetery consisting of forty two graves aligned east-west follows the curve of the enclosure wall, suggesting that it post-dates the wall.[104] Most of the graves are of the lintel type, originally covered with slabs but now mainly not *in situ*. There are also a small number of dug graves. The cemetery was marked out by inscribed pillar stones and centred upon the slab-shrine and perhaps a wooden oratory.[105] This slab-shrine is situated in front of the later oratory and on the same level as the lintel-graves and therefore may have indicated the western boundary and focus of the primary cemetery.[106]

At Reask we can see the importance of the 'sacred core' to the rest of the settlement site. The burial of the saint credited with the foundation is marked in some manner at over thirty sites[107] and the slab-shrine at Reask is of the type described by Thomas.[108] The A-shaped slab-shrine is a common form of monumental tomb and similar examples can be found at a number of south-western Irish sites including Church Island[109] and in a non-Irish context possibly at Ardwall Isle.[110] Several of these structures are contained within a rectilinear enclosure. This combination of A-shaped slab-shrine and rectilinear enclosure is found at several sites throughout the Dingle and Iveragh Peninsulas, including Caherbanagh, Illaunloughan, Killabuonia, Killoluaig, and Kilpecan. Indeed the presence of a slab-shrine without the accompanying rectilinear enclosure elsewhere in Ireland has been seen as a partial importing from the Irish South-West.[111] As we have already observed,

---

[102] For a detailed description of the enclosure wall and its dimensions see Fanning (1981), 98–100; Cuppage (1986), 337, 339.

[103] Fanning (1981), 155; O'Kelly (1958), 76.

[104] Cuppage (1986), 339–340; Edwards (1990), 117.

[105] Fanning (1981), 79, 157–158; Cuppage (1986), 339–340; Edwards (1990), 117.

[106] The structure consists of a small paved area measuring 0.9m × 0.85m surrounded by two erect slabs and two small corner pillars (Cuppage (1986), 340).

[107] Herity (1983), 26.

[108] Thomas (1971), 141–142.
See Fanning (1981), 85.

[109] O'Kelly (1958), 87–90.

[110] Herity (1983), 27; Thomas (1971), 142–143; Thomas (1967), 141, 168–169.

[111] Thomas (1971), 142–143.

Thomas has interpreted these enclosures as direct imitations of Mediterranean *cella memoriae*, dating them as early as *c*.AD600. Of the other elements of note here at Reask the cross-slab situated between the slab-shrine and stone oratory is not in *situ* but the striking cross –inscribed pillar, known as the Reask Pillar, located at the north-eastern corner of the site, would appear to have been in *situ* and may well have marked the northern boundary of the lintel grave cemetery.[112] It is an early cross form found in Ireland whose design could potentially be as early as the sixth or seventh century. It has a Maltese style cross within a circle and bears the inscription DNE (*Domine*) in an early form of Irish script.[113]

Some 2 metres to the south of the slab-shrine and on the same level are two post-holes. While this might indicate the priority of a wooden structure, possibly an oratory, pre-dating the extant stone structure this remains highly speculative.[114] The relative chronologies of wooden and stone churches are complex and we shall discuss the matter in greater detail in a later chapter but whatever its pre-history the erection of the small stone oratory over some of the early lintel graves marked the beginning of the second major phase of building on the site.[115] The small dry-stone structure at Reask is aligned east-west and constructed of fairly small stones. It measures 3.5m × 2.7m internally and the walls are on average 0.9m thick surviving to a height of 0.45m. Interestingly the external corners at the eastern end are rounded whereas the western end would appear to have been sharp angled in plan. This would suggest that the structure originally had a corbelled roof like the beehive huts rendering it somewhat different in style from the Gallarus-type oratory.[116] However, in size and general plan the oratory has parallels with those on Skellig Michael (de Paor (1955), figs. 8 and 9) and at Inishtooskert and Kildreelig. The oratories at Gallarus, Kilmalkedar, Ballymorereagh, Valentia, Church Island, Temple Cashel, and Killabuonia are bigger and of larger plan.[117] At the same time as the oratory was built an internal dividing wall was also constructed crossing the site from the south-west in a curve, dividing the enclosed area into two parts. This wall has an average basal width of 1.4m (2m at its widest) with a break halfway along probably to allow

---

[112] Fanning (1981), 86; Edwards (1990), 117.

[113] Fanning (1981), 139–141, 152; Cuppage (1986), 342.

[114] Fanning (1981), 86; Edwards (1990), 117.

[115] Fanning (1981), 158.

[116] Fanning (1981), 76–78; Cuppage (1986), 340.

[117] Fanning (1981), 149.

access from cells A and B to the oratory.[118] It clearly post-dates the occupation deposits and post-holes of the central area and was almost certainly built to portion off the sacred area from the habitation area. A similar feature is present at other Kerry sites including Gallarus, Killabuonia, Illaunloughan and Loher and elsewhere such as Inishmurray in County Sligo, Caher Island in Co. Mayo and High Island off the coast of Co. Galway.[119] As noted in earlier discussion the presence of paving leading from cells A and B, through the gap in this wall, to the oratory echoes similar finds on Church Island and Skellig Michael.[120]

The dating of the site at Reask is no less challenging than Skellig Michael. The dating of the oratory at Reask is uncertain because of the lack of any hard archaeological evidence but it probably dates from midway in the development of the cemetery and so could lie anywhere on a spectrum stretching from the early seventh or eighth century to as late as the twelfth century. Attempts have been made to date the oratory more closely using Gallarus as a benchmark, but are doubtful as the generally accepted eighth century date for that oratory is not based on solid evidence. If the presence of Romanesque features can be taken

---

[118] Fanning (1981), 78–79; Cuppage (1986), 339.

This second phase probably also included the building of cells A and B. Built into the enclosure wall on the northern side these two conjoined clochans post-date the primary enclosure wall (Fanning (1981), 90–92). They may well have been situated at the original entrance to the enclosure and were enclosed by a later separate dry-stone wall with a basal width of 1.5m. These dry-stone corbelled huts were both circular in plan; Cell A, with an internal diameter of 5.5m and an average wall thickness of 1m is slightly smaller than B whose internal diameter was 6.1m with average wall thickness of 1.3m. The internal diameter of Cell A would suggest that it had a thatched roof whereas Cell B shows signs of corbelling in its upper walls (Cuppage (1986), 339–340) although Fanning has suggested that the large diameters of both structures would indicate a thatched roof (Fanning (1981), 90). As noted above, both cells were surrounded by an *annulus* (Cuppage (1986), 340; Fanning (1981), 89–90).

Also built into the primary enclosure wall, and therefore post-dating it, were two further conjoined cells C (ovoid; internal diameter 3.6–4m, average wall thickness of 1.15m) and D (circular; internal diameter 4.5m, average wall thickness of 1.1m) (Cuppage (1986), 340). Cells C and D structurally predate A and B and may well date from later on in the first phase (Fanning (1981), 158).

Another structure built into the primary enclosure wall in the southern sector is cell E, a small rectilinear structure measuring 5.5m × 2.8m internally with an average wall thickness of 1.4m. There is no dating evidence available for structure E other than it is later than the main enclosure wall (Cuppage (1986), 340; Fanning (1981), 94–96, 154).

[119] Fanning (1981), 150; Cuppage (1986), 339.

[120] Cuppage (1986), 338, 339; Fanning (1981), 78–79, 150, 158; O'Kelly (1958), 75–76; Horn, Marshall, and Rourke (1990), 40.

as a possible indicator of a later date the lack of any extant Romanesque features on the Reask oratory alongside its smaller and more primitive form might suggest that it is relatively early but this remains speculative.[121] However the building sequence at Reask would support Harbison's theory that stone oratories were far from being the primary structures that Leask and others believed them to be.[122] More helpfully carbon-dating of charcoal from a hearth in the primary central area of the enclosure has given a radiocarbon determination of AD385 plus or minus 90 years and Bii ware sherds from both the central occupation levels and from the upper fill of the slab-shrine in the burial area indicate a *terminus ante quem* of before c.AD600.[123]

As to typology and function Reask is arguably more securely typical of its land-based class of small religious settlement than Skellig Michael is of island monasticism. Despite poor and often non-existent documentary evidence Ó Carragáin has identified 66 typologically similar settlement sites in the western extremes of the Iveragh and Dingle peninsulas.[124] Interestingly, Fanning entertained the possibility of Reask as 'a mainland version of the monastic enclosures on Skellig Michael and Church Island' although he does register some reservations about the comparison.[125] He also recognized that the settlement boasted characteristics which fitted both the 'developed cemetery' model posited by Thomas and the confident monastic taxonomy of Rahtz.[126] Yet as we acknowledged earlier the origins of the site are unclear and whether its history was predominantly ecclesiastical or secular, let alone monastic, remains uncertain.[127] The presence of Bii imported pottery might indicate an ecclesiastical usage and the discovery of pottery remains found on the site including Bii amphorae and E ware (Gaulish) potentially date occupation to between the late fifth and seventh centuries.[128] The absence of grave goods and the context, plan and alignment of this cemetery would also indicate an early Christian origin within a fifth to seventh century band. The spatial relationship with both the slab-shrine (contemporary with the lintel graves and

---

[121] Fanning (1981), 150–151; Harbison (1970), 57–58.

[122] Harbison (1970); Leask (1955), 21.

[123] Cuppage (1986), 338, 340.

[124] Ó Carragáin (2003), 127–129.

[125] Fanning (1981), 158, 159–160.

[126] Thomas (1971), 51; Rahtz (1973), 126; Fanning (1981), 158.

[127] Edwards (1990), 118.

[128] Thomas (1981), 13, 24; Campbell (2007), passim.

containing a piece of Bii ware) and the cross and spiral pillar which appears to be *in situ* and whose design could potentially be as early as the sixth or seventh century would support this early dating.[129]

Whether Fanning is correct in his tentative suggestion that Reask might indeed represent the very earliest phase of monastic activity in Ireland dating from the sixth and seventh centuries[130] or whether Reask is simply a 'proprietary church',[131] the domain of a hereditary church family and similar in type to Church Island,[132] rather than a monastic or eremitic settlement there is convincing material evidence to confirm that the layout of the site conformed to a pattern echoing that found elsewhere in south-western Ireland on both island and mainland sites. Ó Carragáin notes that of the 66 substantial sites detected by him the majority boasted similar dimension and elements to that at Reask including an enclosing feature of approximately 37 metres in diameter and various diagnostic features such as domestic buildings, a cross-slab, burial ground and dry-stone church at the east end.[133] Further the siting of the Reask oratory at the east end of the enclosure may also be interpreted as indicative of a planning consistency. In this case the siting of the oratory is almost certainly determined by the location of the primary cemetery. This would indicate that the location of the oratory was determined by the locus for the primary cemetery and not *visa versa* and a similar building sequence can be seen on several sites including Church Island and Ardwall Isle.[134] Although it is possible that this settlement pattern was a regional aberration restricted to the Iveragh and Dingle peninsulas Ó Carragáin and Herity among others are keen to place it within a wider context, arguing that the 'canon of planning' traced out by the remains of these small remote south-western settlements is also visible on the larger eastern mainland sites.[135]

Our fourth site to be considered is therefore that at Clonmacnoise in Co. Offaly, the very embodiment of the prosperous midland monastic settlement. The earliest plan of this monastery in existence is an engraving from the second edition of James Ware's *De Hibernia et*

---

[129] Cuppage (1986), 340; Fanning (1981), 152; Edwards (1990), 117.

[130] Fanning (1981), 160.

[131] Mytum (1992), 63.

[132] Ó Corráin (1981), 339; Hurley (1982), 324.

[133] Ó Carragáin (2003), 128–129.

[134] Fanning (1981), 150; O'Kelly (1958), 62 fig. 2; Thomas (1967), 139 fig. 26.

[135] Ó Carragáin (2003), 147; Herity (1977), 15.

antiquitatibus eius disquitiones published in London in 1658.[136] The enclosure and structures depicted are much as we would recognize them today although three of the churches marked no longer survive and only two crosses, including the Cross of the Scriptures, are shown.[137] The site at Clonmacnoise is focused upon the stone church at its centre, the *Daimhliag Mór*.[138] Known also as the cathedral, the earliest significant commentary on the *Daimhliag Mór* by Petrie correctly dated the foundation of the present building to the year AD909 as attested to by the *Chronicum Scotorum*.[139] The historicity of the site at Clonmacnoise is however obscure. The settlement was founded by Ciarán who died *c*.AD549, possibly of the yellow plague, although there is no contemporary literary evidence to corroborate these events. We do know that it was important enough by the early seventh century for its abbot to be listed by Cummian among those consulted by him prior to sending his pastoral letter to Abbot Ségéne of Iona concerning the Easter controversy.[140] Certainly by the end of the seventh century it had developed into one of the major midland coenobitic settlements and was clearly regarded by Tírechán, writing *c*.690, as a rival to Armagh in the midlands.[141] It was also significant enough to warrant a visit from Columba during the abbacy of Alither (AD585-599); a visit which was recorded for posterity by Adomnán,

---

[136] This plan is reproduced in a volume of *Archaeology Ireland* (Manning (1994b), 18). For a useful photograph and an up-to-date and much more detailed plan see Manning (1994a), 56–57.

[137] Manning (1994b), 18–19.

[138] The unusual proportions of the *Daimhliag Mór* attracted the attention of Harold Leask. Seemingly adhering to an atypical 2 to 1 ratio as opposed to the more usual and chronologically prior 1.5 to 1, the greater length-width proportion of *Daimhliag Mór* (measuring 18.90m × 8.75m internally) led Leask to argue that it was not as early as its counterpart at Glendalough (Leask (1955), 72) despite the fact that the simple single-cell plan found at Clonmacnoise would appear to be chronologically earlier in design than the more elaborate two-cell plan at Glendalough (Radford (1977), 3). Manning has more recently suggested a four phase developmental chronology for the cathedral which helps to explain this apparent anomaly. Starting with its foundation by Abbot Colmán and the high-king Flann in AD909 the building underwent a series of extensions and it was during the third phase some time in the late thirteenth century that the displacing of the south wall of the *Daimhliag Mór* by some 2m altered the original internal measurements of 18.8m × 10.7m internally, giving a more normal length-width ratio of 1:1.75 and thus fulfilling Leask's criteria (Manning (1994a), 86; Manning (1995a), 31–32).

[139] Petrie (1845), 271, 275.

[140] Cummian, *De controversia Paschali*.
See Charles-Edwards (2000), 251.

[141] Tírechán, *Collectanea*, 25, 47.

providing the sole literary reference to the existence of a *vallum* at Clonmacnoise.[142]

Despite this textual evidence for enclosure at Clonmacnoise the history of its practice on the site is elusive. Although the site is dominated at its heart by the *Daimhliag Mór* with a constellation of other churches and structures radiating out in a dispersed pattern which would suggest a probable inner enclosure the search for substantive material evidence has been frustrating and to some extent inconclusive.[143] Early attempts by Charles Thomas to locate a rectilinear enclosure on the site can now be discounted.[144] However more recent findings by Heather King's team have produced evidence of a substantial feature which was probably in-filled during the late eighth to early ninth century as part of a major expansion of the settlement thus indicating a possible original excavation date in the sixth to seventh century.[145] This dating horizon would accord with evidence from other sites such as Tullynish, Co. Down where the enclosing ditch has been radiocarbon dated to the seventh century and similar examination of peat and brushwood material found in ditches at Armagh and on Iona have yielded dates as early as the sixth century.[146] This ditch may well represent some of the earliest activity on the site and is probably part of the early monastic enclosure, potentially encompassing an area of some 13 hectares.[147] It is quite likely however that this enclosing ditch was replaced during the eighth/ninth century enlargement by a more extensive feature possibly at the same time as the bridge was constructed across the Shannon in *c.*AD804.[148] Further traces of a much larger enclosing feature to the south and east of the Esker ridge are also visible although this may well be of much later date than the ditch mentioned above.[149]

What remains unclear is whether the tripartite enclosure pattern suggested by the above for Clonmacnoise indicates zoning and multivallation. If this were so it would of course be resonant of the *schema*

---

[142] *VC*, I, 3.

[143] Murphy (2003), 20.

[144] Thomas (1971), 30–31; Mytum (2003), 37.

[145] Murphy (2003), 19.

[146] Ivens (1988), 55–56; Gaskell Brown and Harper (1984), 112–117, 158; RCAHMS (1982), 12, 36–39.

[147] Murphy (2003), 21–22.

[148] Timbers recovered from this site have been dendrochronologically dated to *c.*AD804 (O'Sullivan, A. and Boland (2000), 148–149; Boland (1996), 75–76).

[149] Murphy (2003), 21–22.

outlined by Doherty,[150] and embodied in a site such as Nendrum. The apparent tripartite division may however simply reflect differing stages in the development of the site. The issue is further complicated by the need to consider whether even such an iconic site as Nendrum, with its trivallate enclosure pattern, is really a material paradigm of the gradation of sacred space as expressed within the textual evidence, or rather an example of a site recast and interpreted by its excavator(s) to affirm a particular spatial model. There can be a temptation to interpret such material evidence, no matter how putative, through the prism of a preferred planning *schema* which in turn may well have been initially over-reliant on the textual evidence. Nevertheless, it is evident that a pattern can be recognized at Clonmacnoise, based around an inner enclosure coterminus with the present graveyard wall, an intermediate enclosure represented by the backfilled ditch and an outer enclosure following the Esker ridge.[151] Certainly Donald Murphy was content to acknowledge the possibility of a very large enclosing feature at Clonmacnoise and to interpret the findings on the ground within the context of Doherty's biblically based Levitical 'city of refuge' model and the accompanying zoning as depicted within the *Hibernensis* but he was cautious as to possible dating parameters for the various putative enclosures.[152]

Within the enclosure the presence of settlement complexity at Clonmacnoise is suggested by the excavations within the area known as the New Graveyard which have produced evidence of eighth to tenth century occupation including the remains of a round-house, a rectilinear structure and a large hearth situated to the north under which were found post-holes and habitational refuse.[153] John Bradley has suggested that this area would have formed part of the eastern *trian*, recorded in the *Annals of the Four Masters* as being sacked in AD1082.[154] Traces of leather-working and other various craft activities alongside traces of E-ware in this area, coupled with this documentary evidence, would indicate the possible presence of internal divisions and service areas in the Clonmacnoise complex at least by the second half of the eleventh century.[155] Relying on this relatively late eleventh

---

[150] Doherty (1985), 57, 59.

[151] Murphy (2003), 23.

[152] Murphy (2003), 20, 23; Doherty (1985), 57, 59.

[153] King (1997).

[154] *Annals of the Four Masters, s.a.* 1082.11.

[155] Bradley (1998), 45–47.

and twelfth century documentary evidence Bradley has then extrapolated this evidence back to argue for settlement activity at a much earlier date.[156] Undoubtedly the evidence of service areas within the settlement complex of Clonmacnoise at least in the eleventh century is paralleled with that from other major sites including Armagh[157] but there is not sufficient evidence to speak confidently and in detail of how this internal planning might have been arranged or to argue for a more general occurrence of a nucleation of population within larger ecclesiastical settlements as early as the seventh and eighth centuries.[158]

Those who would seek to postulate a topographical consistency across a range of similarly large sites have found rich pickings among the abundance of extant structures on the site at Clonmacnoise. It was Herity who first made the case for a planning consistency between the remote ascetic settlements of the west and the earlier settlement layout of the much larger eastern foundations. Using Clonmacnoise as one of his examples he initially suggested that the Cathedral, the *Daimhliag Mór* (presumed to be on the site of the original oratory), the *Teampull Chiaráin* (traditionally reputed to be Ciarán's tomb), and the Cross of the Scriptures (dated AD909 but, according to Herity, probably replacing an earlier cross-slab) represented the early sacral core of the monastery strongly paralleling the format found on the western sites.[159] He then developed this model by suggesting that, contrary to the western situation, the oratory in the larger eastern settlements was usually placed centrally rather than in the eastern sector of the ecclesial core. Thus the early ninth century South Cross and what he terms the 'North Pillar' were to be considered boundary markers placed around the cathedral marking out, with a third no longer extant cross, a central area of some 70m in diameter. It also meant that the commissioning of the Cross of the Scriptures in the early tenth century represented a new development in monastic planning with the cross marking the centre of a public space (the *platea*) and visible from all sides rather than its traditional function as a boundary marker.

While it might seem unsafe to draw on such a restricted evidential base to argue for the emergence of a widespread monastic planning *schema* Herity claimed that a similar canon of siting could be detected

---

[156] Bradley (1998), 50.
[157] Lynn (1977); (1988).
[158] Swift (1998), 116–119.
[159] Herity (1977), 17.

at Durrow, Kells and Tuam among others.[160] However, the discovery
of an earlier wooden structure, probably a cross, beneath the Cross of
the Scriptures at Clonmacnoise along with evidence of burials and
occupation in the immediate vicinity has since effectively undermined
Herity's postulated 'innovative' canon of siting.[161] Further, as Herity
himself points out, the crosses of the Barrow Valley group, including
that at St Mullins, which were probably erected slightly after the Cross
of the Scriptures between AD925 and AD1000, followed the traditional practice of using crosses for boundary marking.[162] Rather more
cautiously, and based upon more recent excavation work, Harold
Mytum proposed a model for the settlement pattern of large monasteries, including a comprehensive list of diagnostic elements, and
sought to bring it to bear upon the material evidence from Clonmacnoise but was disappointed to be able only to affirm both extensive
and intensive activity on the site and not the presence of zones of activity demarcated by enclosing features such as walls, banks or ditches.[163]
Like Bradley, he too was forced to recognize that much of the extant
material evidence under discussion was eleventh century in provenance
and thus any theory about earlier topography remained conjecture.[164]

Nevertheless, despite the relative paucity of the documentary and
archaeological evidence it would appear that enclosure and zoning
existed at Clonmacnoise, both materially and at a conceptual level.
Indeed the possibility that the boundary may in parts have been a spiritual boundary rather than a ditch or other more substantial physical
structure has been recognized.[165] Further Herity's tendency to overstate
his case should not blind us to the clear parallels between the layout and
constituent elements of a range of sites across a wide spectrum of size
and location.[166] Mytum has helped to identify a number of diagnostic
features which he regards as indicative of large scale monastic settlement. These include concentric rings of settlement activity, potentially
divided by banks, ditches or other markers; a 'sacred core' containing a
church or churches, crosses and a burial or burials; outer occupation
areas in which various supporting activities took place such as craft and

[160] Herity (1983), 42–51; (1984), 60; Doherty (1985), 60.
[161] King (1995); see also Swift (1998), 116.
[162] Herity (1983), 50–51.
[163] Mytum (2003), 37–38, 53–57. See also 39 Table 1.
[164] Mytum (2003), 53–57.
[165] Murphy (2003), 21.
[166] Herity (1984), 60–61.

cultivation and radially divided areas of non-ritualistic activity.[167] Many
of these are also indicative of much smaller scale religious settlement; a
view supported by the aerial and cartographic analysis by Leo Swan of
several Irish mainland monastic sites including Armagh, Kells, Kildare
and Tuam, which strongly suggests that these larger sites followed a set
pattern of layout similar to that found in the west.[168] The evidence from
our own analysis of four very different sites would seem to accord with
this contention. Whilst it is clear that not *all* features are found on *all*
sites there is sufficient evidence to suggest that 'most monasteries, even
small settlements, displayed similar features in the layout of their buildings and internal spaces'.[169]

Certainly some key design principles can be detected. The oratory or
small church, accompanied by a saint's relics perhaps contained within a
slab-shrine, and a cross-slab or more rarely a free-standing cross, forming
a 'sacred core' provided the settlement focus. There was nearly always an
enclosing structure, often a primary feature, such as a wall or ditch
encompassing the entire site and often an additional internal enclosure
to divide off the 'sacred core' from the rest of the enclosure. Close by the
oratory, usually at its west end, there was an open space across which the
monks or hermits would walk to reach the oratory. Supporting activities
such as cultivation or craft work or the entertaining of guests were usually confined to the periphery of the settlement site. It may seem that at
one level the intensity of activity and the accompanying relative afflu-
ence of Clonmacnoise was a world away from the hard ascetic life being
lived out by the residents of Reask and especially by the monks on
Skellig Michael but the material evidence would suggest that the world
created by them through the organisation and form of their monastic
architecture evidenced the same spiritual understanding and aspirations.

2.B. *The Anatomy of Settlement: A Literary Context*

2.B.1. The Praxis of Enclosure

The settlement evidence at Clonmacnoise is particularly significant
for our discussion because it provides a rare convergence between

---

[167] Mytum (2003), 54.
[168] Swan (1985).
[169] Bitel (1990), 58.

archaeology and hagiography. As we have noted, here at Clonmacnoise we have explicit textual reference in Adomnán's testament to the existence of a *vallum* in the late sixth century[170] which we are able to set alongside the material evidence for enclosure on a significant scale emerging from the ongoing archaeological exploration of the site. However, a number of problems remain. First, it is seldom possible to convincingly marry textual and physical evidence. Secondly, both material and textual evidence may provide 'snap-shots' around which settlement models may be constructed but one must always be careful not to over-extrapolate the evidence.[171] Thirdly, and most importantly, the literary evidence, most of which is primarily hagiographical in style and content, is of greatly varying reliability.

For our purposes this evidence comes in three forms. First, reference to the layout and ordering of historically known sites, such as Iona and Clonmacnoise among others, where the archaeology can potentially corroborate the literary description. Secondly, the often idealized accounts of the choosing and marking out of sacred sites, often now unknown or no longer visible, which we encounter in the numerous saints' lives. Finally, the canonical regulations for the ordering of religious space enshrined within the *Hibernensis*. However, a particular difficulty arises when considering the hagiographical evidence of the *vitae sanctorum*. While the dating horizons of key texts, including the anonymous *Vita S. Fursei* and Jonas of Bobbio's *Vita S. Columbani* (both mid-seventh century), and Adomnán's *Vita S. Columbae*, Muirchú's *Vita S. Patricii*, Tírechán's *Collectanea*, and Cogitosus's *Vita S. Brigidae* (all late seventh century) are comparatively secure within a mid to late seventh century milieu the provenance and dating of other *vitae* are much less certain.[172] Richard Sharpe has identified a core group of a further nine or ten Latin Lives which he believes, on orthographical and textual grounds, to be also early, dating from no later than *c.*AD800.[173] The other Latin Lives and the corpus of Irish Lives are, however, most likely to be significantly later in date. Sharpe suggests that many of these other *vitae* may date from the eleventh century at the earliest and the *Bethada* from the tenth to eleventh century at

---

[170] *VC*, I, 3.

[171] Loveluck (2001), 121.

[172] Sharpe (1991), 8–14.

[173] See Sharpe (1991), 297–338. See also Stalmans (2003). For a critique of Sharpe's analysis see Breatnach (2005).

the earliest.[174] This means, of course, that evidence from saints' lives must be treated with caution as it is potentially unreliable. A wide spectrum of hagiographical material has been employed below, including some of the less well known and chronologically later *vitae* (for example, that of St Samthann, an obscure figure who did not die until AD739), and the Irish Lives, but there remains a significant core of textual evidence whose provenance and dating is relatively secure and early.

So despite these caveats, the textual evidence can provide a conceptual framework within which we can begin to interpret and understand better the extant morphology of religious settlement as long as its limitations are properly understood and acknowledged. In an Irish context we do have a significant number of literary references which address some of the issues around layout and enclosure. We have already touched upon the textual evidence for enclosure relating to a number of historically known sites including of course Adomnán who, in his *Vita S. Columbae*, makes reference both to the enclosure at Iona as well as to that at Clonmacnoise.[175] We can also be certain that the Irish monk Columbanus practised enclosure within his own Frankish monasteries even if the material evidence has now disappeared.[176] However, many of the textual references to enclosure are much harder to place in an historical context. An example is provided in the early ninth century text, *Navigatio S. Brendani*,[177] where the monastery of St Ailbe which is visited by Brendan and his companions is described as having a gate guarding the entrance and mention is made of a number of buildings including a refectory, an oratory, and individual cells clearly depicting a recognisable monastic layout. In this most idealized of forms the praxis of enclosure and zoning has on occasion to be inferred. So we witness Brendan examining the shape and dimensions and layout of the church in a manner highly resonant, albeit in a much more abbreviated form, of the detailed scriptural descriptions of the layout of the Temple in Jerusalem.[178] Further on in the same text

[174] Sharpe (1991), 385–386.

[175] *VC*, 2, 29; 1, 3.

[176] Columbanus, *Regulae coenobialis*, 8; Columbanus, *Paenitentiale*, 26; Jonas, *Vita S. Columbani*, 33.

[177] Carney dates the composition of this text to *c*.AD800 or a few decades later although he proposes the existence of a primitive Latin account as early as the seventh century (Carney (1963), 46, 51). Dumville has argued strongly for a date no later than the third quarter of the eighth century (Dumville (1988)).

[178] *Navigatio S. Brendani*, 12.

For the description of Solomon's Temple see 1 Kings 6 and for that of the post-exilic Temple see Ezekiel chs 40–48.

we encounter the crystal pillar and this time we witness Brendan measuring the opening of the net surrounding the pillar and then entering with his companions and measuring each of the four sides of the pillar which was a perfect square.[179] Again this may well represent an attempt to portray allegorically the paradigm of the perfect monastic enclosure.

We do, of course, have more direct and unambiguous textual reference to the praxis of enclosure. The Irish Life of Saint Mochuda provides a detailed account of the marking out and blessing of the boundaries of the settlement of Lismore.[180] It was essential that, once chosen, a site was ritually blessed and this would include the enclosure and the buildings within. The Latin Life of St Bairre provides ample evidence of the blessing, and signing with the cross, of settlements and their buildings in order to secure their safety. We are told explicitly that the monks of Cork could rest easy knowing that St Bairre had blessed their enclosure.[181] We are also told that the saint fasted and prayed before building in order to enhance the sanctity of the site.[182] The Irish Life of St Bairre also recounts the fasting of the saint prior to the siting of the church[183] but attributes the choosing and marking out of the site to an angel.[184] Another Irish vernacular text, *Bethu Phátraic* (referenced here by its Latin title, *Vita tripartita*),[185] provides further, if somewhat historically unreliable, evidence of the ritualized marking out of the new enclosure,[186] and in addition depicts clergy and other

[179] *Navigatio S. Brendani*, 22.

[180] *Betha Mochuda*, 27, 45.

I have cited all primary texts (unless otherwise indicated) by using Arabic numbers for chapter headings. For those Irish Lives contained within Plummer's 1922 edition which contain both Latin and Arabic numerals I have simply normalised the Latin numerals and followed them with the bracketed numbers inserted by Plummer. So, for example, *Betha Mochuda*, xxvii, (45) is cited as *Betha Mochuda*, 27, 45.

[181] *Vita S. Barri*, 6.

[182] *Vita S. Barri*, 12.

[183] *Betha Bhairre Ó Chorcaigh*, 13, 28.

[184] *Betha Bhairre Ó Chorcaigh*, 14, 30–15, 31.

[185] The dating of *Vita tripartita* is uncertain. Dumville has argued for a range between c.AD900 to c.AD1100 (Dumville (1993), 255–258). Sharpe has suggested a tentative tenth century date (Sharpe (1991), 20) but more recently Charles-Edwards has argued for an early ninth century setting for the earliest known recension of the text, perhaps reflecting an even earlier but no longer extant Latin version (Charles-Edwards (2000), 11–12).

[186] Anon., *Vita tripartita*, 140.

(Extracts from *Vita tripartita* are cited by the page number of the Irish text in *The Tripartite Life*, ed. Stokes.)

local worthies walking the boundaries of new settlements to bless both its internal space and its parameters.[187] We are also informed that at Druimchaili Patrick, carrying his *bachall* (clerical staff or crozier), blessed Armagh and measured out the enclosure and buildings in procession with angels, elders of the community, and his retinue.[188] The material evidence of course has shown us that these boundaries were not always substantial in form. The literary evidence suggests that often they were not even physically marked.

For example, as we have already noted in relation to MacDonald's work on Adomnán and Iona, the *Vita S. Columbae* reflects a theological meta-narrative about the enclosure and sanctification of religious space. So here, and in *De locis sanctis*, we encounter a systematic attempt to sanctify the topography of the whole of the island of Iona; a process which would appear to have begun not long after Columba's death. Adomnán's description of the sacred landscape of Iona in the *Vita* is predicated upon an understanding that the physical world of Columba is divided into zones with varying degrees of holiness, where the *loci* of key events in the saint's life are marked by crosses and other memorials; what the anthropologists Eade and Sallnow have referred to as 'the spatialisation of charisma'.[189] Thus the whole island is declared sacred space with the island foreshore as the outer boundary and the monastic enclosure and the church enclosure providing the middle and inner boundaries.[190] So, for example, penitents such as Féchna are greeted at the harbour before being allowed to proceed further inland[191] and the impenitent and the truly wicked are not even permitted to set foot upon the island. Thus the sinner guilty of fratricide and incest is ordered to be set ashore on Mull 'so that he may not set foot upon the sod of this island'.[192] Equally, at the physical and spiritual heart of the community in the area around the church admission is prohibited to lay people unless they are prospective monks,[193] or penitents such as Librán who subsequently becomes a monk.[194] But the boundaries marking out these zones were not man-made structures

[187] Anon., *Vita tripartita*, 230.
[188] Anon., *Vita tripartita*, 236.
[189] Eade and Sallnow (1991), 8.
[190] MacDonald (2001), 15–19.
[191] *VC*, 1, 30.
[192] *VC*, 1, 22.
[193] *VC*, 1, 32.
[194] *VC*, 2, 39.

such as walls or ditches but rather lay in the landscape such as the foreshore or the Sound of Iona.[195] Cogitosus's late seventh century description of Brigit's enclosure of Kildare would also appear to be pertinent for here we have invisible borders within which no enemy or attack is to be feared.[196]

Sometimes the boundaries were marked out by simple crosses such as those marking the spots beside the path where Columba's uncle Ernán died and where the saint himself was standing at that moment, interpreted by MacDonald as having an apotropaic property.[197] A further cross beside a path is mentioned by Adomnán and this too seems to have a significant position halfway between the monastery and the nearest barn.[198] We are told that a cross stood at the doorway of the church of St Bairre at Cork[199] and that a cross could guard such diverse locations as the path to the southern chapel at Druim Moccu Blaí[200] and the door to a shed outside the protection of the enclosure on Iona.[201] The First Life of St Fintan, Abbot of Tech Munnu, tells how, following an encounter with three men in white robes (presumably angels) he marked out the chosen site for his settlement with crosses.[202] We have already noted that free-standing High Crosses were also used as boundary markers at Clonmacnoise and a similar use of crosses as boundary markers for some smaller hermitage sites such as Angus the Culdee's settlement at Disert Bethech is also suggested by the poetic literature. Here Disert Bethech is described as a 'pious cloister behind a circle of crosses' where the only protection against the outside world would appear to have been totemic rather than substantive. The same poem also makes reference to 'Clonenagh of many crosses', once again suggesting that this settlement was similarly to be distinguished by the presence of several marker crosses.[203] Some have, as we have already noted, detected a similar pattern in the diagrammatic *schema* contained within a colophon of the *Book of Mulling*.[204] We shall

---

[195] MacDonald (2001), 15, 17.

[196] Cogitosus, *Vita S. Brigidae*, 32.

[197] *VC*, 1, 45; MacDonald (2001), 16.

[198] *VC*, 3, 23.

[199] *Betha Bhairre Ó Chorcaigh*, 17, 33.

[200] Anon., *Vita tripartita*, 240.

[201] *VC*, 1, 45.

[202] Anon., *Vita prior S. Fintani*, 19.

[203] Anon., *On Angus the Culdee*. See also Herity (1983), 48.

[204] Henry (1940), 102.

discuss this document in detail in chapter four and so we simply note here its potential as a further textual corroboration of a material phenomenon.

Although it would appear that secular Irish Law could cope with the concept of territory marked out with invisible boundaries it clearly much preferred clarity.[205] Legal fines for trespass were much higher if the boundaries were properly marked while some types of trespass over unmarked limits brought no legal sanction at all.[206] The ecclesiastical canons would appear to be much firmer in their advocacy of the need for clearly marked territorial boundaries, both externally and within the enclosed space. The seminal text here is the early eighth century *Hibernensis*; without doubt the single most significant source for early Irish ecclesiastical organisation.[207] According to the *Hibernensis* the enclosing of the sacred space, the *termon* was to be consecrated by king, bishop and people and to be clearly marked out by crosses and/or boundary stones.[208] Much debate has centred on the exact nature and extent of the *termon*, some of which we have already rehearsed. It has been suggested that the *termon* could designate an area of some considerable size such as the whole land over which a church had jurisdiction.[209] The *termon* ascribed to the Cork saint, Molagga, in the eponymous Life in the Book of Fermoy, was several kilometres across[210] and a similar area has been suggested for St Finán's[211] settlement at Church Island on Lough Currane.[212] The description of Armagh's *termon* in the late seventh century *Liber Angeli* as 'most vast' stretching 'from the top of *Mons Berbicis* to Slíab Miss; from Slíab Miss to Bri Erigi; from Bri Erigi to Drummai Breg' also appears to suggest that the *termon* could encompass a huge area. Indeed the angel of the Lord declares to Patrick that 'a vast *termon* is being established by the

---

[205] Bitel (1990), 64.

[206] *Corpus Iuris Hibernici*, 1.68

[207] Etchingham (1999), 47.

[208] *Hibernensis*, 44, 3.
Item: *Tres personae consecrant terminum loci sancti: rex, episcopus, populus.*
Likewise: three people consecrate the boundary of a holy place: a king, a bishop, a people.

[209] Etchingham (1999), 158.

[210] *Betha Molaga*, 9.

[211] There is some confusion as to which St Fínán, Fínán Cam or Fínán Lobhar, may being referred to here. Ó Carragáin has suggested that it is likely that both Fínáns derive from a single cult (Ó Carragáin (2003), 134 n. 9).

[212] Ó Carragáin (2003), 137.

Lord for the city of Armagh.[213] This angelic declaration has led to this
termon being seen as perhaps equivalent to a diocese[214] or a province.[215]
The material evidence, while not perhaps supporting such an extensive
termon, would suggest that the areas contained within could be substantial. We have already noted the very large enclosure tentatively recognized by Hill at Whithorn which may encompass an area of
approximately 230 hectares although nothing quite as impressive as a
diocese or province.[216] The recent excavations of the monastery at
Portmahomack in Easter Ross (possibly founded by Columba in the
late sixth century) have led the excavators to suggest that a series of
decorated cross-slabs found on several neighbouring sites may possibly
demarcate the area of jurisdiction of the eighth century monastery.[217]
The area enclosed would have been considerable and comparable to
the *termon* now being suggested for Church Island. At Killinaboy in
north Clare the area enclosed would appear to have been almost two
kilometres in radius.[218]

These inordinately sized *termons* may reflect a seventh century
extension to the area of sanctuary previously commonly claimed[219] but
their expansive dimensions sit uneasily with the more forensic definition of the *termon* reflected in Cogitosus's late seventh century description of Brigit's Kildare as a *civitas refugii*[220] and with the forensic use of
terminus/termon as found in the *Hibernensis*.[221] We find a similar
understanding in the Irish vernacular laws[222] where the *termon* must
surely rather signify that area of sanctuary, the *civitas refugii*, in relative
proximity to the church.[223] Here we find a natural extension of the secular notion of sanctuary which related to a freeman's *les* (the ring of a

---

[213] *Liber Angeli*, 7.
See Doherty (1985), 56.
[214] Binchy (1962a), 60–61.
[215] Doherty (1991), 66–68.
[216] Hill (1997), 6 fig. 1.4; Lowe (2001), 7–8.
[217] Carver and Spall (2005), 183–184; Carver (2004), 26.
Carver has since somewhat revised his view that Portmahomack might be a
Columban foundation (Carver 2004, 183). Instead he has suggested that the settlement represents an indigenous religious expression, independent of either Iona or
Jarrow (Carver 2008, 196–198).
[218] Sheehan (1982), 37.
[219] Doherty (1985), 57.
[220] Cogitosus, *Vita S. Brigidae*, 32.
[221] *Hibernensis*, 44, 2; 44, 3; 44, 5; 44, 8.
[222] *Corpus Iuris Hibernici*, 50.28.
[223] Etchingham (1999), 158.

ring-fort or boundary) to encompass ecclesiastical notions of sanctuary embodied in the concept of the *civitas refugii*.[224] As we have seen above, much of the hagiography depicts a similarly restricted understanding. In the shorter Irish Life of Máedóc of Ferns the saints cursed those who sought to defile this space with theft, assault and murder. Facing an assault upon his settlement Máedóc and all the people of the district withdrew within his *termon* and Máedóc then drew a line with his *bachall* around the cattle which were being rustled by the invaders and the invading army stopped except for one chief who died as soon as he crossed the line.[225] The *termon* was a place of sanctuary and thus those who defiled that sanctuary deserved to be severely punished. Further, although there is evidence to suggest that the *termon* could indeed denote an area of some considerable size such as all the land over which a church had jurisdiction, the extent of the *termon* claimed for Armagh by the *Liber Angeli* would seem to be atypically large and almost certainly the result of propaganda. Ó Carragáin has stated that the ecclesiastical enclosure designated by the word *termon* was usually from 30m to 300m in diameter[226] and certainly the material evidence from our survey of sites and much of the textual evidence would support such dimensions. One explanation for this variation in scale is that as time passed the notion of *termon* as sanctuary metamorphosed into something more akin to protected space with its consequent increase in the area affected.[227] However, it is the more geographically limited understanding of *termon*, predicated upon the concept of a finite area of enclosure and sanctuary, rather than the potentially much larger sphere of influence of a particular saint or religious foundation which is of key significance for the present discussion. It is this notion of *termon* which we encounter reflected within the material evidence we have examined and in relation to a discussion of the nature of enclosed settlement space the more pertinent. We will discuss the internal organisation of the *termon* in greater detail below.

2.B.2 The Anatomy of the Enclosed Space

If we accept the definition of the *termon* as a discrete area of enclosure and sanctuary then we need next to consider how the space, once

---

[224] Charles-Edwards (2000), 119–120.
[225] *Betha Máedóc Ferna* (I), 18.
[226] Ó Carragáin (2003), 137.
[227] Davies, W. (1992), 4–5.

enclosed, might be successfully divided up, the rules of admission established and the function of each area or zone made clear. The process of zoning, like the laying down of the enclosing feature itself, would appear to have been part of the ritual act. Thus we are told in a highly composite and relatively late Life of Máedóc of Ferns that when St Máedóc, on founding Druim Lethan in the sixth century, blessed the site he carefully measured out the internal space and allocated the various buildings to their proper place.[228] Once the enclosed area had been divided up rules would have been required to enforce the subdivision of the enclosed area into zones of various degrees of sanctity and to protect the ritual integrity of the enclosure, not just from profanation by criminals and undesirables but by the laity as a whole. This would have been especially necessary given the role of the *termon* as a place of sanctuary for those accused of crimes and misdemeanours.[229] For this more forensic approach to the internal ordering of the enclosure we can turn for guidance to the *Hibernensis* which gives us explicit and detailed reference to the structured use of the enclosed space although the evidence and the topography thus described is not always consistent. So for example in Book 17 in a discussion of the food needed within ecclesiastical establishments, we appear to have depicted a fourfold, rather than the normative threefold, division of space.[230] Nor was the scriptural precedent claimed by the *Hibernensis* always accurate and reliable.[231] In Book 44 the depiction of the division of the holy space around

---

[228] *Betha Máedóc Ferna* (II), 20, 55.

The buildings listed include round towers which did not appear in Ireland until the tenth century (Bitel (1990), 62).

[229] Charles-Edwards (2000), 120.

[230] *Hibernensis*, 17, 4.

De quatuor oblationibus ecclesiae Dei.

In lege quatuor cibi sacerdotum erant: primum Aaron tantum et filii ejus comedebant in tabernaculo, secundum filii Aaron tantum manducabant in ostio tabernaculi, tertium uterque sexus manducabat in atrio, quartum enim in ostio familia tota manducabat cum vernaculis et empticiis.

On the four offerings in the house of God.

In the Law, there were four types of food for the priests; first those that Aaron and his sons used to consume in the *tabernaculum*; secondly, those that the sons of Aaron used to consume in the *ostium* of the *tabernaculum*; thirdly, those that either sexused to eat in the *atrium* and fourthly, those that the whole household used to eat in the *ostium* with the servants and the purchased people (for translation see Swift (1998), 107).

[231] Swift (1998), 108–109.

Mt Sinai[232] is much more elaborate than that found within the scriptures which simply note that priests and people were kept outside the boundaries laid down by the Lord around the mountain.[233] The dissonance with the account in Exodus is clear. The hierarchical division of space depicted within the *Hibernensis* is not found with the scriptural text.[234] However, allowing for some textual corruption, and occasional overly liberal interpretation of the scriptural text by the compilers, Book 44 effectively advocates a threefold division of the sacred space into gradations of holiness, holiest, holier and holy, *sanctus, sanctior, sanctissimus*, radiating out from the central core[235] with severe penalties for violating these sacred boundaries[236] for not only was movement restricted into the *termon* but also within its boundaries. Thus according to a more detailed textual variant of the same extract from Book 44 of the *Hibernensis*, while only clerics could enter the sanctuary, the second most holy area was a space (*plateas*) into which laity 'who have not

---

[232] *Hibernensis*, 44, 6a and 6b.
De loco sancto a malis non tangendo.

> a. Lex: *Mons Sina, in quo Lex dabatur, jubetur, ne tangere illum omnis populu et pecora, et posuit terminum inter se et Moysen, et inter Moysen et Jesum, et inter Jesum et seniores, et inter seniores et vulgus populi.*
> b. Item: *Inter tabernaculum et populu tribus Levi intervallum fuit, et in atriis familia sacerdotum, et inter tabernaculum et sancta sanctorum.*

Concerning a sacred place not to be touched by sin.

> a. In the Law it states: at Mt Sinai, on which the Law was given, it was ordered that all the people or their cattle should not touch it, and the Law placed a boundary between them and Moses, and between Moses and Joshua, and between Joshua and the elders, and between the elders and the common people.
> b. Likewise: there was a space between the *tabernaculum* and the people of the tribe of Levi, and in the *atria* there was the household of the priests, and also between the *tabernaculum* and the Holy of Holies.

[233] Exodus 19:23–24.
[234] Swift (1998), 108.
[235] *Hibernensis*, 44, 5.
De numero terminorum sancti loci.
Eadem Sinodus [i.e. Sinodus Hibernensis]: Quatuor terminos circa locum posuit: primum, in quem laici et mulieres intrant; alterum, in quem clerici tantum veniunt. Primus vocatur sanctus, secundus sanctior, tertius sanctissimus. Nota nomen quarto defecisse.
Concerning the number of boundaries of a holy place.
Likewise the synod [i.e. the Irish synod] has placed four boundaries around a place: the first, in which the laity and women may enter; the other (second?) into which only clerics may enter. The first is called holy, the second holier, the third holiest.
The name of the fourth part was not known.
[236] *Hibernensis*, 44, 7 and 8.

surrendered to any great wickedness' and the third, and least holy area, was somewhere where access would appear to have been denied to very few.[237] This pattern of internal zoning resonates strongly with that advocated within Isidore of Seville's early seventh century *Etymologiae*[238] which was certainly known on Iona and clearly served as a textual source for the *Hibernensis*.[239] Book 15 of *Etymologiae*, *On Sacred Buildings*, makes unequivocal reference to the subdivisions of a temple based on degrees of sanctity and to the restricted access to the 'sancta sanctorum', the 'holy of holies'.[240] This partitioning almost certainly

[237] *Hibernensis*, 44, 5 [Ms.6 variant].

Sinodus: Duo vel tres termini circa locum sanctum debent fieri: primus in quem praeter sanctorum nullum introire permittimus omnino, quia in eum laici non accedunt, nec mulieres nisi. nisi clerici; secundus, in cujus plateas plebium rusticorum catervas non multum nequitiae deditas intrare sinimus; tertius, in quem laicos homicidas, adulteros permissione et consuetudine intra ire non vetamus.

Inde vocantur primus sanctissimus, secundus sanctior, tertius sanctus, deferentes honorem discrepantibus.

Nota quod deficit nomine tertio.

Synod: there should be two or three boundaries around the sacred place: the first into which we permit absolutely no one to enter except of the saints, for laity may not enter, nor women unless they are clergy; the second, into whose area we allow to enter the group of ordinary folk who have not surrendered to any great wickedness; the third, into which we will not prevent laity guilty of murder, adulterers and prostitutes, from entering by permission and custom.

Therefore, we denote the first as most sacred, the second holier, the third sacred, conferring honour to each differently. The name of the third is not noted.

[238] The *Etymologiae* or *Origines* probably date from the period between AD610 and 620 (see O'Loughlin (1998), 244 n. 124).

[239] O'Loughlin (1994), 52; Hillgarth (1961), 451.

[240] Isidore, *Etymologiae*, 15, 4, 2.

(I am grateful to my colleague David Thomson for this translation.)

Sancta iuxta veteres exteriora templi sunt. Sancta autem sanctorum locus templi secretior, ad quem nulli erat accessus nisi tantum sacerdotis. Dicta autem Sancta sanctorum quia exteriori oraculo sanctiora sunt, vel quia sanctorum conparatione sanctiora sunt; sicut Cantica canticorum, quia cantica universa praecellunt. Sanctum autem a sanguine hostiae nuncupatum; nihil enim sanctum apud veteres dicebatur nisi quod hostiae sanguine esset consecratum aut consparsum. Item sanctum, quod extat esse sancitum. Sancire est autem confirmare et inrogatione poenae ab iniuria defendere; sic et leges sanctae et muri sancti esse dicuntur.

According to the ancients the outer parts of a temple are holy. The holy of holies, however, was a more secret place of the temple, to which there was access for no-one except only the priests. It was called the holy of holies because it is more holy than the outer *oraculum* or because among the holy places they are by comparison more holy, just as the Song of Songs is so called because it excels all other Songs. *Sanctum*, however, takes its name from the blood (*sanguis*) of the victim, for nothing was called holy among the ancients unless it had been consecrated by or sprinkled with the blood of the victim. Again, that is *sanctum* which stands consecrated (*sancitum*), for to consecrate is to strengthen and by invocation of a penalty to defend from injury: so also laws are called holy and walls holy.

reflects both established praxis within religiously inspired early medieval Irish settlement and a conceptual tradition stretching back to scriptural roots as we shall discuss further in the next chapter.

As we have already noted from our discussion of the archaeological evidence the focus of religious settlement was evidently the cross-slab marking the founding saint's final resting place or the slab-shrine containing the saint's remains, usually accompanied by an oratory. We have also seen that this 'sacred core' was frequently partitioned off from the rest of the enclosure. We should be in no doubt that the saint's relics were of the utmost importance and of great attraction to both monk and pilgrim. Cuthbert, when approaching his death on the Great Farne, asked that his remains be left there and not translated to Lindisfarne for he feared that 'the presence of my bones will prove very irksome', attracting 'the influx of fugitives and every other kind of malefactor which will otherwise result. They will flee for refuge to my body, for, whatever I might be, my fame as a servant of God has been noised abroad'.[241] Indeed there is ample hagiographical testimony to how monks and religious went to great and often rather dubious lengths to secure the presence of relics within their settlement, whether it was amongst the grandeur of Cogitosus's Kildare, where Brigit was buried in great splendour, or the simplicity of Tempul Crónáin in Co. Clare, where Crónán was buried outside of the church in a simple slab-shrine.[242] The *Liber Angeli* relates how the monks of Armagh compensated for the fact that they did not actually have Patrick's body by amassing a veritable collection of apostolic remains.[243] The nuns of Cell Eochaille implored their patron Senán to provide them with the relics of a monk, any monk, to protect them and their church.[244] As we have seen above in the case of St Cuthbert, saints themselves were anxious to ensure that their remains were treated with dignity and in accordance with their wishes. St Máedóc of Ferns left a truly impressive list of relics to his various foundations at Ferns, Drumlane and Ros Inbir and his own 'beauteous' remains he bequeathed to Ros Inbir, cursing in anticipation those who might fail to carry out his wishes.[245] Ciaráin of Saighir, having gone all the way to Tours in a successful attempt to secure the relics of St Martin, asked to be buried with his

---

[241] *VCB*, 37; see also *HE*, 4, 29.

[242] See Bitel (1990), 67–69.

[243] *Liber Angeli*, 19.

[244] *Betha Shenain meic Geirginn*, 2472.

[245] *Betha Máedóc Ferna* (II), 72, 231–233.

relics, including those of St Martin, in a 'secret place'.[246] Once the precious relics had been buried they had to be protected and it would seem that the threat was real. The recounting of the strange tale of the desecration of the grave of Báitán in the burial place of the monastery at Derry is of course not only proof that the practice of separating differing grades of enclosed space including that for burial was known in Adomnán's day but that even the most sacred of spaces was vulnerable.[247] Certainly the textual evidence of the *Hibernensis* would attest both to the especially sacred nature of the burial place of the saints and martyrs and to the need to protect such spaces from violation.[248] If further proof were needed of the sanctity of the 'sacred core' then the punishments for their despoliation listed in Book 44 should serve to clarify[249] and the greater the number of relics the greater the crime.[250]

Alongside the saint's remains was situated the oratory, a key diagnostic element in establishing the religious credentials of a settlement site.[251] We have discussed in some detail the physical evidence for the recurring presence of the oratory at the heart of religious sites and have already highlighted the numerous references to the presence of oratories in much of the hagiography. It is also clear from the written sources that by the seventh century many prestigious mainland sites such as Clonmacnoise and Glendalough contained several churches. The late seventh century texts, Muirchú's *Vita S. Patricii* and the *Liber Angeli*, make reference to more than one church at Armagh.[252] When Máedóc founded his settlement at Ros Inbir he built 'a strong and ample oratory, and a fair-built quadrangular regular church in

---

[246] *Betha Ciaráin Saighre* (II), 32, 64; 34, 74.

[247] *VC*, I, 20.

[248] *Hibernensis*, 17, *De oblationibus ecclesiae Dei*; 42, *De ecclesia et mundo*; 43, *De locis*; and 44, *De locis consecratis* all deal with this subject to a greater or lesser extent.

[249] *Hibernensis* 44, 7 and 44, 8.

[250] *Hibernensis* 44, 9.
De tanto graviore pollutione sancti loci. quanto plures in eo sancti.
Patricius ait: Quicumque Diis, hoc est martyribus detrahit, Deo detrahit, quanti enim cumque martyres in eo humanti sunt loco, tantum Deo detrahit.
Concerning the fact that the more saints in them, the more serious the pollution of holy places.
Patrick said: whoever dishonours the divine ones, that is the martyrs, dishonours God and the more martyrs that are buried in that place the more God is dishonoured.

[251] Henry (1957), 45–46, 154–156; Herity (1984), 57.

[252] Muirchú, *Vita S. Patricii*, 110; *Liber Angeli*, 16.
See also Hamlin (1985), 283. For the dating of these texts see Charles-Edwards (2000), 439.

preparation for his resurrection'.[253] Certainly the physical and literary evidence is clear that the oratory was at the very heart of the 'sacred core' of religious settlement.

Yet while we may express some confidence that the composition of the 'sacred core' of religious settlement is adequately attested to by both the archaeological and literary evidence, the relationship of that 'sacred core' to the rest of the enclosed space, and what that enclosed space might contain, is still a matter of some debate. For the purposes of our discussion we have employed as a working assumption the idea that the *termon*, a discrete area of sanctuary, denotes the entirety of the enclosed space and that this *termon* is then subdivided into further zones. This *schema* would imply that two of these zones, the *platea* and the *suburbana*, formed an integral part of the *termon* and that the *termon* did not simply designate the area of the 'sacred core' but included all of the enclosed space.[254] This understanding would seem to be reflected in the extant settlement material and to fit with the depiction of settlement layout contained within the *Hibernensis* and other relevant texts. Such a view however would certainly not be universally accepted. The *termon* and the *platea* have been interpreted by some, including Lisa Bitel, as separate areas of settlement with the *termon* denoting the inner most part of the enclosure, the *sanctissimus*, and the *platea* the next most holy sector, the *sanctior*.[255] Ann Hamlin has also explicitly equated the *termon* with the inner area of settlement.[256] However the inclusion of those areas of settlement that might be designated in the hagiography or the canons as *platea* and as *suburbana* within the area of sanctuary, the *termon*, which in turn designates the whole of the enclosed space, must surely be what is implied by the canons. Although such a layout pattern is more easily encapsulated and expressed in a large scale settlement such as Clonmacnoise or Armagh or even Iona the extant physical evidence examined so far from smaller sites would strongly indicate that even there we can see a serious attempt to reflect this 'canon of planning'. This division into zones of varying accessibility does appear to parallel convincingly the material layout of the religious settlements we have examined.

---

[253] *Betha Máedóc Ferna* (II), 58, 157.

[254] Ó Carragáin (2003), 137.

[255] Bitel (1990), 76.

[256] Hamlin (1985), 297.

The difficulty in this debate perhaps results from a scholarly over-familiarity with some of the long-standing forensic terminology which, in turn, has led to an unhelpful and imprecise use of language. A fairly harmless example is provided by the word *vallum*, which properly translated means 'a palisade made from stakes'[257] or in the plural, an 'embankment'.[258] However it is often used in an early medieval context to denote an enclosing structure which included some form of ditch.[259] Such etymological confusion can presumably present potential problems for those in search of the material evidence for settlement. Imprecision within the lexicon of settlement can be more seriously distracting. Particular to our discussion, the Latin word *terminus* from which the Irish word *termon* is derived does not of course refer to an area at all but rather denotes a boundary-mark or limit.[260] Thus the *Hibernensis*, despite the challenge of textual corruption, would appear to advocate that *de minimis* the holy space should be marked out with a visible sign[261] and then subdivided using boundary-markers, *termini*, the number ranging from two to four, and that access to each zone should be restricted according to ecclesiastical status and righteousness of life.[262] So the area we normally describe as the *termon* is marked out by *termini* but it is the *terminus*, the boundary, which is the key defining element and not the area enclosed by that *terminus* or boundary. The adoption of a more precise use of language when discussing enclosure and the nature of the enclosed space would thus enable us to talk more appropriately of the *platea* and the

---

[257] ed. Simpson (1968), 630.

[258] ed. Latham (1965), 504.

[259] Bitel (1990), 58; McCormick (1997), 49.

[260] ed. Simpson (1968), 600.

[261] *Hibernensis*, 44, 3a and 44, 3b.

De termino sancti loci ignoto, terminatoque tribus personis.

    a. Sinodus Hibernensis: Terminus sancti loci habeat signa circa se.
      [MS 6 reads for this: *Sinodus: Omnes sanctorum locorum termini consecrati debent habere signa circa se, ut a plebilem agris separentur*]
    b. Sinodus dicit: Ubicunque inveneritis signum crucis Christi, ne laeseritis.

Concerning sacred places enclosed by an unmarked boundary and demarcated by three people.

    a. The Irish Synod: the boundary of a sacred place shall have a sign around it.
      [MS 6 reads for this: Synod: all boundaries of consecrated sacred places ought to have signs around them in order to separate the common people]
    b. Synod says: wherever you find the sign of the cross of Christ, you should not trespass.

[262] *Hibernensis*, 44, 5.

suburbana being enclosed within *termini*. This would eradicate the difficulty encountered when trying to establish how areas such as the *platea* and the *suburbana* might relate to *termini*, which are essentially boundaries not areas. However for the purposes of this debate and for the sake of clarity we will adhere to the established practice of using the term *termon* to denote an area.

To return to the internal composition of the enclosure, the widespread presence of the *platea* or *plateola* on both large and small sites from an early stage of development has been argued for convincingly.[263] Herity has suggested that on the early hermitage sites the *plateola* denoted a private space for the hermit only which developed eventually in larger monasteries into an open area, the *platea*, to which the public might have access.[264] Adomnán also refers to both a *plateola* and a *platea* at different times within his *Vita S. Columbae* although it is hard in either reference to discern any intention to imply a difference in size by terminology.[265] Clearly the *platea* could be a significant space because it served as an area of ceremonial contact between the saint and his monks and the laity. Adomnán knew of such an arrangement for he tells us that it was *in platea monasterii* that Columba received the food offerings from the people at Cúil Rathain [Coleraine].[266] Further, although the literary evidence for the presence of a *plateola* on small sites is admittedly only implicit it would seem reasonable to infer that even on the smallest of sites there would have been a space separating the visitor from the hermit or monk. The existence of such a space on a very small eremitic site is implied in Bede's *Vita S. Cuthberti* in the account of Herefrith visiting Cuthbert on Farne. Here we are told that on arrival Herefrith would give a signal to let Cuthbert know he had arrived.[267] Again in the same work we are told how Cuthbert would 'go out' if his brother monks came over from Lindisfarne to see him.[268] Indeed it has been suggested that one of the functions of the *platea* was to separate the 'sacred core' from the domestic and other buildings of the settlement and that these buildings were actually arrayed around the *platea*.[269] This would accord to some extent with the ninth century

[263] Herity (1984), 60–61.
[264] Herity (1984), 64.
[265] *VC*, 3, 6; 1, 50.
[266] *VC*, 1, 50.
[267] *VCB*, 37.
[268] *VCB*, 18.
[269] Herity (1983), 29–30; MacDonald (1984), 296; Bitel (1990), 76.

glossary, *Sanas Cormaic*, where the *platea* is compared to the Irish *faitche*, the open green before a fort or church,[270] defined in Irish Law as 'the extent of a lawful green . . . as far as the sound of a [church] bell or the crowing of a cock reaches'.[271] The *platea* would also seem to have been used in Hiberno-Latin texts synonymously with the term *atrium* as a place where not only outbuildings could be situated but also an area where people might congregate. It is also possible that the *platea* was an area of habitation; this would parallel the reference within the *Hibernensis* to the *atrium* as a place of dwelling for the priests.[272] Iona obviously boasted a *platea* but although Adomnán mentions a number of elements of settlement such as the church or oratory,[273] a guest-house,[274] a refectory,[275] a barn,[276] a 'large building' or 'great house',[277] and a number of huts,[278] he is frustratingly reticent about the topography of the monastic layout on Iona, making little comment about how these elements might have spatially interrelated or where they were located in relation to the *platea*.

The relationship of the *suburbana* to the rest of the settlement is more problematic and this lack of clarity has at times been reflected in the scholarship. Hamlin's attribution of the label *termon* exclusively to the innermost enclosure, the *sanctissimus*, as distinct from the *suburbana* which she places firmly on the outer edges of the settlement area would appear to arise from a misreading of Doherty's monastic planning *schema*.[279] Her confusion can be forgiven for Doherty's explanation of the relationship of the *suburbana* to the rest of the *termon* is perhaps at times ambivalent. His apparent locating of the *suburbana*

---

[270] *Sanas Cormaic*, 628, 1073.

[271] *Bechbretha*, 46.

See Bitel (1990), 76.

[272] *Hibernensis*, 44, 6b.

Item: Inter tabernaculum et populu tribus Levi intervallum fuit, et in atriis familia sacerdotum, et inter tabernaculum et sancta sanctorum.

Likewise: there was a space between the *tabernaculum* and the people of the tribe of Levi, and in the *atria* there was the household of the priests, and also between the *tabernaculum* and the Holy of Holies.

See Swift (1998), 111.

[273] *VC*, 1, 8; 1, 22; 1, 32; 2, 13; 2, 45.

[274] *VC*, 1, 4; 2, 31–32.

[275] *VC*, 2, 13.

[276] *VC*, 3, 23.

[277] *VC*, 1, 29; 3, 15.

[278] *VC*, 1, 25; 1, 35; 3, 15.

[279] Hamlin (1985), 297.

outside of the area of sanctuary and refuge seems to imply that the *suburbana* might indeed lie outside the *termon*.[280] However while Doherty is clear that the *suburbana* were outlying areas, service lands, and that the most holy area lay at the centre of the site he does not equate that central core exclusively with the *termon*.[281] He also explicitly states elsewhere that the area of sanctuary, the *termon*, was to include the *suburbana*.[282] Unfortunately the hagiography does not bring much clarity to the discussion. The outer limits, the *suburbana*, of the larger settlements, would appear, according to the *Hibernensis*, to have included the pasture-lands supporting the monastery.[283] Adomnán however appears to distinguish the farmlands on Iona, which arguably equate to Doherty's *suburbana*, from the monastic settlement. Thus the farm buildings such as the barn are apparently to be found *outside* the *vallum monasterii*.[284] Further, in his account of Columba's visit to the monastery at Clonmacnoise Adomnán tells us that some of the brothers were working in the fields *outside* the *vallum monasterii*.[285] Interestingly Hamlin in her pictorial depiction of eighth-century large scale monastic settlement has placed the pasture-lands of her monastic exemplar firmly within the enclosure walls. Chris Lowe has done likewise in his pictorial depiction of the Anglian settlement at Hoddom.[286]

The available textual evidence concerning the location of the *suburbana* mainly relates to larger settlement sites and it could be cogently argued that to talk of *suburbana* in the context of small eremitic settlement sites such as Reask, Church Island or High Island or even Skellig Michael is inappropriate. The term is more helpfully restricted to the description of larger scale settlements such as Clonmacnoise and Iona. However both the extant archaeology and hagiography would indicate that a number of ancillary and support functions such as craft and agriculture were located on the periphery of even the smallest

---

[280] Doherty (1985), 57.

[281] Doherty (1982), 302.

[282] Doherty (1985), 70.

[283] *Hibernensis*, 44, 2b.

Item: *Omnis civitas sacerdotibus data cum suburbanis suis xv milia longitudinis, et latitudinis x milia alendis pecoribus sacerdotum fuit.*

Likewise: every town shall give to the priesthood an area *within* its suburbs measuring 15000 cubits long and 10000 cubits wide for rearing its flocks.

[284] *VC*, 3, 23; MacDonald (1984), 280.

[285] *VC*, 1, 3.

[286] Hamlin (1985), 298; Lowe (2006), 195 fig. 9.1.

of sites. At Reask two of the cells on the edge of the settlement were used for iron-smelting and a corn drying kiln was placed just outside the enclosure wall.[287] The remains of a watermill found close by the enclosure on High Island suggest both technical sophistication and considerable arable activity on a remote island site.[288] Indeed the hagiography provides evidence that watermills were known at a number of larger settlements sites including Brigid's Kildare and possibly on Adomnán's Iona.[289] It has also been argued that Adomnán's use in his *Vita S. Columbae* of the Latin word *canaba* to denote a shed situated on the periphery of the settlement refers rather to a grain-drying kiln which if correct would indicate the use of water-powered milling on Iona.[290] Certainly Adomnán supplies textual evidence of the presence of grain in large quantities on Iona[291] and if the references cited above to a watermill and to the putative grain-drying kiln are reliable then we can reasonably deduct that there was agrarian activity being conducted on the island.[292]

Another topographically peripheral activity on all sites was the offering of hospitality, a vital part of the activity of any Irish settlement, religious and secular. The putative remains of guest-houses have been located on the outer perimeter of several sites, again including small eremitic ones such as High Island,[293] Church Island,[294] and even on Farne where Bede's *Vita S. Cuthberti* tells of Cuthbert constructing a house near the landing-place in which visiting monks might stay.[295] On a rather larger scale Adomnán makes several references to the presence of a guest-house on Iona,[296] including its construction from withies,[297] where the numerous visitors to Iona could stay, occasionally

---

[287] Fanning (1981), 71 fig. 2.

[288] Marshall and Rourke (2000), 188 fig. 142a, 189 fig. 143, 203.

[289] Cogitosus, *Vitae S. Brigidae*, 8; *VC*, 3, 23.
See Thomas (1971), 210–211; Marshall and Rourke (2000), 202.

[290] *VC*, 1, 45.
See Marshall and Rourke (2000), 202; Sharpe (1995), 308 n. 195.

[291] *VC*, 3, 23.

[292] It would appear from the early Irish documentary sources that the presence of a barn, watermill and kiln were functionally related (Mytum (1992), 195) and therefore the presence of one or more of these elements is of significance.
See Marshall and Rourke (2000), 209.

[293] Marshall and Rourke (2000), 51.

[294] O'Kelly (1958), 124–125.

[295] *VCB*, 17.

[296] *VC*, 1, 4; 1, 31; 1, 32; 2, 39.

[297] *VC*, 2, 3.

for considerable periods of time.[298] Guesthouses were also mentioned in relation to the monastery of Luchen and Odran, brothers of Ciaran of Clonmacnoise, at Isel Ciarain, but here they appear to have been situated outside the enclosure.[299] Once again, the pictorial depiction of monastic life provided by Ann Hamlin very clearly places the guesthouse at the entrance to the settlement but within the enclosure,[300] unlike those located on High Island[301] and Church Island[302] which are situated just outside the enclosure which the archaeology would suggest was the usual arrangement.

2.c. *Conclusion*

The foregoing survey would suggest that we can be confident that we have direct physical and documentary evidence that in the early medieval Irish church religious space was regarded as holy space and that this holy space was delineated by some form of enclosing feature or boundary sign. Indeed in the examples explored in detail in our survey all the settlements were enclosed within significant built features and in some cases, such as High Island, the scale of this feature could be very impressive. Yet the primary function of the enclosure would appear to have been a theological one; to enclose the holy space and to act as a spiritual boundary. Enclosures were intended to separate the enclosed holy space from outside profane or secular space with the emphasis on its apotropaic rather than its physical or defensive properties. This is suggested by the fact that enclosure was practised even on the remotest of sites and on islands such as Skellig Michael, and High Island where there was no obvious need to enclose for security or other purposes. Interestingly we can also see in the case of Church Island an enclosure being constructed *after* the main settlement. If safety and defence were prime concerns here it is likely that the construction of an enclosure would have been paramount.

[298] *VC*, 3, 7.
[299] Anon., *Vita S. Ciarani de Cluain mic Nois*, 23.
See Marshall and Rourke (2000), 51.
[300] Hamlin (1985), 298.
[301] Marshall and Rourke (2000), 47 fig. 29a.
[302] O'Kelly (1958), plate xvii.

Once enclosed the internal space was often subdivided or 'zoned' to denote areas of varying importance based upon holiness or sanctity. We encounter this spatial organisation even on small sites such as those at Reask, Gallarus, Killabuonia, Illaunloughan, Caher Island, and on High Island where internal dividing walls have been built to enclose the 'sacred core'. The practice of zoning is also clearly visible on much more developed sites, most famously perhaps at Nendrum but more convincingly on such sites as Clonmacnoise or on Iona. There is also sound evidence of the presence of what I have labelled a 'sacred core' with the same recurring diagnostic elements across a range of settlement sites regardless of location and size. All of the sites examined contain at least one oratory, sometimes several as at Clonmacnoise, accompanied by a slab-shrine as at Reask, and/or a cross-slab(s) as at the main settlement site on Skellig Michael, possibly indicating the presence of the founder's tomb. At Skellig Michael we even have a further reliquary shrine situated on the almost inaccessible South Peak hermitage. This holiest area was normally located at the centre of the settlement exercising a centrifugal force upon the less holy areas and activities which tended to be situated around the periphery of the site, both within and without the enclosing boundary. Again the literary and material evidence which makes clear that activity such as crafts and agriculture or the provision of hospitality, while of importance, are nevertheless located on the edge of settlement. We can see this both on hermitage sites such as Cuthbert's Farne, small island sites such as High Island and Church Island, and on much larger sites such as Iona.

In the case of sites such as High Island and Skellig Michael it would appear that the vagaries of the terrain did not deter the planners from seeking to adhere to a basic pattern. The circular or sub-circular form of the enclosure would appear to have been integral to this. Certainly both the hagiographical and the canonical material depict the circular or sub-circular enclosure form as normative. The religious significance of the curvilinear layout would appear to be confirmed by the story of the foundation of the settlement of Cell Áir (Killarney) in the Latin Life of St Aed where an enormous boulder, '*ingens saxum*', which was blocking the proposed line of the enclosing feature was miraculously moved by the saint in order to avoid any deviation from the planned circular form.[303] However on occasion some accommodation to the landscape clearly had to be made. We have seen that the enclosing wall

---

[303] Anon., *Vita S. Aidi*, 25.

on several sites including Skellig Michael, High Island, and Reask deviated from the usual circular or sub-circular form to allow for the natural topography. Again on Church Island the terrain of the island and the harsh conditions prevailing there appear to have dictated to some extent the settlement topography but this deviation from the norm is noteworthy because it is so unusual. Almost always the basic 'canon of planning' would appear to have been followed as faithfully as possible.

In this chapter I have pursued the problem of the present lack of clarity with regard to the forensic language of settlement. We have looked at ways in which this imprecision has overflowed into the archaeology and hindered clear debate. We have sought therefore to recover the original meaning of key diagnostic terms such as *vallum* and *terminus/termon* and to reference them back to recognisable topographical features. This has obviated circular arguments about the nature of the spatial relationship between the various areas of enclosure and has enabled us to establish a clear topographical model for how enclosed space might have been ordered.

The material expression and literary depiction of Irish religious settlement examined above demonstrate a general Christian understanding of what holy space might look like. The main task of the next chapter will be to determine what this 'understanding' might have been and its origin. We will consider its influence upon the Irish context through what I have referred to in this study as a 'canon of planning'. In the final chapter we will then consider the extent to which this canon impacted upon the theology and form of religious settlement within the early medieval Irish church. In particular we shall ask to what extent was this 'canon' counter-balanced by the impact of other factors and whether in the end what was produced on the ground was in fact a compromise between ideal and reality.

3. 'FROM THE TABERNACLE TO THE NEW JERUSALEM' : AN EXPLORATION OF A BIBLICAL HERMENEUTIC FOR THE TOPOGRAPHY OF RELIGIOUS SETTLEMENT

It is being argued in this study that the principal determinant of spatial layout within Irish religious settlement was external rather than vernacular. It was also not particular but reflected a broad understanding of what built holy space might look like. This 'understanding' or 'canon' will be seen to be essentially scriptural in inspiration.

We have already noted some initial forays into this question for the Irish and Anglo-Saxon churches by Charles Doherty and John Blair. Drawing on key legal and hagiographical texts, a number of biblical exemplars for planning have been suggested, including the Levitical 'cities of refuge' in the Heptateuch,[1] the description of the Levitical city in Ezekiel chapter 48[2] and the New Jerusalem of the Book of Revelation with its strong Temple imagery.[3] A key text in signposting these scriptural references in the context of early Irish religious settlement, in particular the idealized description of the restored post-exilic Temple of Jerusalem envisaged by the prophet Ezekiel in chs 40 to 48, is the *Hibernensis*.[4] To understand more fully the significance of the Temple for the morphology of early Irish religious settlement we need first to

---

[1] Doherty (1985), 57, 59.
[2] Doherty (1985), 59.
[3] MacDonald (1984), 297; Blair (2005), 196–198, 248.
[4] See MacDonald (2001), 29–30.

consider the influence of the Temple motif upon the depiction of holy space within scripture itself, from the Garden of Eden in the Book of Genesis through to the New Jerusalem of the Book of Revelation.

There is an extensive critical literature focusing upon the Temple motif in its earliest Jewish context as well as its influence upon Western theology but very little of any substance within an early Irish setting. The aim of this chapter will be to establish the importance of such a Temple hermeneutic in decoding the literary and material evidence for religious settlement within an Irish context and to begin to ask whether or not the Temple might have provided not only an interpretative framework for early Irish religious settlement but may also to a greater or lesser extent served as its inspiration.

3.A. *The Bible and the Sanctification of Space*

The Old and New Testaments are full of stories about what we would term sacred or holy places. Such places can perhaps be divided into three main types. The first grouping consists of those that are located in real time and space; places such as Bethel, Gilgal, and Sinai. These were made holy usually by being the *locus* of a hierophany, an irruption of the divine into the material world so as to transform that place into something qualitatively different.[5] This irruption could take the form of a theophany, or manifestation of God, such as experienced by Abram at Shechem[6] or by Jacob at Bethel[7] or a place may be made holy by being the site of a miraculous happening or sign.[8] Indeed the Holy Land itself is so-called because it was the *locus* for Jesus's earthly ministry whose very presence sanctified the land.[9] One possible example of such a location within an early Irish setting would be Iona, the scene of several direct and indirect encounters between Columba and God.

There are other biblical holy places that are described as if they too exist within the physical world but which in truth essentially belong to the world of faith and are not geographically locatable. Obvious biblical examples of these are the Garden of Eden and Heaven.[10] In the Insular

[5] Eliade (1959), 26–27.

[6] Genesis 12:6–7.

[7] Genesis 28:12–19a.

[8] Genesis 22:13–14.

[9] Davies, D. (1994), 44.

[10] Davies, D. (1994), 33–35.

context a number of the destinations within *Navigatio S. Brendani* provide an apposite if not exact parallel. Such sacred places operate at both a literal and an allegorical level. The believer can view them as real, as though they exist in some physical sense. Non-believers, or even perhaps some believers, could view them rather as metaphors, with spiritual meaning but not a physical *locus*, although such a rather neo-Platonist perspective is countered by Augustine (AD354-430) who, when discussing the Garden of Eden in his epic work *De civitate Dei*, argued that there could be no questioning of the reality of the Garden of Eden. So while he acknowledged that the Garden of Eden accounts in Genesis could be interpreted allegorically he insisted that its temporal and physical reality were also affirmed.[11]

This brings us to the third significant category of holy space encountered within scripture; that of the man-made, constructed, holy *locus*, the Tabernacle or Temple; a particularly significant category for our discussion of early Irish topography. There is here clearly an overlap with our second category of holy space. So, for example, the Temple of Jerusalem is at one level typologically distinct from *loci* such as the Garden of Eden or Heaven in that it has unarguably a verifiable physical reality but it too has a metaphorical or allegorical function. So at one and the same time the *locus* of the Temple is where God dwells among his chosen people, the Jews, but it serves also as the paradigm of the heavenly kingdom as described in the Book of Revelation.[12] Here the earthly beauty of the magnificent Temple of Solomon serves as a pre-figuring of the heavenly perfection of the New Jerusalem. The Tabernacle of Moses is described as being but a 'sketch and shadow of the heavenly one'[13] and the Holy of Holies has been replaced by a heavenly sanctuary 'not made with hands'[14] which is the dwelling place of God.[15]

The Temple of Jerusalem was the apotheosis of a long association between the Jewish people and a temple culture which itself reflected the wider temple culture within the ancient world. The Egyptians and the Babylonians both created extensive temple precincts which manifested many of the signature features of the Jewish temples including

[11] Augustine, *De civitate Dei*, 13, 21.
See also Eucherius of Lyons, *De laude eremi*, 15.
[12] Revelation 21:1–2.
[13] Hebrews 8:5.
[14] Hebrews 9:11–12.
[15] O'Reilly (1995), xx–xxi.

the enclosure and gradation of sacred space.[16] Indeed the first biblical account we have of a temple complex is that found at Babel (the Hebrew name for Babylon) which serves as a form of pagan anti-Temple.[17] The Temple motif is, of course, part of a scriptural sub-text from the very beginning.[18] So we have in the description of the Garden of Eden many of the core elements of the Temple ideal, such as the theme of creation, the waters of life, a tree of life and celestial guardians; elements which continue to resonate throughout both the description of the Temple of Solomon and the Temple of Ezekiel's vision to the account of the New Jerusalem of the Book of Revelation. More explicitly in terms of the biblical narrative there are also numerous references in the Old Testament to cultic centres, temples, altars and holy places including of course the Moysian Tabernacle. The location of the Tabernacle appears to have changed several times during the course of its Exodus history, perhaps originating at Shechem and then moving on to Bethel and then Gilgal, ending up finally at Shiloh where its presence is well attested.[19]

In addition to the presence of the Tabernacle at Shiloh where Eli was the priest[20] and Samuel grew up[21] the Books of Judges and Samuel tell of the presence of what scholars such as Barker are happy to label synonymously as temples or altars but which were in reality probably merely altars rather than fully developed temples.[22] Others would wish to draw a much clearer distinction between the two[23] and argue that the evidence for the presence of actual temple sites is strictly limited, especially given the paucity of material evidence to support any textual suggestion of Temple activity.[24] Indeed some scholars have questioned whether the eastern Mediterranean society of c.1000BC had the capacity to build such a structure as the Temple.[25] Others have argued that

---

[16] Hamblin and Seely (2007), 10–11.

[17] Genesis 11:1–9.

[18] This observation should not be read as an uncritical endorsement of Margaret Barker's view of the centrality of Temple theology to almost all other theology. However, there is no doubt that the Temple was a key motif in biblical reflection upon the nature of holy space.

[19] Joshua 18:1.
See also Judges 18:31.

[20] 1 Samuel 1:3.

[21] 1 Samuel 3:2–3, 3:21.

[22] See Barker (1991), 14, 17.

[23] Haran (1978), 15–17.

[24] Haran (1978), 26–27.

[25] Hurowitz (2005), 63.

not only did the ability exist in Israel[26] but that it was unlikely that Solomon's Temple was the first to be built in Jerusalem for when his father David entered the Jebusite city of Jerusalem he would in all probability have found a cult and temple already established there.[27] It has been suggested that the Melchizedek of the Abraham cycle is a memory of the Canaanite god El Elyon in Jerusalem[28] and certainly, in an archaeological context, there is some evidence to suggest that the Temple of Solomon was typologically similar to other Syrian and Canaanite temples of the period.[29] In Syria two ancient temples have been uncovered, Tell Tayinat and Ain Dara, which have significant material physical resonances with the suggested architecture of Solomon's Temple.[30] The evidence from a possible third site at Arad in Israel is much more insecure[31] and the fact remains that the archaeological evidence from putative temple sites is often ambiguous. Claims by archaeologists to have uncovered material evidence of several other possible Israelite temples not recorded in scripture such as that at Megiddo, Arad, Lachish and Beersheba must therefore be treated with caution.[32]

However, if we are content to accept scriptural testimony to certain types of cultic activity as a possible indicator of a temple site[33] then the textual evidence would indicate that there was a temple at a number of sites including Gilgal where Saul was made king,[34] at Dan and Bethel where Jeroboam placed two gold calves for the Israelites to worship,[35] and at Mizpah where Samuel deposited the book of the rights and duties of kingship before the Lord.[36] It was the priest of the temple at Nob (probably containing the Tabernacle which had been transferred from Shiloh) who gave David and his men the bread of the Presence to eat.[37] Indeed the Bible lists in all around a dozen sites that could be identified as shrines dedicated to Yahweh, including Shiloh, Dan, Bethel, Gilgal,

---

[26] Albright (1959).
[27] Barker (1991), 14–15.
[28] Barker (1991), 15.
[29] Hamblin and Seely (2007), 30.
[30] Monson (2000).
[31] Hurowitz (2005), 66.
[32] Hamblin and Seely (2007), 33; Haran (1978), 26–27.
[33] Haran (1978), 26.
[34] 1 Samuel 8:14–15.
[35] 1 Kings 12:28–29.
[36] 1 Samuel 10:17, 25.
[37] 1 Samuel 21:1–6.

Mizpah, Hebron, Bethlehem, Nob, Ephraim, Ophrah and Gibeah.[38] The extent to which such sites actually contained temples, and their structural and topographical relationship to the Temple in Jerusalem, remains unresolved but the textual evidence available would suggest that by the time Solomon brought the Ark into the Holy of Holies[39] in the tenth century BC the role of the temple within Jewish religious life was pivotal. It is to this textual witness that we now turn our attention.

3.B. *The Tabernacle and the Temple: A Textual Depiction of Sacred Topography*

There are, of course, a number of scriptural and non-scriptural descriptions of both the Tabernacle and the Temple in their various manifestations.[40] These include the biblical descriptions of Moses's Tabernacle found in Exodus, chs 25–31 and 35–40 and the descriptions of Solomon's Temple found in 1 Kings, chs 6 to 7 and in 2 Chronicles, chs 3 to 4. We also have Ezekiel's visionary description of a Temple,[41] the depiction of the Temple layout contained within the Temple Scroll, one of the Dead Sea Scrolls,[42] which describes a temple complex unlike any other known,[43] and the descriptions of both the Tabernacle and the Temples of Solomon and Herod supplied by Josephus.[44] Since nothing remains

---

[38] Hamblin and Seely (2007), 33; Haran (1978), 27–39.

[39] 1 Kings 8:4.

[40] We know of three separate Jewish Temples built in Jerusalem. The first was built by Solomon (*c.*970–930BC) and is described in 1 Kings 5–8 and in 2 Chronicles 3–4. This was destroyed by the Babylonians in 586BC (2 Kings 25:8–17) and its rebuilding was envisaged by Ezekiel (40–48). The Second Temple of Zerubbabel, built largely at the instigation of Haggai and Zechariah, was completed in 515BC (Ezra 3:8–13; 6:16–18). No description of the Temple survives in the Old Testament. It was desecrated by Antiochus Epiphanes in 167BC (2 Maccabees 6:1–6) and rededicated by Judas Maccabaeus in 164BC (1 Maccabees 4:36–59). The Third Temple, which was of course that known to Jesus, was largely the work of Herod the Great which he began in *c.*20BC. The Temple was finally destroyed by the Romans in AD70 (Barker (1991), 1, 9–10; Hamblin and Seely (2007), 23).

[41] Ezekiel chs 40–48.

[42] The Dead Sea Scrolls is the name given to a series of scrolls and fragments discovered between 1947 and 1960 at seven caves on the shores of the Dead Sea, eleven caves near Qumran, and several other caves at various locations. The eponymous scrolls are thought to have once belonged to the library of the Jewish community of the Essenes based on a large settlement at Qumran (eds. Cross and Livingstone (1997), 457).

[43] Barker (1991), 12.

[44] Josephus, *Antiquitates Iudaicae*, 3, 6; 8, 3; 15, 11.
The Temple of Herod is also described in Josephus, *De bello Iudaico*, 5, 5.

in material terms of Solomon's Temple or of the Second Temple and very little of Herod's Temple we are totally dependant upon the literary evidence for their pattern and layout. This is not a significant issue for our discussion as we are concerned primarily not with the physical reality of the Temple layouts but rather their biblical depiction. It is the textual witness rather than any material evidence which shaped the early Irish church's understanding of the Temple's sacred topography.

Similarly, the unravelling of the complex relationship between a particular piece of textual evidence, biblical and non-biblical, and a particular Temple may be a challenge for biblical scholars but is of less importance for us. Whether Ezekiel's description of the restored post-exilic Temple reflects his own recollection of the Temple of Solomon towards the end of its days when he was a priest within its environs or whether it was the template for an earthly restoration of the pre-exilic Temple is of secondary importance for our discussion.[45] Its significance for us is that it represents an ideal; its historical physicality ultimately not as pertinent as the model of religious topography it represents.[46] We recognise, of course, that the more detailed account of the construction and layout of Solomon's Temple in 1 Kings is corrupt in places,[47] and that the parallel account in 2 Chronicles includes significant material not found in 1 Kings, perhaps reflecting the differing attitudes of the authors to the Temple.[48] It is also clear that both these biblical accounts do not reconcile easily with the description of Solomon's Temple given by Josephus.[49] Nevertheless, what can be

[45] Haran (1978), 45; Barker (1991), 11, 23.
Both the authorship and dating of the Book of Ezekiel have been matters of scholarly contention but a convincing case can be made for a sixth century BC date predating the restoration of the Second Temple (Joyce (2005), 146). This would allow for the possibility that the Temple description of the Book of Ezekiel was intended to serve as some form of ideal for a restored Temple.

[46] A similar issue arises with the Temple as described in the Temple Scroll. Is the Temple plan described in the Temple Scroll a blueprint for the earth bound Temple demanded by God of the Israelites and to be built by the Israelites or is it an ideal Temple, to be built by God on earth at the 'End of Days', as possibly was the case with Ezekiel's vision, or is it the plan for a heavenly Temple, again built by God? It would seem that the instructions for the layout of the Temple contained within the Temple Scroll were delivered to Moses in much the same way as the original ordinances for the Tabernacle were in the Book of Exodus and so the academic consensus would suggest that the intention was to depict the earthly man-made Temple rather than an eschatological or heavenly one (Yadin (1985), 112–115; Hamblin and Seely (2007), 56–57).

[47] Hurowitz (2005), 67.

[48] Barker (1991), 2.

[49] Josephus, *Antiquitates Iudaicae*, 8, 3.

affirmed with some confidence, despite warnings that Ezekiel's account is so factually unreliable that it must be treated with extreme caution,[50] is that there is a notable descriptive continuity between the Temple as envisaged by Ezekiel and that described in 1 Kings.[51] Thus our inability to link much of the extant textual evidence to a specific point in the Temple's history and development[52] should not seriously impact upon our deliberations with reference to religious layout in early historic Ireland. What is of primary interest for unravelling Irish conceptions of sacred space is the idealized depiction of holy space encapsulated within the Temple descriptions, rather than specific detail of architectural development or even particular stages in the Temple's development and history. As long as we can be confident that the generic concept of an idealized layout represented by the Temple did not change significantly within the time span of the early Irish period we can examine the literary evidence without needing to establish an exact chronology or even a correlation between specific textual evidence and a particular Temple.

Of course, not all of the scriptural and non-scriptural evidential sources listed above would have been available to the early Irish church,[53] but we can be confident that the Book of Ezekiel was well-known and viewed by the Irish church as a significant text in discussions about the organisation of religious space.[54] We know from texts such as the *Hibernensis* that the biblical descriptions of the topography of both the Tabernacle[55] and the Temple[56] were referenced within the

---

[50] Hurowitz (2005), 67–68.

[51] Joyce (2005), 150.

[52] Barker (1991), 11–12.

[53] O'Loughlin has provided a very helpful summary of the non-biblical texts that might have been available in the Library of Iona during Adomnán's abbacy (O'Loughlin (1994), 52).

[54] Such a contention is given support by the influence of Ezekiel on the tenth century Irish poem *Saltair na Rann* whose detailed architectural description of heaven (the *ríched*) is based on three major sources; Adomnán's *De locis sanctis*, a text of the apocalyptic work *Visio Pauli*, and an Old Latin translation of Ezekiel, part of which has survived as a fragment in a St Gall manuscript of *c.*AD900.
See Carey (1986), 103; (2000), 108–119.

[55] *Hibernensis*, 44, 2e.
Item: Tabernaculum Moysi circa se atrium habuit.
Likewise: The Tabernacle of Moses had around it a hallway.

[56] *Hibernensis*, 44, 2d.
Item. Templum Salomonis habuit septum circa se, in quo qui malum faceret periret.
Likewise: The Temple of Solomon had an enclosure about it, in which anyone who did evil would perish.

context of discussion about early Irish religious settlement patterns. What we need to understand is the nature of the scriptural understanding of holy or sacred space embodied in these structures and buildings, and as the Tabernacle precedes the Temple, at least within the context of the biblical narrative, we begin there. It is in the description of the Tabernacle found in Exodus chs 25 to 31 and 35 to 40 that we initially encounter the formulaic depiction of holy space reflected within the biblical Temple descriptions. It will be argued that this biblical model in turn prefigures the lexicon of religious topography found within the early Irish textual witness to sacred layout.

The Tabernacle has of course long been regarded by many scholars as an idealized retrojection of the chronologically later Temple created by a redactor with a clear ecclesiological and political agenda.[57] The dating of this P source (the term used to refer to the material produced by the priestly redactor(s) who probably wrote Leviticus and much of Genesis as well as providing the Tabernacle descriptions within Exodus) is problematic. Traditionally scholars have argued for a late exilic or post-exilic milieu for P in which an image of Solomon's Temple was projected back on to the Tabernacle accounts.[58] If it is indeed a product of the post-exilic Jerusalem priesthood, the catalyst for its creation may well have been the need to establish the credentials of the Temple because the Temple was under attack and in need of justification.[59] Other theories include the suggestion that the description of the Tabernacle represents a phase in the development of the Temple somewhere on the continuum between the original Temple and that envisaged by Ezekiel.[60] Certainly the description of the Tabernacle found in Exodus depicts a most unlikely structure for a nomadic people to be able to construct and deconstruct with ease. It has thus been further argued that the Tabernacle as depicted by P is unlikely ever to have existed and that the layout depicted is more likely to reflect the layout of the Temple of Solomon rather than being an accurate depiction of the original desert shrine.[61] It is of course possible that the description of the Tabernacle has been influenced by a residual memory

---

[57] Bright (1960), 146; Barker (1991), 11.

[58] Noth (1962), 17.

[59] Barker (1991), 11–12.

[60] Hurowitz (2005), 68.

[61] Haran (1978), 189.

of the traditions surrounding the tent-shrine erected by David[62] which was itself probably modelled upon the earlier pre-monarchic desert shrine known as the Tent of Meeting[63] and that therefore the account in Exodus contains within it a substratum of ancient and quite genuine material. If this is so then the description of the Tabernacle as we now have it represents the fusing together of two disparate design elements, that of the tent sanctuary and that of the Jerusalem Temple.[64] The possibility that this might give us access to a relatively primitive exemplar for the organisation of holy space is clearly of interest and may provide substantive textual evidence of an ancient and biblical 'canon of planning'.

The resolution of these textual issues happily resides outside our immediate concern. What is pertinent for us in our consideration of the paradigmatic role of the Tabernacle and Temple in the creation of the sacred landscape of early historic Ireland is that the discussion above would clearly suggest that the Tabernacle as depicted in scripture is itself little more than a reflection of a Temple paradigm. Thus its primary significance for us lies in what its topography can tell us about the layout of the later Temple. Our only biblical source for the layout of the Tabernacle is that given in the Book of Exodus although there are further references elsewhere within the Old Testament to its migration and eventual arrival in the Temple at Jerusalem.[65] It is probable that it was destroyed with the burning of the Temple in 586BC; an event described in Psalm 74.7.

The most striking feature of the Tabernacle was, of course, the fact that it was portable and, at least originally, in the form of a tent-shrine intended for use by a transient people.[66] It was to be a place where Yahweh would 'tabernacle' or 'pitch his tent' among his people.[67] The description of the construction ordinances in Exodus chs 25–27, which were laid down by God and given to Moses, start with the Ark and

---

[62] 2 Samuel 6:17.

[63] Exodus 33:7.
See Bright (1960), 146.

[64] Noth (1962), 211.

[65] Exodus 25–31 and 35–40.
We do also have the benefit of a fairly detailed description provided by Josephus (*Antiquitates Iudaicae*, 3, 6).

[66] Bright (1960), 146–147.

[67] Noth (1962), 211.

work outwards. However, we shall begin our discussion of the Tabernacle complex at ch. 27 (vv. 9-18) with the regulations for the perimeter and work inwards.[68] The entire complex was orientated on an
east-west axis (with access from the east, unlike the usual Christian
pattern) and enclosed by a partition of white linen curtains suspended
from poles covering an area of 100 cubits long and 50 cubits wide;
some 150 × 75 feet (46 × 23m). This area was basically made up of two
equal squares, one constituting the Outer court in which the laver and
altar were situated (see fig. 7). The other half of the complex contained
the actual Tabernacle. The Tent of Meeting was 45 × 15 feet (13.7 ×
4.6m), and was further divided into two distinct sections; the Holy
Place (measuring 20 × 10 cubits, 30 × 15 feet, or 9.1 × 4.6m) and the
Holy of Holies (a perfect cube of 10 cubits, 15 feet or 4.6m). The Holy
Place contained three sacred objects; the incense altar, the table of the
bread and the lampstand. Inside the Holy of Holies was the gold-
plated chest decorated with two golden cherubim known as the Ark of
the Covenant.

With regard to access regulations and prohibitions a veil divided
the Holy Place from the Holy of Holies, and the Holy of Holies
with its golden Ark was accessible only to the High Priest while the
Holy Place was open to the priestly class as a whole. Any ritually
clean Israelite could enter the Outer Court. The increasing sanctity
of the areas through which one progressed on the journey into the
complex was reflected not only in the restriction of access to the various parts of the complex but in the quality of the materials used for
construction. As we shall see, this circulatory control was not only a
feature of the Temple it is also clearly embodied in the canonical
injunctions regarding the protection of the differing areas of religious settlement in an early Irish context. Further, while conscious
of the danger of being distracted by the somewhat tedious recital of
the materials to be used, the measurements given in the scriptural
account are of particular interest because they enable us to make
some form of comparison with the dimensions of Irish settlement
patterns. If, as we have already noted, Ó'Carragáin is correct in his
advocacy of an average enclosure size of 37 metres in diameter for a
significant number of south-western settlements then we can see
that the Tabernacle complex was comparable in size, measuring only

---

[68] For an analysis of the layout and dimensions of the Tabernacle see Hamblin and
Seely (2007), 19–22.

46 × 23m.[69] In terms of the elements contained within the complex we can see that the dimensions of the Tent of Meeting (13.7 × 4.6m) are considerably greater than those of the oratories (and cells) found in an Irish context where for example the two oratories found at Skellig Michael only measure 3.65 × 2.45m and 2.45 × 1.85m internally.[70] Even the *Daimhliag Mór* at Clonmacnoise initially measured only 18.90 × 8.75m internally.[71] However the dimensions of the Holy Place (9.1 × 4.6m) and the Holy of Holies (4.6 × 4.6m) correspond much more closely to the scale of religious architecture found within an Irish context. So it would appear that if it was the Tabernacle, or indeed the much larger Jerusalem Temple, which served as an exemplar for Irish religious topography then scale was not a key concern. What was being copied was something other.

Without the material supplied by the Exodus account of the Tabernacle the accurate reconstruction of the Temple complex(es) would be a much more challenging task. We have already rehearsed some of the inadequacies of the textual witness to the First Temple and also the difficulties in tying up various textual descriptions, biblical and non-biblical, with a particular stage in the Temple's history. Further the evidence for the layout of the Second Temple is very sparse with only short passages from Ezra and Nehemiah giving us a scripturally based insight into what this manifestation of the Temple might have looked like although there is a description of the Temple, and the vestments and vessels used there, in a text of the second century BC known as *The Letter of Aristeas*.[72] This 'letter' from a Jew close to the Egyptian court named Aristeas to his friend Philocrates purports to give a detailed description of the glories of the Second Temple.[73]

These admittedly limited literary witnesses would indicate that the Second Temple was built to the same proportions as the original but we also know that it must have been disappointing in comparison with the magnificence of the original because we are told that those who had seen the glory of Solomon's Temple wept when they beheld its

---

[69] Ó'Carragáin (2003), 128–129.

[70] O'Sullivan, A. and Sheehan (1996), 283–284.

[71] Manning (1995a), 32.

[72] *The Letter of Aristeas*, 83–120.

[73] For an assessment of the text's provenance and reliability see Porter (2001), 104–105.

replacement.[74] Our most complete picture of a Temple complex is undoubtedly that of the Third Temple,[75] ascribed to Herod. It is relatively well attested to by the literary evidence of both Josephus[76] and the third century rabbinic text, the *Mishnah*.[77] Although at times the evidence from the two sources does not coalesce well this discrepancy may result simply from the changing layout over time.[78] There are also, of course, a number of tangential allusions to the topography of this Temple within the New Testament[79] although none of them very helpful for our discussion. What is clear is that the dimensions of the Temple constructed by Herod are significantly greater than those of previous Temples[80] and there is no doubt that much of the grandeur of Solomon's Temple was recaptured in that built by Herod.[81] Its destruction in AD70 marked the end of its earthly existence but bestowed upon it a mythic and iconic status which was to have far reaching consequences for both the Jewish and Christian religions.

Although, as we have noted, the chronological relationship between the various textual depictions of the layout of the Temple is far from resolved it is clear that the scriptural depiction of the layout and spatial organisation of the Tabernacle may be used to decode the sacred topography of the Temple form. So within the Temple building itself (the 'house') we find that all three iterations of the Temple maintained the tripartite division of space first encountered in the Tabernacle. Indeed the Tabernacle has been confidently described by one scholar as a 'miniature version' of the Temple; the former to be studied for what it can tell us about the latter[82] and undoubtedly the Temple of Solomon was in many ways simply a larger version of the Tabernacle, built now in stone rather than in wood.[83] Like the Tabernacle the 'house' was orientated east-west with its gate in the east end. It was rectilinear and

---

[74] Ezra 3:12.

[75] Yadin (1985), 164.

[76] Josephus, *Antiquitates Judicae*, 15, 11; *De bello Iudaico*, 5, 5.

[77] The *Mishnah* is a collection of oral law made by Rabbi Judah ha-Nasi in the early third century AD (Barker (1991), 182).

[78] Goodman (2005), 460.

[79] For example Acts 3:2.

[80] Jeremias (1969), 22; Goodman (2005), 460.

[81] Jeremias (1969), 23–25.

[82] Barker (1991), 10–11.

[83] Hamblin and Seely (2007), 25; Hurowitz (2005), 69.

divided into three distinct sections; the porch or vestibule (*ulam*), the Holy Place (*hekhal*) and the Holy of Holies (*debir*) which contained the Ark guarded now by the addition of two giant free-standing cherubim[84] and separated now from the Holy Place by a door rather than a veil.[85]

Although the external measurements of the Temple of Solomon are not given[86] it is clear from the account in 1 Kings ch. 6 that the Temple complex was, like the Tabernacle, built to precise mathematical measurements and proportions. According to the biblical description the 'house' was internally 60 cubits long and 20 cubits wide and 30 cubits high, that is, approximately 90 feet long, 30 feet wide and 45 feet high (32 × 9.1 × 13.7m) with a porch or vestibule at the front, 20 cubits wide and 10 cubits deep (30 × 15 feet or 9.1 × 4.6m). [87] This would make the Temple building approximately 105 feet or 32m in length.[88] The Holy Place also adhered to the strict design proportions, measuring 40 × 20 × 30 cubits or approximately 60 × 30 × 45 feet (18.3 × 9.1 × 13.7m).[89] The inner sanctuary, the Holy of Holies, was, again like that within the Tabernacle, a perfect cube, this time measuring 20 cubits square, approximately 30 feet or 9.1m square.[90] As already suggested, these measurements would indicate that the Temple was constructed on a significantly greater scale than anything in Ireland in the period under discussion and so if the Temple layout prefigured that for Irish religious settlement the replication of the ideal was not dependant upon similarity of scale or indeed of architectural form.

We have already remarked that the Second Temple, although a pale imitation of the former, was similar in size to that built by Solomon and that the Third Temple, Herod's Temple, was significantly larger. In Herod's complex the Temple itself was 172 feet (52.4m) long and 34.5 feet (10.5m) wide compared to the 105 × 30 feet footprint of the Temple of

---

[84] Bright (1960), 197.

[85] 1 Kings 6:31.

[86] Hurowitz (2005), 69.

[87] 1 Kings 6:2–3.

[88] I have used the imperial and metric equivalents given by Hamblin and Seely (2007), 25–26 as a basis for my discussion of the relative dimensions of all three Temples. A cubit is roughly equal to 1.5 feet or 45cm.

[89] 1 Kings 6:16–17.

[90] 1 Kings 6:20.

Solomon.[91] Once again the Temple space was divided into three with a porch, the Holy Place and the Holy of Holies. As in the Tabernacle and as in Solomon's Temple the Holy Place contained a seven-branched lampstand, the table for the bread of the Presence and an incense altar. Also once again the Holy of Holies was a perfect cube (34 feet or 10.4m) only this time of course the Ark and accompanying cherubim were gone.

With regard to the layout of the two 'ideal' Temple layouts, that of Ezekiel and that found within the Temple Scroll, again we encounter the same emphasis upon the structured division of the enclosed holy space.[92] While it has to be acknowledged that the author of the Temple Scroll focused upon the structure and layout of the courts rather than upon that of the 'house'[93] it is still evident that the main Temple building was to be constructed on traditional lines.[94] According to Ezekiel, the 'House' is to be partitioned into three zones reflecting the divisions within the Tabernacle, the *Ulam* (the vestibule),[95] the *Hekal* (the 'Holy'),[96] and the *Debir* (the 'Holy of Holies').[97] In terms of the relationship of the Temple building to the various courts within which it was placed the Temple complex of Ezekiel's vision clearly also adhered to the threefold division found within the actual sanctuary building. So, not only do we have reference in Ezekiel to a wall enclosing the entire Temple area[98] but also mention of an

---

[91] Hamblin and Seely (2007), 46–48.

For Josephus's detailed but complex description of Herod's Temple see his *Antiquitates Iudaicae*, 15, 11 and *De bello Iudaico*, 5, 5. Interestingly Jeremias more cautiously estimates the Herodian Temple as being only 150 feet in length (Jeremias (1969), 24). What is clear however is that the Third Temple was significantly bigger than both its predecessors.

[92] We have already noted that the relationship between these 'ideal' Temple formats and layout of the actual Temple complexes is problematic but there are clear similarities between the Temple as envisaged by Ezekiel and that described within the Temple Scroll. It is possible that the author of the Temple Scroll drew upon several sources including Ezekiel for his plan (Yadin (1985), 169) whilst still managing to create a Temple plan that was significantly different from any other, ideal or actual (Barker (1991), 12). It has even been suggested that Josephus based his description of Solomon's Temple upon that found within the Temple Scroll (Yadin (1985), 168). This latter contention must be treated with caution.

[93] Yadin (1985), 117.

[94] Yadin (1985), 122.

[95] Ezekiel 40:48–49.

[96] Ezekiel 41:1–2.

[97] Ezekiel 41:3–4.

[98] Ezekiel 40:5.

Outer Court,[99] an Inner Court[100] and the Temple.[101] This repeating layout pattern[102] is significant for our discussion in relation to Insular religious planning because the segregation of the enclosed holy space into courts based on holiness and/or gender not only mirrors the tripartite division of the Temple itself but also once again prefigures early Irish praxis where both tripartite zoning and a concentric spatial pattern would appear to have exercised a significant influence upon the religious topography.[103]

It is clear that the various biblical and non-biblical descriptions of both the Tabernacle and the Temple were predicated upon the need to divide the holy space into areas of increasing holiness, both within the Temple building and within the wider Temple complex. This gradation was respected in all of the Temple plans, both actual and ideal. So, for example, it would appear that each of the Temples contained separate areas or courts, for priests, for men, and for women, arranged around the 'sacred core' of the Temple 'house'; the 'sacred core' being situated at the heart of the complex. This gradation of the holy space was reflected not just in the topography of the Temple complex but also within the 'house' in the subdivision of the internal space and in the quality of the materials used within the various parts of the Temple building.[104]

[99] Ezekiel 40:17–27.

[100] Ezekiel 40:28–47.

[101] Ezekiel 40:48–41.26.

[102] In a fascinating chapter in his book on the place of ritual in religion, undertaken from the perspective of a comparative study of religion approach, Jonathan Z. Smith argues that the topography of the Temple of Ezekiel was designed to reflect a number of 'hierarchies of power', each of which was essentially based upon a sacred/ profane dichotomy (Smith (1987), 47–73). Within this framework there were a 'series of segmentations' in which each constituent part of the entire Temple complex, and indeed the world beyond, was placed within a sacred/profane hierarchy. So for example, the land outside was judged profane in comparison with the Temple Mount but the Temple Mount was judged 'profane' in relation to the Temple building, and so on (Smith (1987), 56–57). This apparently shifting *locus* of sanctity perhaps sits somewhat uneasily alongside the more objective biblical understanding of what is, and what is not, holy. Nevertheless, Smith's work brings an interesting sociological perspective to bear upon the biblical depiction of Ezekiel's Temple and highlights the significance of the division of sanctified space within the Temple model.

[103] Although some scholars would favour a predominantly concentric model for all the Temple complexes, a model which would accord with both the biblical description of the Tabernacle layout and with Josephus's description of the Temple of Solomon (Josephus, *Antiquitates Iudaicae*, 8, 3, 9) and with the ideal temples of Ezekiel and the Temple Scroll (Barker (1991), 22–25), Josephus's depiction of the Temple of Herod (Josephus, *Antiquitates Iudaicae*, 15, 11, 5) has been interpreted as allowing at least the possibility that the courts were adjacent rather than concentric (Yadin (1985), 168).

[104] Hurowitz (2005), 88–90.

Further, movement within both the Temple complex and the sanctuary was, as with the Tabernacle, strictly controlled.[105] The transgression of these access restrictions or any form of misbehaviour could provoke not only a severe popular reaction[106] but also a fatal punishment inflicted by its 'lethal aura'.[107] These various prohibitions and punishments threatened to those who might trespass these boundaries are again contained within the early Irish textual witness where the consequences of the violation of holy space are also potentially deadly.[108]

This enclosure, division, and gradation of the holy space would appear not to have been unique to the Temple in Jerusalem. Of course, we know that the Temple of Solomon was designed by a Tyrian architect[109] after a pattern thought to have been common in Palestine and Syria at that period.[110] The archaeological exploration of the disputed temple site at Arad also provides material evidence of a similar layout *schema* but, as we noted earlier, this evidence is of uncertain value. Nevertheless, the presence at Arad of three rooms within the shrine does reflect the form of other shrines in polytheistic Syro-Palestine such as that at Tell Tayinat and Ain Dara which, as we also acknowledged earlier, offer significant architectural parallels to the Solomonic Temple.[111] In addition,

[105] Ezekiel 44:4–5.
[106] Acts 21:27–28.
[107] Leviticus 10:1–2.
See Haran (1978), 187–188; Hurowitz (2005), 98.
[108] *Hibernensis*, 44, 7.
De violatione templi Dei cum septis punienda.

> a. *Paulus: Si quis violaverit templum Dei, disperdet illum Deus.*
> b. *Hieronimus: Quicumque peccaverit in locis sanctis, dignus morte, et quicumque violaverit munda, dignus penitentia.*
> c. *Item Hieronimus: Quicumque loca sancta polluerit, duplicia persolvet.*
> d. *Hiermias: Polluisti templum Domini, ideo super vos mala vestra reddam.*
> e. *Agustinus: Nolite tangere sacra, non solum interiora, sed etiam exterior.*

Concerning the punishment of the violation of God's temple and enclosures

> a. Paul: if anyone violates God's house, God will destroy him.
> b. Jerome: whoever sins in sacred places deserves death and whoever violates earthly things deserves penitence.
> c. Likewise Jerome: whosoever pollutes a sacred place, will pay for it twofold
> d. Jeremiah: if you have polluted God's house for that reason all your sins will rebound on you.
> e. Augustine: refuse to touch any sacred places, not only the inside but also the outside.

[109] 1 Kings 7:13–14.
See also Josephus, *Antiquitates Iudaicae*, 8, 5, 3.
[110] Bright (1960), 196.
[111] Hamblin and Seely (2007), 30, 33–34.

Egyptian and Babylonian temples such as that at Marduk in the sixth century BC also clearly demonstrate the gradation of holy space which is centripetally arranged upon a central holy of holies.[112] Interestingly, in a Jewish/Israelite context the concept that religious space could be divided up into areas of differing sanctity would appear to have extended beyond the Temple and its courts into the wider world. In Ezekiel we encounter an understanding of holiness that moves beyond a sharp focus upon a defined holy place such as the Temple to encompass a much wider geographical area such as a mountain top[113] or the whole of the land occupied by the Zadokites.[114] This diffusion of holiness is also found elsewhere. In the *Mishnah*, we encounter an understanding of the gradation of holy space on a grand scale based upon the premiss that the whole land of Israel is to be regarded as holy.[115] Within the area encompassed by

[112] Hamblin and Seely (2007), 10–11.

[113] Ezekiel 43:12.

[114] Ezekiel 48:11–12.
See Joyce (2005), 156–157.

[115] *The Mishnah, Kelim*, I. 6–9.
(*Keilim* (literally 'Vessels') is the first tractate in the Order of Tohorot in the *Mishnah*. It contains thirty chapters, making it the longest tractate in the entire *Mishnah*. The tractate discusses the laws of ritual purity and impurity pertaining to all types of vessels. I have cited the relevant passage here in full because of its strong resonance with the early Irish material.). See also Barker (1991), 25.
There are ten degrees of holiness. The Land of Israel is holier than any other land . . .
The walled cities [of the Land of Israel] are still more holy, in that they must send forth the lepers from their midst; moreover they may carry a corpse therein wheresoever they will, but once it is gone forth [from the city], they may not bring it back.
Within the wall [of Jerusalem] is still more holy, for there [only] they may eat the Lesser Holy Things and the Second Tithe.
The Temple Mount is still more holy, for no man or woman that has a flux, no menstruant, and no woman after childbirth may enter therein.
The Rampart is still more holy, for no gentiles and none that have contracted uncleanness from a corpse may enter therein.
The court of women is still more holy, for none that had immersed himself the selfsame day [because of uncleanness] may enter therein, yet none would thereby become liable to a Sin offering.
The Court of the Israelites is still more holy, for none whose atonement is incomplete may enter therein, and they would thereby become liable to a Sin offering.
The Court of the Priests is still more holy, for Israelites may not enter therein save only when they must perform the laying on of hands, slaughtering and waving.
Between the porch and the altar is still more holy, for none that has a blemish or whose hair is unloosed may enter there.
The sanctuary is still more holy, for none may enter therein with hands and feet unwashed.
The Holy of Holies is still more holy, for none may enter therein save only the High Priest on the Day of Atonement at the time of the [Temple-] service.

Israel there are to be areas of varying holiness. These areas are to be marked out by a series of concentric circles radiating out from the Holy of Holies, out into the sanctuary areas of the Temple building itself, and then out into its various courts, and then out further into the city of Jerusalem, and eventually out to the borders of Israel.[116] This, of course, not only mirrors the understanding of the Holy Land as sacred space which we encounter in the Old Testament.[117] It resonates also with the developing model of the early Irish *termon* as an area of land which could potentially embrace a much larger area than just the geographically restricted 'sacred core' originally assumed by scholars.

It is evident from scripture that the guiding principle behind the layout of Tabernacle and Temple was the desire to provide an appropriate space for God to dwell among his people and in which humankind could encounter the divine. In order to achieve this, the holy space was ordered according to a sacred plan given by God to his people. The layout of the Tabernacle,[118] and the Temple after it,[119] was divinely ordained, to be constructed to a pattern given by God, to reflect the perfection of Heaven.[120] Likewise the Temple foreseen by Ezekiel is to be built to a divine *schema*.[121] Accordingly such a space must necessarily be protected from improper or profane intrusion and thus the chosen space was first enclosed and then subdivided into areas of differing levels of holiness; access to which was restricted according to ritual status. This gradation of space was marked by external and internal boundaries and zones of different sanctity were marked out by the use of materials of increasing and decreasing value. What is more, the concept of holy space and the idea that it might be encountered in varying degrees of intensity or sanctity seems not to have been restricted simply to a single holy *locus* or even multiple holy *loci* but to have been applied to much larger areas and even whole lands. Much of the above clearly prefigures the interpretation and praxis of enclosure which we encounter in the literary and material evidence within an Irish setting and the temptation is therefore to reference Irish religious

---

[116] Jeremias (1969), 79.

[117] Davies, D. (1994), 44.

[118] Exodus 25:8–9; Exodus 25:40; Hebrews 8:5.

[119] 1 Chronicles 28:19.

[120] Hebrews 8:5.
See also Exodus 25:40.

[121] Ezekiel 43:10–11.
See Joyce (2005), 155–156.

topography directly back to its biblical roots. However, the Irish literary depiction of religious settlement patterns is not simply a rehearsal of the scriptural account but rather reflects a more theologically developed sense of 'holy' or 'sacred' space. We turn our attention now to the intellectual context for this development.

3.c. *The Temple Motif within Patristic Exegesis*

The fall of the Temple in AD70 changed forever the relationship of the Jewish people to the Temple and transformed the way in which both Jews and Christians viewed it. There was no realistic expectation that it might again be rebuilt and certainly within Christian circles at least its destruction was seen as a sign of God's displeasure with his so-called chosen people among whom, at this early stage, the Christians were numbered. Christ had foretold the destruction and now that the prophecy had come to pass their faith was confirmed.[122] Some were of course openly hostile to the Temple and what it stood for. Stephen's blistering critique in Acts ch. 7 of the arrogance of Solomon in presuming to build the Temple in the first place is simply one end of a spectrum of growing unease within both Jewish and Christian circles with the Temple and its role within religious life. This discomfort was nothing new. The rebuilding of the Second Temple had not been universally welcomed and Jesus's outburst during the cleansing of the Temple was a plea for much needed reform if not actually for abolition. Further, the emphasis in the account of the cleansing of the Temple appears to be on the Temple as a house of prayer rather than as a cultic and ritual centre.[123] This reflects the fact that by the time of Jesus and the ongoing construction of the Third Temple by Herod the cultic language of the Temple was beginning to be transferred to individual and corporate notions of holiness which were increasingly free of a need for a ritual *locus*.[124] This process was inevitably quickened by the fall of Jerusalem and the destruction of the Temple and we can see during the first century the development of a Temple theology which extends far beyond cultic and ritual needs. Stephen's attack upon the religious *status quo* included the implication that the Temple itself was

---

[122] Mark 13:1–2; Matthew 24:1–2.
[123] Matthew 21:12–13.
[124] Rowland (2007), 469–470.

a form of idolatry[125] and in the writings of the New Testament we encounter a definite theological shift away from the significance of the Temple as a building and a holy *locus* towards a much more sophisticated allegorical interpretation of Temple imagery.

The Temple as place, however, remained significant within the religious life of both Jew and Christian. We are told that Paul continued to worship there and it would seem that Paul saw no dissonance between his continued religious observance in the Temple and his developing allegorical understanding of its true spiritual meaning.[126] In a complex mix of allegory Paul equates the Temple under the new dispensation both with the body of the individual believer[127] and with the body corporate of the church.[128] To defile the living Temple was as great a crime as desecrating the Temple in Jerusalem.[129] We can also see in Paul's writings the emergence of the concept of a heavenly Temple as 'a house not made with hands, eternal in the heavens'[130] of which the earthly Temple was but a pale reflection.[131] This dualism between the heavenly and the earthly was to be further developed by the author of the Epistle to the Hebrews and within the Book of Revelation. Hebrews, with its emphasis upon the Tabernacle rather than the Temple and its strong eschatological tenor, draws an unfavourable comparison between the heavenly and earthly sanctuaries and is unequivocal that the religion of the Tabernacle is defunct, rendered obsolete by the sacrifice of Christ.[132] We can also see in Hebrews the sanctification of Jerusalem into a heavenly city, the New Jerusalem,[133] where temple and city are synonymous; a coming together which culminates in the description of the New Jerusalem in Revelation chs. 21 and 22. For St John the Divine, in a description resonant of Ezekiel's eschatological Temple, there is now no need of a Temple because Almighty God and the Lamb are the Temple, and the whole city of the New Jerusalem is permeated by

---

[125] Acts 7:48–50.

[126] Acts 21:26.

[127] 1 Corinthians 3:16.

[128] Ephesians 2:19–22.
See also 1 Peter 2:4–10.

[129] 1 Corinthians 3:17.

[130] 2 Corinthians 5:1.

[131] Hamblin and Seely (2007), 99; Rowland (2007), 476.

[132] Hebrews 9:24.
See Rowland (2007), 477.

[133] Hebrews 12:22.

the divine glory.[134] God's eternal presence makes the whole city a Holy of Holies.[135] Here there are clear resonances in this motif of the New Jerusalem with Adomnán's later depiction of the island of Iona as a holy place. The idea that the earthly Temple has been replaced by the divine glory is also found implicitly in the Logos theology of the opening chapters of John's gospel.[136] Here Jesus assumes the place of the Temple and acts as the intermediary between earth and heaven; a role reinforced by the clear reference to Jacob's vision at Bethel.[137] The body of the incarnate Christ is the new Temple and as such is the *locus* of the divine presence.[138]

This strongly allegorical approach to scripture extended beyond the confines of the writers of the New Testament. The difficulty of interpreting the different literary styles within the scriptures was recognized from the time of Clement of Alexandria (c.AD150-c.215) and Origen (c.AD185-c.254), and the scholastic notion of the 'literal' and the 'allegorical' senses of scripture originates from this period. Of the great writers of the fourth and early fifth centuries both Jerome (c.AD345-420) and Augustine (AD354-430) described their exegetical process and both Jerome and Cassian (c.AD360-after 430) were concerned to move beyond the Pauline 'letter' of scripture to discover its 'spirit'.[139] This analysis was to some extent mirrored by Augustine who, in his *De utilitate credendi* acknowledged the various levels of meaning to be found in scripture[140] but there were significant differences in his approach not least in the number and nature of the differing understandings of the scriptural sense. It is thus important to note that patristic exegesis was not a uniform entity.[141]

Theological reflection of the early medieval period, and biblical criticism in particular, owed much to the influence of several major figures including of course Augustine of Hippo and theologians such as Isidore of Seville (c.AD560-636). Although it has been argued that it

---

[134] Ezekiel 40–48; Revelation 21:22.

However, reference is also made to those outside of the holy city, and thus beyond God's grace; see Revelation 21:8.

[135] Rowland (2007), 478.

[136] Rowland (2007), 472.

[137] John 1:51.

[138] O'Reilly (1995), xxii.

[139] O'Loughlin (1998), 218.

[140] Augustine, *De utilitate credendi*, 5–7.

[141] O'Loughlin (1998), 211 n. 18.

was primarily Augustine who bequeathed to the high medieval period the formal hermeneutical device of the 'four-fold sense of scripture' known as the *Quadriga* it is Jerome's methodology, later adopted by Cassian in his *Collationes*, which has been long regarded as the classic model.[142] For our purposes, it is sufficient simply to understand that what this new hermeneutic meant was that in addition to the literal sense of scripture, three spiritual senses were to be discerned: the *allegorical* or *typological*, which concerns what is believed, the *anagogical*, which concerns what is hoped for, and the *tropological*, which concerns moral conduct. Thus the literal or historical meaning might refer to the Temple as a physical entity; the allegorical or typological meaning to the Temple as a symbol of Christ or the church; the anagogical or mystical to the celestial Temple; and finally the moral or tropological to the Temple as a symbol of the human soul as a dwelling place for the Holy Spirit.[143] The literal sense always had priority, as we noted at the beginning of this chapter in our discussion of Augustine's interpretation in his *De civitate Dei* of the Garden of Eden accounts in Genesis, but the use of the other senses allowed difficult or contradictory pieces of scripture to be harmonized. This desire to illustrate that all scripture, and in particular the gospels, could indeed be harmonized provided the impulse behind another of Augustine's works, *De consensu evangelistarum* (a work which we know was a source for Adomnán's *De locis sanctis*) which sought to prove not only that the gospels were consistent and congruent but that they were also free from error.[144] What all exegetes were agreed upon was the necessity for all of scripture, especially the gospels, to be reconciled for it was inconceivable that the word of God might be seen as contradictory or even illogical.

For the early church fathers the New Testament figurative and allegorical interpretation of the Temple and the vision of the coming of the New Jerusalem were key influences upon patristic exegesis. Within the Jewish world Philo (*c.*20BC-*c.*AD50), a first century Platonist and exegete, had already explored the allegorical potential of both the Tabernacle and the Temple in cosmological terms.[145] Flavius Josephus (*c.*AD37-*c.*100), the Jewish historian, had also written of the veil of the

[142] O'Loughlin (1998), 217.
[143] Hamblin and Seely (2007), 116.
[144] Augustine, *De consensu evangelistarum*, I, I.
See O'Loughlin (1997b); (1999), 147.
[145] Goodenough (1954), Vol. 4, 130–132; (1964), Vol. 12, 56.

Temple in similarly cosmic terms, comparing its material to the four elements.[146] Now in a Christian context the Alexandrian theologian Origen argued that the Tabernacle was an allegory for the church as a whole as well as for the individual believer in whom God could dwell. The earthly Temple was viewed as simply a type of the heavenly one.[147] Augustine recognized that the motif of Jerusalem ideally lent itself to several layers of exegesis for it clearly points beyond itself.[148] Thus in the works of Origen (c.AD185-254/5), Ambrose (c.AD339-97), Jerome (c.AD345-420), Augustine (AD354-430), Cassian (c.AD360-after 430), Gregory the Great (c.AD540-604) and, of course, eventually Bede (c.AD673-735) and Adomnán (c.AD624-704) we encounter an increasingly systematic development of the allegorisation of the role of the Temple which had begun within the pages of the New Testament.[149]

As part of this process we can also see the continuing conflation of Temple imagery with the apocalyptic vision of the New Jerusalem of the Book of Revelation.[150] For Gregory the Great, in one of his homilies on Ezekiel ch. 40, the measuring out of the heavenly city in Revelation (21:15–17) clearly called to mind the visionary Temple of Ezekiel.[151] By the time Adomnán came to write *De locis sanctis* Jerusalem as the heavenly city, the embodiment of all that the Temple had represented, was already well-established as an exegetical model, first by Jerome in his *Commentarii in Ezechielem*, then by Augustine in his *De civitate Dei* and of course later by Cassian in his *Collationes*.[152] So, for example, for Jerome and Cassian the word 'Jerusalem' had four meanings, only one of them historical. For Jerome these were (1) the city that could be burnt down, (2) the heavenly city, (3) the church and (4) the believer's soul.[153] For John Cassian, the various interpretations differed slightly so 'Jerusalem' is (1) the Jewish city, (2) the church, (3) the

---

[146] Josephus, *De bello Iudaico*, 5, 5, 4.

[147] Origen, *In Exodum homiliae*, 9 (*De Tabernaculo*), 13.
See Farr (1997), 58 and Hamblin and Seely (2007), 99–100.

[148] Augustine, *De civitate Dei*, 15, 2.

[149] As O'Reilly makes clear the allegorisation of the Temple in early Christian thought had its roots within the New Testament and was not simply a product of later patristic exegesis (O'Reilly (1995), xxiii).

[150] O'Reilly (1995), xxvii.

[151] Gregory the Great, *Homiliae in Ezechielem*, 2, 1.

[152] O'Loughlin (1992), 41.

[153] Jerome, *Commentarii in Ezechielem*, 4, 16.

heavenly city and (4) the human soul. [154] It is against this background of an increasingly complex and sophisticated allegorical understanding and interpretation of scripture as a whole that any discussion about the ongoing significance of the Temple for the early church, and its possible role as a theological inspiration or even a blueprint or exemplar for an ecclesial layout *schema* within Ireland in particular, must be conducted.

3.D. *The Temple Motif within Early Irish Exegesis*

Although by the time of the New Testament the Temple as a *locus* of the divine presence had been made redundant and much of the cultic language of the Temple transferred to describe individual and corporate piety the ongoing importance of the Temple as a building remained 'in the theological bloodstream of early Christians'. With the creation of Christianity as the official religion of the Roman Empire church buildings began to grow in number and scale with an ever increasing degree of spatial sophistication and architectural complexity which echoed rather the Temple than the synagogue. [155] In the earliest extant description (*c.*AD325) of a Christian church– the festival oration on the building of churches, addressed by Eusebius to Paulinus, the Bishop of Tyre[156] – the heavenly Jerusalem and the celestial Temple are clearly the models for the patterns created by men on earth.[157] The layout, the precincts, the very fabric of the church had become symbols of the body of the faithful. Paulinus is compared to Bezalel,[158] Solomon,[159] and Zerubbabel,[160] in turn the builders of the Tabernacle and the First and Second Temples and, like Solomon's Temple, the new church is built according to the 'heavenly types in symbolic fashion'.[161] The Temple was to be revered because it represented a divinely ordained prefiguring of the heavenly Temple and as

---

[154] John Cassian, *Collationes*, 14, 8.

[155] Rowland (2005), 479.

[156] Eusebius, *Historia ecclesiastica*, 10, 4.

[157] Doherty (1985), 47.

[158] *Eusebius, Historia ecclesiastica*, 10, 4, 3 and 10, 4, 25.

[159] Eusebius, *Historia ecclesiastica*, 10, 4, 45.

[160] Eusebius, *Historia ecclesiastica*, 10, 4, 36.

[161] Eusebius, *Historia ecclesiastica*, 10, 4, 25–26.
See Hamblin and Seely (2007), 103.

such its material structure could and should be studied with advantage and of course as we have seen above the descriptions of the heavenly Temple within the scriptures were greatly circumscribed by knowledge and experience of its earthly types.[162]

In an early Irish and Anglo-Saxon context the ongoing significance of the Temple as a holy place is clear. In an Irish context we find within the margins of the early ninth century *Liber Ardmachanus* an instance where its scribe, Ferdomnach, writing in AD807, draws an admittedly somewhat enigmatic parallel between the sacking of Iona by the Vikings in AD801 and the fall of the Temple by placing the name of the then abbot of Iona, Cellach, in the margin alongside the Marcan account of Jesus's prophecy of the destruction of the Temple.[163] More explicitly, and this time within an Anglo-Saxon setting, the exegetical work of Bede bears rich testimony to the centrality of the Temple as an ecclesial motif. Within a range of works including *De Templo* and *De Tabernaculo* mentioned above but also encompassing works such his *De locis sanctis*, *In Regum Librum XXX quaestiones*, and his commentary on Ezra and Nehemiah, the Temple is a constant focus of scholarly attention. Indeed the responses to questions eleven to thirteen of *In Regum Librum XXX quaestiones* provide the reader with a detailed written plan of the layout of the Temple and its complex.[164]

This interest in the appearance and layout of the Temple building is also evidenced in pictorial form within both Insular and Anglian biblical exegesis. Most famously the Lucan Temptation scene in the *Book of Kells* contains what has generally been interpreted as a detailed artistic depiction of the Temple in the Irish vernacular form of an ornate wooden church with a shingle roof and gable finials.[165] Another Irish visual expression of the Temple is found in the aforementioned *Liber Ardmachanus* where the diagram of the heavenly Jerusalem at the end of the Book of Revelation provides a detailed plan of the layout of the heavenly city described in Revelation ch. 21.[166] This diagram,

---

[162] O'Reilly (1985), xxi.

[163] Henry (1940), 154: Bieler (1979), 2.

[164] Bede, *In Regum Librum XXX quaestiones*, 11–13.

[165] Edwards (1990), 122; Henry (1940), plate 33; Farr (1997), 33 plate 1.
For a detailed discussion of whether this drawing does indeed represent the Temple see O'Reilly (1994), 390–397.

[166] Farr (1997), 56–57; O'Loughlin (2000c).

depicting Christ himself as the Temple, functions as a form of exegesis in its own right,[167] and is almost certainly related to a diagram found within the earlier *Codex Amiatinus*.[168] The *Codex Amiatinus* is of Anglo-Saxon origin, produced at the monastery of Wearmouth-Jarrow during the time of Bede (*c*.AD673-735) and under the abbacy of Ceol-frith (AD688-716). It contains a diagram of what has been regarded variously as either the Temple or the Tabernacle. This drawing is, in turn, believed to have been copied from a diagram in the sixth century *Codex Grandior*, an Old Latin pandect, produced by Cassiodorus and seen by Bede at Monkwearmouth-Jarrow to where it had been brought by Ceolfrith.[169] Despite the scholarly uncertainty as to whether the *Codex Amiatinus* drawing represents the Temple or the Tabernacle or even a hybrid exemplar the detailed exposition of the layout is striking and the fact that time and skill was invested in creating this diagram within such a document is testimony to the continued interest in, and significance of, the Temple structure within the Insular churches.[170] Alongside this illustrative evidence we can also place the evidence from the early to mid eighth century Northumbrian Franks Casket with its depiction of the sack of Jerusalem and its Temple by Titus.[171] This con-cern to create a visual image to sit alongside the scriptural description of the Temple clearly extended beyond the Celtic and Anglian worlds. The tenth and eleventh century manuscript iterations of the eighth century text *Commentarium in Apocalypsin*, composed by Beatus of Liébana (d. AD797), evidence much more elaborate visual depictions of the Temple for which the image within the *Liber Ardmachanus* might possibly have provided an early and even subconscious proto-type.[172]

The extent to which this predominantly monastic interest in the Temple or Tabernacle permeated the wider early Irish religious mindset is, however, harder to determine. We have already highlighted in our earlier discussion a significant amount of early Irish textual evidence

---

[167] O'Loughlin (2000c), 24–26, 29 n. 13 (4).

[168] Farr (1997), 57.

[169] Bede, *De Templo*, 2, 17.2; *De Tabernaculo*, 2, 12.

It has been suggested that what Bede actually saw was only a copy of the *Codex Amiatinus* diagram placed in another work by the same author. For a detailed discus-sion of the possible relationship between the two codices see Holder (1994), 92 n. 1.

[170] O'Reilly (1995), lii–lv; Farr (1997), 56.

[171] Farr (1997), 56–57.

[172] O'Loughlin (2000c), 35–36.

which resonates with, or indeed parallels, scriptural depictions of the Tabernacle and Temple. So, for example, the hagiographical evidence (which is also probably mainly 'monastic' in origin) pertaining to the marking out of holy space which we encounter in the various saints' lives or the vivid description by Cogitosus of the glory of Brigid's church at Kildare would appear to recall clearly the divine spatial ordering of the Temple.[173] Yet the extent to which this reflects a contemporary and conscious theological understanding or is rather a reading back, either on our part or on the part of a particular author or both, of a later planning model inspired by a developed Temple theology is problematic. Certainly I would argue that it is not until the opening chapters of Book 44 of the *Hibernensis*[174] that the depiction of the Insular ritualized marking out of holy space is placed explicitly within a scriptural context; with the accompanying angelic or divine ordinance and precise measurement that so dominates the biblical narrative. Here

[173] Cogitosus, *Vita S. Brigidae*, 32.
[174] *Hibernensis*, 44, 2.
De debito termino circa omnem locum sanctum.

    a. Omnis civitas refugii cum suburbanis suis posita est.
    b. Item: Omnis civitas sacerdotibus data cum suburbanis suis XV milia longitudinis, et latitudinis X milia alendis pecoribus sacerdotum fuit.
    c. Item: Ezechiel metiens civitatem aliquando metitur mille passus, aliquando milia passuum in orientem sic et reliq.
    d. Item. Templum Salomonis habuit septum circa se, in quo qui malum faceret periret.
    e. Item: Tabernaculum Moysi circa se atrium habuit.
    f. Item Ezechiel: Vidi angelum habentem arundinem in manu, ut metiret civitatem in circuitu et plateas ejus foras.
    g. Item in apocalipsin: Venit angelus, ut metiret civitatem et plateas ejus.
    h. Item in Zacharia: Quando reversi sunt a Babilone, aedificaverunt templum et circumseptum ejus et reliqua.

Concerning the necessary boundary around every holy place.

    a. Every town of refuge is laid out with its *suburbana*.
    b. Likewise: every town shall give to the priesthood an area within its suburbs measuring 15 000 cubits long and 10 000 cubits wide for rearing its flocks.
    c. Likewise: Ezekiel measuring the city at one time measured 1000 paces and then at another time measured 1000 paces to the east etc.
    d. Likewise: The Temple of Solomon had an enclosure about it, in which anyone who did evil would perish.
    e. Likewise: The Tabernacle of Moses had around it a hallway.
    f. Likewise Ezekiel: I saw an angel with a rod in his hand with which to measure the perimeter of the city and its *plateae* outside.
    g. Likewise in Revelation: the angel came to measure the city and its *plateae*.
    h. Likewise in Zechariah: when they had returned from Babylon they built the temple and its enclosure and so forth.

in the *Hibernensis* we find explicit reference to the measuring out of the Levitical cities,[175] including the 'cities of refuge', and to the accounts of the layout and dimensions of the Tabernacle of Moses and the Temple of Solomon and of their idealized successor the Temple of Ezekiel. Further, the ritual significance of the act of measuring, and the need to be accurate, is attested to by reference to the angelic role in a number of biblical accounts, including the measuring out of the Temple of Ezekiel's vision,[176] the measuring out of the New Jerusalem recounted in the Book of Revelation,[177] and the measuring out of Jerusalem as depicted in the Book of the prophet Zechariah.[178] Despite the confused nature of some of the biblical allusions and the difficulty in securing an exact origin for some of the scriptural references the reader is being reminded here that the Tabernacle and the Temple were divinely ordained, that they were to be constructed to a pattern given by God, and should reflect the perfection of Heaven.

The creation within the *Hibernensis* of a scriptural context for religiously inspired enclosure also influenced the text's depiction of the *internal* layout of the enclosed space. Its threefold division of the internal space clearly suggests a Temple or Tabernacle model as a possible paradigm and again it is primarily within the *Hibernensis* that we encounter a systematic attempt to place this spatial organisation within a scriptural and theological context. Drawing heavily upon both scriptural descriptions of the Tabernacle and Temple, and upon the pattern of internal zoning advocated within works such as Isidore of Seville's early seventh century *Etymologiae*, the *Hibernensis* provides a scriptural and patristic framework within which the morphology of Irish religious settlement might be interpreted. We have already observed that the Temple has been suggested as an exemplar for the religious topography of Iona based primarily on the tripartite division of the sacred landscape of the island perceived within the text of Adomnán's *Vita S. Columbae*.[179] Here the whole island is declared sacred space with the island foreshore as the outer boundary and the monastic enclosure and the church enclosure providing the middle and inner boundaries.[180] We have further noted that the divine

---

[175] Numbers 35:3–5.
[176] Ezekiel 40:3.
[177] Revelation 21:15.
[178] Zechariah 2:1–2.
[179] MacDonald (2001), 29–30.
[180] MacDonald (2001), 15–19.

topography of the city of Jerusalem depicted in detail within Adomnán's other key work, *De locis sanctis*, has also served as a metaphor for the Ionan landscape and indeed prefigures Adomnán's description of Iona found in the later *Vita S. Columbae*.[181] So we are left facing the question as to why the author(s) of the *Hibernensis* and of the *Vita S. Columbae* and *De locis sanctis* were so anxious to employ the exemplar of Jerusalem and the Temple as an extended metaphor for Irish religious settlement, and for Iona in particular.

One obvious answer would be to assert that it was natural for any Christian writer to wish to identify his community with Jerusalem and the Temple and if we are correct in our belief that the Temple as a holy *locus* was paradigmatic for Christian settlement not only in Ireland but across the Christian world then we should not be surprised at the systematic attempt in these texts to make that crucial identification. However, it is also possible that there were other rather more worldly concerns lying behind the creation of these texts and so the answer to our question as to why the identification with Jerusalem and the Temple was so important is potentially less straightforward than might initially be assumed.

To explore this possibility further the first task is to establish the nature of the relationship, if any, between the *Hibernensis* and the two works we know to have been written by Adomnán, the *Vita S. Columbae* and *De locis sanctis*. The provenance of the *Hibernensis* is far from settled but despite the proliferation of continental versions of the *Hibernensis* it has been a scholarly given that Recension A at least is Irish in origin and no serious contrary opinion has prevailed.[182] Its

---

[181] O'Reilly (1997), 86.

[182] Kenney (1929), 248.

For a detailed discussion of the putative Irish origins of the *Hibernensis* see Dumville (1994), 86–89.

The origins of Recension B have proved more elusive. The colophon in Recension A, even if genuine and accurate, does little to shed light on the authorship of Recension B (Davies, L. M. (1997), 213). Despite Dumville's cautious suggestion that it might possibly be Breton Sheehy is clear that B was also Irish in origin representing a development of Recension A (Dumville (1994), 89; Sheehy (1982), 534). Charles-Edwards, whilst admitting the likely Irish genesis of the A-text and its chronological priority, also sees in the A-text a work in progress but rejects the notion that it provided a preparatory text for B which he views as more likely deriving from a text with fewer mistakes than A. One explanation offered is that the A-text represented the culmination of the work of the southern half of the collaboration between Ruben and Cú Chuimne and that after the death of Ruben Cú Chuimne completed the task using a more accurate copy. This would still place the B-text firmly in an Irish milieu where the A-text was known (Charles-Edwards (1998), 236–237). The question effectively remains unsettled.

'Irish-ness' is attested by a number of factors including its form and likely provenance and authorship. In terms of its form and provenance parallels can be made with other contemporary ecclesiastical and secular writings including native law texts. Although the Latin used is at times cumbersome and frequently inadequate to the task of capturing the essence of orally based Old Irish concepts in an alien idiom the linguistic style and didactic structure adopted places the *Hibernensis* within a broad insular/Irish cultural and legal context. The use of Isidorian etymologies in the B-text of the *Hibernensis* is resonant of what one scholar has referred to as the 'pseudo-etymological analysis' of native Irish Law glosses.[183] Distinctive features such as glosses, puns, and numerology are reminiscent of eighth century Hiberno-Latin writings and of Irish exegetical literature of the period such as the Ps-Hilarius's *Exposito in vii epistola catholicas*, a text we now know to have been drawn upon by the compilers of the *Hibernensis* and which, in turn, may have drawn upon an earlier 'native etymological tradition'.[184] In addition, the *trium* of chapter headings, *exempla*, and *testimonia* used throughout the *Hibernensis* is paralleled within the Old Irish glosses although the question as to which drove the agenda for the *Hibernensis*, the heading or the evidence, is a vexed one. The truth is probably that both set the agenda at different points of the text.[185] One is also struck instantly by the significant number of references to Irish synods listed under various headings such as *Patricius, Romani, sinodus Romana, sinodus Hibernensis*, forming approximately 120 of the chapter headings in the *Hibernensis*.[186] Further, the methodology of treating canon law by topics was paralleled and almost certainly predated by the practice within Irish vernacular law.

With regard to authorship, the names of the compilers are actually given to us by a colophon, inserted by the scribe Arbedoc, in a ninth century Breton manuscript of the A-text of the *Hibernensis* where they are listed as two Irish monks, Ruben of Dairinis, an island monastery on the Blackwater in Munster, and Cú Chuimne of Iona.[187] Other potential candidates for Irish authorship have included Cummian,

---

[183] Sheehy (1982), 532; Davies, L. M. (1997), 211.

[184] Breen (1984), 213.

[185] Charles-Edwards (1998), 210, 231, 236.

[186] Richter (1999), 222–223.

[187] *Hucusque Ruben et Cu-chuimne Iae et Dairinis* (St Germain text; Paris BN lat. 12021).

See Etchingham (1999), 47.

author of the *Penitentiale Cummeani*, and Adomnán whose *Canones Adamnani* appear alongside the *Hibernensis* in several manuscripts.[188] Serious discussion has revolved around the two monks named in the Breton colophon and a number of objections have been raised to this particular assertion of Irish authorship. David Dumville has pointed out the significance of the fact that the ascription of the work to Ruben and Cú Chimne appears uniquely in this Breton manuscript version and that paradoxically this manuscript version is also one of three manuscripts[189] which contain a preface written in the first person singular which would, of course, argue against dual authorship.[190]

Nevertheless, a number of factors do argue strongly for an early Irish context for the document. The significant overlap with Irish vernacular law and the likely Irish authorship of the *Hibernensis* coupled with the fact that the latest authorities cited are, for Recension A, Theodore of Canterbury (d. AD690), and, for Recension B, Adomnán of Iona (d. AD704), has meant that an early eighth century Irish milieu for the document is generally accepted.[191] It is also generally accepted that Cú Chuimne and Ruben of Dairinis were its authors or compilers.[192] If one of the compilers was indeed Cú Chuimne of Iona a possible *terminus post quem* provided by the date of Iona's adherence to the Roman Easter in AD716 might help to explain the supposedly pro-Roman tone of some of the document. Book 20 explicitly condemns the Britons who 'are contrary in all things to Roman custom and have cut themselves off from the unity of the church . . .'.[193] This pro-Roman, anti-nativist stance was detected by Kathleen Hughes who speculated that the *Hibernensis* might have been born out of a

---

[188] The textual juxtaposition of the *Canones Adomnani* and the *Hibernensis* has certainly helped to convince at least one scholar of the likelihood of Adomnán's authorship (Nicholson (1901), 102).

The manuscripts which include the *Canones Adomnani* are Oxford, Bodleian Library, Hatton 42 (B-text) (written in Brittany in the ninth century and the earliest B-text); Orléans 221; Paris BN lat.12021; Paris BN lat. 3182; Cambrai 625; and London, British Library, Cotton Otho E XIII. Interestingly Cambrai is the only non-Breton manuscript.

See Davies, L. M. (1997), 217 n. 56.

[189] The three texts are Paris, BN lat. 12021 (A-text); Oxford, Hatton 42 (B-text); Rome, BV T.XVIII (B-text). See Davies, L. M. (1997), 213–214.

[190] Dumville (1994), 85–86.

[191] Etchingham (1999), 47.

[192] Richter (1999), 216; Etchingham (1999), 47.

[193] *Hibernensis*, 20, 6.

aut ad Britones, qui omnibus contrarii sunt et a Romano more et ab unitate ecclesiae se abscidunt (see Etchingham (1999), 149).

seventh century struggle between the *Romani* and the *Hibernenses* with the *Hibernensis* being 'a final statement by the *Romani*, setting out canons advocating a Roman type government as well as a Roman type tonsure'.[194] It has even been suggested that the prime objective of the compiler(s) of the *Hibernensis* was to reconcile Celtic usage with Roman practice.[195] This view is undermined by the fact that the *Hibernensis* does not represent a single consistent view point and that Irish sources are much quoted in the work.[196] It would seem therefore that there is very little substantive textual evidence which could help determine the compilers' intentions.[197] What we can assert with certainty is that if Ruben was also one of the compilers then the *terminus ante quem* is given by his obit which is listed in the *Annals of Ulster s.a.* 725.[198]

However, even if the compilers' original motivation remains elusive, Book 44 of the *Hibernensis*, as well as other parts of the work, clearly does reflect a desire, similar to that found within both the *Vita* and *De locis sanctis*, to place Irish ecclesiology within an overtly biblical context; in particular within a clear Temple framework. Further, if we are correct in accepting an Ionan provenance for the *Hibernensis*, on a similar chronological horizon to both the *Vita S. Columbae* and *De locis sanctis*, it is even possible, as Nicholson has suggested, that Adomnán was indeed the creator, or at least the 'overseer', of the *Hibernensis*.[199] This could point to the existence of an 'Ionan school' which potentially produced all three works. To explore this possibility we need to turn our attention to that much overlooked work of Adomnán, *De locis sanctis*, to explore its relationship with the later *Vita S. Columbae*, and to ask the same question of these texts as was asked of the *Hibernensis*; why were they written?

It is important to note at this stage that early Irish exegesis was far from solely preoccupied with the Temple as a physical edifice. Like the rest of western Christendom Irish exegetes had been exposed to the allegorising theology of the Alexandrians and the early church fathers and more particularly to the theology of Isidore of Seville. Certainly, on the basis of the probable contents of the library on Iona, it is safe to

[194] Hughes (1966), 123–133.
[195] Jackson (1978).
[196] Dumville (1994), 86.
[197] Davies, L. M. (1997), 214.
[198] Charles-Edwards (2000), 421 n. 28.
[199] Nicholson (1901).

assume that Adomnán (c.AD624–704) was well aware of the four-fold sense of scripture as systematized by Jerome and Cassian and encapsulated so brilliantly by Isidore.[200] It has been cogently argued that Adomnán's *De locis sanctis* fits comfortably into this intellectual milieu; representing an outstanding example of early Irish biblical criticism.[201] The work draws directly and indirectly upon a number of apposite works, including Isidore of Seville's *De natura rerum* and Jerome's *Liber de situ et locorum*, the influence of which can be found in almost every chapter of Book Two of *De locis sanctis*.[202] More intriguing still, the point has been well made that there are many chapters of the *De locis sanctis* where we have virtually no knowledge of what sources lay behind the text even though it is obvious that other written sources were being employed.[203] This is not to imply that it was simply derivative of other works but rather that it belonged to an exegetical methodology that had a scholarly history. It was essential for any self-respecting exegete to be able to call upon the support of the church fathers to support his interpretation and it is clear from the text of *De locis sanctis* that Adomnán's hermeneutical application fitted into an already established tradition of exegesis.

That said, at first sight *De locis sanctis*, almost certainly written before the *Vita S. Columbae* and the *Hibernensis*,[204] might appear to be little more than a medieval Baedeker; a wistful pilgrim narrative detailing the travels of an unknown Gallic bishop by the name of Arculf around the sights of the Holy Land, written by a Celtic monk who realistically would never visit these places himself.[205] This has certainly been the view of a number of scholars who have dismissed the work as being of little religious significance.[206] As a result the work has not attracted anything like the scholarly attention received by the author's more famous work *Vita S. Columbae*. Yet to his venerable near-contemporary, Bede, the author of *De locis sanctis* was regarded as a scholar of note. Described by Bede in his own *De locis sanctis* as *eruditissimus in scripturis*[207] and *virem*

---

[200] O'Loughlin (1994), 52.
[201] Bullough (1964).
[202] O'Loughlin (1994), 38, 48–49.
[203] O'Loughlin (1994), 51.
[204] Meehan (1958), 4–5.
[205] O'Loughlin (1992), 37.
[206] Smyth (1986), 211, 230; (1996), 283–284.
[207] Bede, *De locis sanctis*, 19, 4; see also *HE*, 5, 15.

venerabilem,[208] Adomnán's reputation appears to have been built not upon the *Vita S. Columbae* but upon *De locis sanctis.*[209] For Adomnán's contemporaries there can be little doubt that *De locis sanctis* was a much more theologically significant work than his now more famous *Vita S. Columbae.* It was the exegetical skill exhibited in the *De locis sanctis* that earned him the title *vir illustris*, not the hagiography of the *Vita.*[210] It is also clear that Adomnán himself viewed the latter work as important for he states at the end of the third book that he has written this text despite the many other pressing calls on his valuable time.[211]

Adomnán's *De locis sanctis* is, without doubt, a much more complex and sophisticated text than might first appear and far from being simply an ecclesiastical travelogue it is in fact a highly developed piece of biblical exegesis.[212] Most importantly for our discussion it is in this intriguing text that we encounter Adomnán's most theologically sophisticated exposition of the significance of the holy place. In particular we can see both through his detailed depiction of the holy city of Jerusalem and in the very form and structure of the work a systematic attempt to identify Iona with Jerusalem. The holy city, to which Adomnán devotes almost half of *De locis sanctis*, was already well-established as an exegetical model and the description of Jerusalem contained within *De locis sanctis* would appear to pre-figure the depiction of Iona as a holy land found in the later *Vita S. Columbae.*[213] As we have already noted, this explicit and thematic biblical referencing is evident elsewhere in Adomnán's work. In the *Vita S. Columbae* he also seeks to highlight the sanctity of the island community, and the religious gravitas of its founder, by drawing a number of typologically similar comparisons between events in Columba's life and various scriptural, mostly Old Testament, exemplars.[214] Thus he draws a parallel between Joshua's deliverance of the Jewish people into the Promised Land and the Saxon king Oswald's Constantinian-style vision of Columba before the battle against the British king Cadwalla.[215] The

---

[208] Bede, *De locis sanctis*, 19, 5.
[209] O'Loughlin (1995).
[210] O'Loughlin (1995), 1.
[211] *DLS*, 3, 6, 5.
[212] O'Loughlin (1992).
[213] O'Reilly (1997), 86.
[214] MacDonald (2001), 28.
[215] *VC*, 1, 1.

Joshua story was already regarded by patristic exegesis as a prefiguring of Christ and his salvific role in leading the new chosen people, the church, into the heavenly promised land and so the fulfilment of Columba's prophecy of Oswald's victory provided a clear parallel between the ministries of Joshua, Columba, and of course, most importantly, Jesus.[216] Again, the story of Columba's pillow-stone recalls Jacob's night at Bethel and in so doing marks Iona out, like Bethel, as an especially holy place where God is revealed.[217] Equally, the account of the taming of the snakes on the island by Columba resonates with the story of the expulsion of the snakes by God from the Garden of Eden marking Iona out not simply as a holy place but as an earthly paradise, a type of the Garden of Eden.[218] Adomnán however also references New Testament material, even drawing a parallel between Columba and Christ himself. This is perhaps most strikingly seen in his telling of the encounter between the saint, his attendant Diormit, and the white horse.[219] In the story the horse senses Columba's impending death and his tears fall freely on to the saint's lap in a clear recollection of the biblical accounts of the anointing of Jesus at Bethany. In these accounts a woman anoints Jesus's feet with costly perfume and is rebuked for doing so by his disciples in much the same way as Diormit rebukes the mourning horse.[220] There is also supporting evidence from an additional textual source potentially located to the same dating horizon as the *Vita* itself which lists the names of twelve companions who are alleged to have accompanied Columba on his voyage to Iona. The use of this apostolic number should perhaps not surprise us but it does nevertheless enhance the Christological credentials of Iona's founding father.[221]

The scriptural referencing employed by Adomnán was not restricted to textual *content*. In terms of textual *structure*, O'Loughlin has argued that the tripartite division of the texts of both the *Vita* and *De locis sanctis* is deliberately intended to mirror the three stage missionary impulse depicted in Luke-Acts.[222] Iona is a holy place, like

---

[216] O'Reilly (1997), 84–85.
[217] *VC*, 3, 23.
[218] *VC*, 2, 28.
[219] *VC*, 3, 23.
[220] Mark 14.3–9; Matthew 26.6–13; John 12.1–8.
[221] Sharpe (1995), 19, 353–354 n. 356.
[222] O'Loughlin (1996), 114.
See especially Acts 1.8.

Jerusalem, but this time situated at the northernmost edge of the Christian world where Christ's redemptive work continues to be articulated through Columba.[223] Iona is also the *ultimum terrae*, the very end of the earth, the eschatological edge of the church's mission, and the third and final stage in the conversion of all humankind.[224] This is again significant for Adomnán because it helps to place the conversion of Ireland and the Iona mission in a scriptural context. Thus the Columban mission was the fulfilling of scripture and Iona the New Jerusalem at the eschatological edge of the church's mission; a *locus sanctus* in direct relationship with Jerusalem, the *locus sanctissimus*.

Accordingly, when *De locis sanctis* is set alongside the *Vita S. Columbae* and the *Hibernensis* they do arguably represent *de minimis* a common ecclesiological and scriptural approach to the understanding and interpretation of the nature of religious settlement based upon the biblical metaphors of the New Jerusalem and the Temple. What I would want to argue here is that the catalyst for the writing of *De locis sanctis* and for the *Vita*, and quite possibly also for the *Hibernensis*, was not purely theological in nature; but that other more worldly concerns were also pressing. Attention has already been drawn by a number of scholars to the possible impact of both ecclesiological and secular concerns upon the work of Adomnán, and upon the *Vita* in particular.[225] Picard has argued forcefully that by the time Adomnán came to write the *Vita* the Columban ecclesiastical primacy was under pressure from a number of quarters. The Roman party in Ireland were in the ascendancy following the Synod of Whitby. The reputation of Columba had suffered as a result of the controversy over the dating of Easter; a debate which had involved a sustained Northumbrian attack upon the sanctity of Columba. Further it would appear that not only was the cult of Cuthbert at Lindisfarne beginning to overshadow that of Columba on Iona there were also the emerging counter-claims to primacy of Armagh and Kildare to contend with.[226] It should however be acknowledged that this interpretation of events is not universally accepted. Herbert has dismissed the suggestion that Adomnán would have viewed either Armagh or Kildare as a serious threat at this time. She also rejects that notion that during Adomnán's life time the fortunes of Iona were on the wane.

[223] O'Reilly (1997), 86.

[224] O'Loughlin (1996), 115–116.

[225] Picard (1982); Herbert (1988); O'Loughlin (1992); Sharpe (1995); O'Reilly (1997); MacDonald (2001).

[226] Picard (1982).

She argues instead that the catalyst for the creation of the *Vita*, although it undoubtedly had its genesis in the events at Whitby, was rather more personal to Adomnán. She suggests that Adomnán, in the wake of his decision to follow the ruling of Whitby and 'convert' to the Roman dating of Easter and to adopt the Roman tonsure, needed to assure his community that he was still loyal to the Columban memory. Herbert further argues that he also felt the need to reassert the orthodoxy of Columba's Christian witness in the face of ongoing Northumbrian criticism.[227] Certainly the *Vita* both in form and content was recognisably orthodox in its portrayal of Columba drawing upon other well-known and unquestionably sound *vitae sanctorum* such as the *Vita S. Martini* of Sulpicius Severus and Athanasius's *Vita S. Antonii* (in the Latin version by Evagrius) as well as upon other standard theological works such as Gregory's *Dialogues*.[228]

Whatever the truth of the matter, it would appear that Adomnán was anxious to ensure that Columba remained where he rightly belonged, amongst the spiritual greats. Adomnán's vision was not bounded by the parameters of his monastic community or of the island of Iona; his perspective was far from insular. Columba was a saint who deserved to be known throughout Christendom. Moreover, set alongside these broader ecclesiological considerations there were also some rather more parochial diplomatic issues at stake. In particular Adomnán was concerned that the Columban *familia* might continue to have a significant role within secular Irish society and especially within the ruling Uí Néill of which, of course, both Columba and Adomnán were members. What Adomnán appeared to want was for Uí Néill rulers to govern with the blessing and the counsel of the successors of Columba.[229] We first encounter this aspiration in the small fragment remaining to us of Cumméne's earlier 'Life' of St Columba, *Liber de virtutibus Sancti Columbae*, which probably dates from the 630s or 640s and remains to us as an insertion into the oldest extant version of Adomnán's *Vita*.[230] In this pericope Columba warns Áedán of the dire consequences for the succession if he or his descendants disobey Columba and his descendants. We can see this desire for an ongoing Columban influence over the Uí Néill kingship affirmed

---

[227] Herbert (1988), 142–148.
[228] Sharpe (1995), 57–59; O'Reilly (1997), 80. See Sharpe (1995), 26–27, 355–356 n. 358.
[229] *VC*, 3, 5.
[230] See Sharpe (1995), 3, 357 n. 360; Herbert (1988), 134–136.

also within the main body of the text of the *Vita* in a number of places, most notably in the enigmatic story of the consecration in AD574 of Áedán mac Gabráin as king by Columba; the earliest known account of sacramental king-making and a story which may well have its genesis in the biblical account of Samuel's anointing of King Saul.[231] A similar example is found in the story of Columba's prophesying the succession of Eochaid Buide mac Áedáin to the kingship; a story which more obviously parallels the biblical account of Samuel's choosing King David to succeed King Saul.[232] From these extracts the reader is left in no doubt that Adomnán was keen to ensure a Columban perennial influence upon the Christian kingship of the Uí Néill. In legislative terms the enactment of the Law of Adomnán in AD697 was probably a step towards achieving this goal.[233] In ecclesiological terms a key element in establishing this Columban legacy was the identification of Iona with the heavenly city, Jerusalem, and of Columba with the figure of Christ.

I would argue therefore that both the *Vita* and *De locis sanctis* reflect a retrospective sanctification of the landscape itself by an author who clearly wished to promote the Columban legacy and the place of Iona both within the wider church and within the secular power structures of his day by making a favourable identification of the holy island of Columban Iona with the holy city of the New Jerusalem of the Book of Revelation. In the case of the *Hibernensis* (a work which I would also place firmly in a Columban and probably in a specifically Ionan setting during the abbacy of Adomnán) I would argue that it too represents a desire to secure the position of the Irish church on the Christian world map. The sheer scale of the task undertaken[234] and the ambitious desire confessed within the

[231] *VC*, 3, 5; 1 Samuel 10:1.

[232] *VC*, 1, 9; 1 Samuel 16:1–13.
Michael Enright has interpreted these two stories (along with *VC*, 1, 36 which describes the murdered Diarmait mac Cerbaill as 'ordained by God') as forming part of a broader exposition of biblical kingship, based upon 1 Samuel, which runs as a theme throughout the *Vita*. Interestingly, he has further argued that this understanding of kingship was a formative influence upon *De regno*, Book 25 of the *Hibernensis* (Enright (1985), 5–78). If he is correct this is yet another connection between the work of Adomnán and the *Hibernensis*.
See Sharpe (1995), 355–356 n. 358.

[233] Herbert (1988), 52.

[234] The scale of the *Hibernensis* is indeed truly impressive. Comprising some 70 books and approximately 750 chapters each chapter is subdivided into 'headings' or rules and 'evidence'; the evidence coming in two main forms; *exempla*, such as events from biblical or ecclesiastical history establishing a rule, and *testimonia*, texts from authoritative sources such the Church Fathers or synods and councils supporting this rule (Richter (1999), 217; Charles-Edwards (1998), 210).

prologue to several of the extant manuscripts to encompass in a single volume the vast range of synodical decrees available to the reader would lead us to presume that in the *Hibernensis* we have a conscious systematic and innovative attempt to encapsulate for the first time canon law into one coherent work[235] and in so doing inevitably bring kudos and influence to the community or communities which produced it.

We do, however, need to be cautious about over-emphasising Adomnán's ecclesiological or secular agenda. By the seventh century Jerusalem was an accepted liturgical motif as the place where God was to be met and as the site of Christ's passion and resurrection and as O'Loughlin has pointed out the language of *De locis sanctis* has many liturgical resonances.[236] In addition, first and foremost, Adomnán was a monk. The reconciling of the scriptures through detailed exegesis was a valid and necessary preoccupation for the church; an important enough task to merit Adomnán's own time. Augustine himself had stated that among the tools of an exegete must be a good book on the geography of Palestine and that he hoped someone would produce one.[237] *De locis sanctis* could be seen as Adomnán's response to that plea. The agenda of *De locis sanctis* is clearly set by Adomnán's exegetical requirements and not by the itinerary of Arculf's travels.[238] There is also clear evidence in *De locis sanctis* that Adomnán was determined to resolve some of the most intractable temporal and geographical conundrums presented by the scriptures. As we have already noted, such exegesis had been identified by no less a figure than Augustine as an essential element in a proper understanding of scripture for the resolution of these scriptural *aenigmates* would help to clarify a text.[239] Adomnán's concern with geographical accuracy ranges from his meticulous description of the holy city at the very beginning of the text to the resolution of exegetical problems by the use of Arculf's eyewitness account of the topography. He tackles a wide spectrum of exegetical issues ranging from major issues such as what we would now call the 'synoptic problem'[240] to the whereabouts of Rachel's *sepulchrum*[241] to

---

[235] Sheehy (1987), 278.
[236] *DLS*, I, 7, 1.
See O'Loughlin (1992), 41–42.
[237] Augustine: *De doctrina Christiana*, 2, 39, 59.
[238] O'Loughlin (1997a), 128.
[239] O'Loughlin (1997a), 128 n. 5.
[240] O'Loughlin (1992), 46–47.
[241] *DLS*, 2, 7.

the importance of Hebron as a biblical location[242] to a discussion of the Dead Sea and its salt content.[243] Essentially, the *De locis sanctis* provides an outstanding example of early medieval exegesis at work and what emerges from the text is the fact that Adomnán was a skilled and meticulous scholar who in many respects was an innovative thinker who set himself the task of solving the scriptural *aenigmates*, highlighted by Augustine, using the best topographical and geographical evidence available to him.

Nevertheless, there is convincing evidence to suggest that Adomnán was also working to a definite ecclesiological agenda centred upon the need to protect the reputation of Columba and thereby ensure an ongoing Columban ecclesial hegemony. A key part of this strategy was the need to draw a convincing parallel between Iona, and its community on the northern edge of the Christian world,[244] with Jerusalem, the heavenly city at the very heart of this world. It was thus essential to firmly locate Iona within the salvific schema outlined in Acts. However, this was not simply a cynical political manoeuvre but stemmed from Adomnán's genuine belief in the sacred character of the island of Iona. As we have already noted, for Adomnán Jerusalem was an archetype for his own monastic community; a holy land on the very outer limits of Christendom which was, like Bethel, a place of God's revelation and, like the Garden of Eden, an earthly paradise.[245] Whilst recognising the force of O'Loughlin's argument that *De locis sanctis* was written with a very definite theological purpose in mind, namely salvation,[246] I would suggest that it was not solely individual, or even corporate, salvation that concerned Adomnán in his writings but also the ongoing credibility of his patron saint in the eyes of the wider Christian church and the future unity and integrity of his own religious community. It was this ecclesiological anxiety which made the achievement of a convincing comparison between Iona and Jerusalem all the more important and which partly explains the strong Jerusalem and Temple centred imagery of both the *Vita S. Columbae* and *De locis sanctis* and ultimately of the *Hibernensis*.

---

[242] *DLS*, 2, 8 and 9/10.
[243] *DLS*, 2, 17 and 18.
[244] O'Reilly (1997), 86.
[245] *VC*, 3, 23; *VC*, 2, 28.
[246] O'Loughlin (1992), 38.

3.E. *Conclusion*

From the Tabernacle to the Levitical cities and from the Temples of Solomon and Ezekiel to the New Jerusalem of the Book of Revelation, the scriptural witness to the demarcation and division of holy space undoubtedly provided an interpretative context for early church theologians to describe contemporary religious topography. This is no less true within an Irish context. Further, there is explicit literary evidence that the Temple in particular was a uniquely significant religious and spiritual *locus* for the early church. In that capacity it served as a key paradigm. Indeed, it can be argued with some confidence that in terms of the Old Testament witness it was the description of the Temple by Ezekiel with its strong eschatological overtones that had the most profound effect upon later Jewish and Christian Temple theologies. Certainly it was the description of the Temple contained within the Book of Ezekiel that most influenced the development of the Temple motif within Christian biblical exegesis, again including within an early Irish context.[247]

The foregoing has drawn attention to the presence of explicit Temple imagery within a number of key Irish texts relating to the layout of Insular religious space and it is clear that MacDonald's admittedly 'very tentative' suggestion that the Temple of Ezekiel might provide the 'ultimate exemplar' for Adomnán's depiction of the sacred landscape of Iona has merit.[248] Further, there is credible evidence within the *Hibernensis*, a seminal text for our discussion, that a significant degree of what might at best be called biblical text proofing was carried out with the specific aim of setting the layout of Irish religious settlement within a Temple context. Of the 1000 direct and many more indirect or elliptical scriptural references contained within the *Hibernensis* many are difficult or indeed impossible to trace. This is partly because, despite warnings in the B-text against the changing of the *sensus scripturae* by teachers and scholars, there is evidence that the compilers were on occasion content to interpret biblical texts rather than translating them. This is particularly true of the *Hibernensis* texts referring to ecclesiastical layout where, as Swift clearly illustrates, the use of the Vulgate text within the *Hibernensis* represents a 'medieval recasting' of the biblical text rather than an accurate recital with clear

---

[247] Hamblin and Seely (2007), 39.
[248] MacDonald (2001), 30.

evidence that biblical material is being used by the compilers of the *Hibernensis* to justify pre-existing Irish ecclesiastical *mores*.[249]

If Swift is correct in her analysis, and I would argue that she is, then despite the Iona-centric nature of a number of the key texts, and the particular ecclesiological concerns of the Columban *familia* which may have influenced their form and content, the spatial *schema* depicted within the *Vita S. Columbae, De locis sanctis* and especially the *Hibernensis* does indeed reflect a wider Irish settlement pattern rather than a specifically Columban template. Certainly the topographical regularity of the extant material evidence, particularly when viewed through the prism of the vernacular literary witness, suggests that there existed some degree of universal understanding about the nature and form of religious settlement.

This brings us back to the vexed question of the nature of the relationship between the textual and material evidence. Determining the extent to which the scriptural witness to the layout of the Temple in particular may have provided not only an interpretative context for understanding the nature of religious topography but also influenced the development of its form, serving perhaps as a catalyst for ecclesiastical architectural design and even innovation, is challenging. Yet the retrospective nature of the textual evidence for a Temple influence provided by much of the relevant literature does not preclude the possibility that not only did the layout of the Temple provide a hermeneutic for the topography of Iona but also served as some sort of 'canon of planning', not just for Iona but for other early Irish religious settlements. The consideration of this possibility is the subject of the next chapter.

---

[249] Swift (1998), 107–109.

4. 'AND WAS JERUSALEM BUILDED HERE?': THE MAKING OF A RELIGIOUS LANDSCAPE

Thus we have established that religious settlement in early Ireland evinces a consistent pattern of enclosure and spatial ordering. The resonance of the archaeology with literary models, most particularly the Temple, has led me to argue for the existence of a scriptural 'canon of planning'.

Some issues remain to be resolved with respect to this contention. If we propose that the topography of religious settlement in Ireland was directly influenced by a 'canon of planning' inspired by a biblical paradigm of holy space, in this case the Temple, then how was this 'canon of planning' transmitted? How was it shared, even 'enforced', to a sufficient degree to have dictated the shape of the religious landscape over a wide and diverse geographical area?

A 'canon' is literally a 'general law, rule, or principle',[1] so I have preferred this term to the concept of a 'plan', which would imply something more finite in form for we need to think carefully about the character and possible extent of what was transmitted. To refer to a later case-study, the extent to which a text such as the Rule of St Benedict was able to be interpreted to produce a normative architecture gives some indication that a minimal witness to conceptions of space might be widely influential if accompanied by a received interpretation in a particular monastic order or tradition. The fact that some scholars

[1] Thompson, ed. (1995), 191.

have imagined a work such as the *Plan of St Gall* to actually have been necessary for planning challenges us to explain with certainty how scriptural exegesis alone might give rise to a normative model.

We also need to take account of other possible influences at work upon the morphology of early Irish religious settlement. Religious settlement anywhere does not emerge in a religious or cultural vacuum and that is equally true for Ireland. In the early medieval period the relationship between the sacred and secular was highly complex and neither can be fully understood in isolation from the other; an assumption of separation is an anachronism before the last centuries of the first millennium.[2] Religious settlement must be assumed to reflect a range of native religious and secular influences. In an early medieval Irish context among these possible 'influences' is the cultural and architectural legacy of Ireland's pagan past and its impact upon the built environment of the emerging Christian religious settlements. In particular, the Irish preference for the typologically distinctive circular or sub-circular form within both secular and religious buildings in Ireland in this period undoubtedly impacted upon the morphology of all types of settlement. Other potentially determinative factors include the ongoing influence of native construction techniques such as corbelled masonry and the extent to which the locally available materials, such as wood and dry-stone, determined form and layout.

4.A. *A Scriptural 'Canon of Planning'*

One of the possible modes of transmission of a 'canon of planning' is a pictorial representation or plan. We shall begin by examining two key documents for any discussion of early medieval monastic plans; the early ninth century Benedictine *Plan of St Gall* and the eighth to ninth century Irish manuscript known as the *Book of Mulling*; both of which we have referred to earlier in our discussion. These provide, albeit with contrasting degrees of certainty and detail, pictorial plans of religious settlements.

The early ninth century Carolingian *Plan of St Gall* is a pictorial depiction which sets out in intense detail the design and construction

---

[2] Turner (2003), 171.

of a Benedictine monastery.[3] In immediate terms the *Plan* was born out of the deliberations of the Synods of Aachen of AD816–817, the first occasion when the nature of the relationship between a monastic rule and monastic layout was actively and formally discussed. Following the synod Louis the Pious, egged on by the ascetically minded Benedict of Aniane, imposed the Benedictine Rule upon all religious houses within the Frankish kingdom. In the longer term the gestation of the *Plan of St Gall* lay within the very same Merovingian and Carolingian monasticism from which the synods arose. The *Plan* was the textual expression of the grandeur and scale of Philibert's monastery of Jumièges[4] and of the giant monasteries of the Carolingian renaissance such as the late eighth century re-buildings at Centula-St. Riquier, near Abbeville, and Fulda.

Benedict himself said relatively little upon the subject of spatial organisation in his monasteries. He did however recommend that monasteries should be constructed in such a way as to contain within their limits all that was necessary for community existence such as watermills, gardens, crafts etc in order that the monks should not have to go outside the enclosure lest their spiritual well-being be imperilled.[5] This injunction was undoubtedly taken to heart by the author(s) of the *Plan of St Gall*. The *Plan* includes within its *schema* all of the facilities required by Benedict, and includes a reserved area around a central courtyard in which the monks might live and pray.

Walter Horn argued that the *Plan* was an idealized model.[6] It is certainly highly unlikely that the creator of the *Plan* ever intended it to serve as a plan fit for use and there is no evidence that this exemplar was ever built.[7] It has been suggested that the *Plan* did not so much provide a template for a particular building but rather a menu from

[3] The document, possibly a creation of the monastery at Reichenau under Abbot Haito (AD763–836), dates from *c.*AD820 and represents the oldest known monastic building plan (Dimier (1964), 67–68). It is reproduced in Lorna Price's beautifully produced summary of the magisterial three volume work on the *Plan* by Walter Horn and Ernest Born (Price (1982), xii).

[4] Looking to the past Jumièges may well represent the coming together of both Irish and Gallo-Roman architectural styles in the one monastery but, looking forward; it has also been seen as a possible bridge between the more explicitly eremitic layout of the early Merovingian monasteries and the highly stylized form represented by the Benedictine St Gallen *Plan*. As such it was not a work of late antiquity but a product of the Carolingian renaissance (Braunfels (1972), 28, 36).

[5] Benedict, *Regula monachorum,* 66.

[6] Horn (1973), 13.

[7] Braunfels (1972), 37.

which an Abbot could pick and chose when constructing a monastery.[8] However, the *Plan* was clearly intended to influence *future* Benedictine monastic layout.[9] Not perhaps as some sort of platonic ideal to be copied in total but rather as the embodiment of a Benedictine ideal to be emulated, at least in part.

So how does such a plan compare with the only extant early Irish pictorial evidence; the colophon diagram in the *Book of Mulling*? This diagram shows what has been interpreted as a circular monastic enclosure surrounded by a number of crosses dedicated to the evangelists and the four prophets.[10] The 'enclosure' contains within its area five or six further crosses including those dedicated to the 'Angels from above', the 'Holy Spirit' and 'Christ with his Apostles'.[11] The potential significance of the Mulling drawing was first explored by H. J. Lawlor who tentatively suggested that it might represent the plan of the monastery of St Mulling.[12] Following on from that initial observation Françoise Henry suggested that what was being depicted here in the colophon diagram was a combination of free-standing cross and circular enclosure which was thought to be a common feature of eighth century monasteries.[13] A similar view of the diagram has since been

[8] Sullivan (1998), 267–268.

[9] The monastery at St Riquier, completed by Angilbert in AD788 and influenced by Jumièges, was destroyed by the Vikings a century later and rebuilt once again between AD1071 and AD1097. Here we find a monastery still significantly divergent in layout from that envisaged in the *Plan of St Gall* but we can detect the beginnings of an attempt to conform to the *Plan* such as clustering the places regularly used by the monks around the cloister (Dimier (1964), 69–70). In the majestic grandeur of Cluny II completed by Abbot Odilo during the late tenth and early eleventh centuries we find three of the four main monastic areas as outlined in the *Plan of St Gall*, the *claustrum* or monastic enclosure, an open area to receive guests and to house the school and the Abbot's house, and an area for the novices and the sick. The domestic buildings were largely omitted at Cluny but again we have the cloister with the conventual buildings situated around it in accordance with the St Gallen plan (Braunfels (1972), 41–42). With the coming of Cistercian reform in the early twelfth century we find this standardising tendency taken to its ascetic extreme. The strict regularising of life within the Cistercian monastery brought about a standard Cistercian plan which in time became essentially a Bernardine plan inspired by the foundation at Clairvaux upon which all new Cistercian foundations were to be based (Braunfels (1972), 68; Dimier (1964), 137–143).

[10] One of the best reproductions of the colophon drawing remains that found in Françoise Henry's 1940 work, *Irish Art in the Early Christian Period* (Henry (1940), 102). A more recent reproduction is provided by Lawrence Nees in his 1983 article on the drawing (Nees (1983), 69).

[11] Henry (1940), 101–102; Thomas (1971), 39; Herity (1983), 42.

[12] Lawlor (1897), 167–185.

[13] Henry (1940), 101–102.

taken by several scholars including Charles Thomas, Vincent Hurley, and more recently Lisa Bitel.[14]

Concrete examples of the Mulling *schema* have been discerned within the material evidence. Michael Herity has postulated that the sites at Kilkieran and Ahenny where a number of crosses potentially encircled a primitive oratory and at Castlekieran in Co. Meath and Ferns in Co. Wexford where groups of crosses surround the churches represent the material expression of the canon which is schematized in Mulling.[15] A similar claim was made by John Sheehan in relation to a number of church sites in north Clare including Temple Cronan where the small stone crosses surrounding the site were in addition to the newly discovered enclosure.[16] He sees these as explicable in terms of the Mulling canon.

However, despite Bitel's confident assertion that this drawing does indeed represent an eighth or ninth century Irish monastic layout,[17] others have been more reserved in their conclusions. Kathleen Hughes places the drawing in a somewhat earlier, seventh century, context. She is also more cautious in her analysis, suggesting that the drawing *might* represent an 'ecclesiastical city' compatible with the planning parameters of the *Synodus Hibernensis*.[18] A more substantive word of caution has come from Lawrence Nees who argues for a later, mid-ninth century, milieu and warns against an over-simplistic interpretation of the diagram. He also disputes the assumption that the drawing in the Mulling colophon offers a reliable guide to the arrangement of early Irish monasteries by suggesting that it owes its genesis to Carolingian iconography and manuscript illumination rather than to an attempt to accurately depict the layout of an early Irish monastery.[19]

Nevertheless, the Mulling *schema* clearly has resonances in extant monastic layouts. It would, however, be a leap to argue that such a minimalist *schema* is itself a 'blueprint' to be worked from. Certainly to attempt to build a monastery based on the information contained within this document would be a challenge.[20] The potentially late dating

---

[14] Thomas (1971), 38–40; Hurley (1982), 320; Bitel (1990), 59.

[15] Herity (1983), 43.

[16] Sheehan (1982), 37.

[17] Bitel (1990), 59.

[18] Hughes (1966), 149.

[19] Nees (1983), 90–91.

[20] Nees (1983), 70.

would suggest that it was a product of, or a representation of, a physical reality rather than its inspiration. Lisa Bitel's comment that 'no plan of St Gall exists for early Ireland' is thus true.[21] It is, of course, a rare survival from a period for which only a few manuscripts are extant but there is no evidence to suggest that a Hibernian counterpart to the *Plan of St Gall* ever existed. What we see in an Irish context described in the literature, and reflected in the extant settlement archaeology, is not the result of adherence to a drawn plan. It is, rather, the embodiment of an ideal. An ideal based on a biblically inspired understanding of holy space; an ideal based upon the sacred topography of the Jerusalem Temple. This 'canon of planning' is perhaps best described as 'received wisdom' rather than as a technical blueprint. What I am thus suggesting is that the builders of early Irish religious settlements had a defined concept of what holy space might look like based upon the scriptural accounts of the most holy of earthly sites, the Temple. This is made explicit in *Hibernensis* 44 but is also implicit in much of the other available hagiographical documentation concerning the marking out and ordering of enclosed space. The material evidence from the period also reflects such a 'concept' in its extant topography. It is manifested both in the grandeur of scale of an iconic site such as Nendrum or Iona and in the much smaller eremitic sites such as Reask and Skellig Michael; in the latter case adapted to a space where symmetrical or simple geometric patterns would be impossible.

All of the above brings us back to our original question regarding the possible mode of transmission of any 'canon of planning', scriptural or otherwise, across such a range of typologically diverse sites and, by early medieval standards, over such a huge geographical area. How was this biblical 'canon of planning' or 'received wisdom' communicated from one religious settlement to the next, and so effectively that it left behind a distinctive spatial arrangement and accompanying literary witness? The most straightforward explanation for the relative material regularity of Irish religious topography would have been the existence of a vernacular planning *schema*, written or oral, which was then adopted by an ecclesial or monastic network. We have discussed already why we think this scenario to have been unlikely. What I am suggesting instead is that it was exposure to scriptural depictions of the Temple which provided the inspiration for this normative early Irish religious topography.

---

[21] Bitel (1990), 74

Our discussion has established that the textual witness to the Temple as found in the Book of the prophet Ezekiel was readily accessible to the Irish through Scripture. We have seen that the Temple was an iconic building for the early Irish church. Further, we have noted that the topographies of both the Tabernacle and the Temple were mentioned within the context of discussion about early Irish religious settlement patterns, including within the seminal text, *Collectio canonum Hibernensis*, which illustrates clearly the influence of both the biblical descriptions of the Moysian Tabernacle and the Temple layout of the Book of Ezekiel in helping to provide a lexicon for the discussion of sacred space.[22]

In terms of Irish exposure to wider developments within scriptural exegesis we have also already established that the early Irish church was well acquainted with patristic scholarship and exegesis, and thus with the idea of the Temple as metaphor and paradigm for a range of Christian activity. The literary connections between Ireland and the European mainland have been well-rehearsed elsewhere.[23] Interestingly we know, for example, that a number of recensions of the *Hibernensis* were circulating in a European context possibly as early as the eighth century,[24] and more certainly in Brittany by the ninth century.[25] This raises questions as to the singular direction of transmission. John Blair has posited a shared monastic/ecclesial model in north-west Europe.[26] The 'canon of planning' evinced in *Hibernensis* 44 was clearly already available over a wide area by the ninth century.

Most importantly of all, a biblical and/or theological perspective was part of the everyday currency of the early medieval monastic life. Early medieval 'religious' lived and breathed scripture in a way which we no longer can fully comprehend. No pictorial depiction or planning blueprint would have been necessary to promote an exegesis of

---

[22] Further evidence of the influence of the Book of Ezekiel upon medieval Irish religious thought is provided by the tenth century Irish poem, *Saltair na Rann*, whose detailed architectural description of heaven (the *ríched*) is based on three major sources; Adomnán's *De locis sanctis,* a text of the apocalyptic work *Visio Pauli*, and an Old Latin translation of Ezekiel, part of which has survived as a fragment in a St Gall manuscript of *c.*AD900.See Carey (1986), 103; (2000), 108–119.

[23] Hillgarth (1961); (1984); James (1982).

[24] Gittos (2002), 206–207.

[25] Dumville (1994), 87.

Dumville is, however, rightly cautious about extrapolating this Breton provenance to substantiate a pan-Francia or even a pan-European availability for the *Hibernensis* as early as the eighth century (Dumville (1994), 90–91).

[26] Blair (2005), 3, 73–74.

spatial arrangement of the Temple. There was no need of a formal plan other than scripture itself.

As one stands today within the material remains of early Irish religious settlement one is not, however, struck immediately by a Temple analogy. This is for two reasons. First, it was the spatial 'ideal' encapsulated within the Temple rather than its actual form which the buildings were to reflect. There was no serious attempt to re-create the actual Temple building within an Irish setting. The literary and material evidence bear witness to the significance of a biblical planning motif; not to the structure and form of the Temple building itself. Secondly, the scriptural 'canon of planning' was the predominant but not the only determinant in the creation of early Irish religious topography. As we shall see, Irish religious settlement patterns were influenced to varying degrees by the experience of other Christian communities including those of the Middle East and Gaul. Nearer to home, our 'canon of planning' also had to accommodate the impact of non-Christian and potentially competing influences. For example, any biblical topographical model would have had to be mediated through a vernacular Irish architectural style using native materials and methods. All of this served to create an undoubtedly unique sacred landscape but one in which the influence of the paradigm of the Jerusalem Temple might not be immediately apparent. We now turn our attention to the discussion of these 'other' factors; how they interacted with a scriptural planning *schema*, and the impact they had upon the religious topography of early medieval Ireland.

4.B. *An Eremitic Inheritance*

4.B.1. The Egyptian Desert

There is no doubt of the circulation throughout Europe of some of the Middle Eastern texts already mentioned such as *Vita S. Antoni* by Athanasius (*c.*AD296-377) and of the accounts of the activities of some of the home-grown saints such as *Vita S. Martini* by Sulpicius Severus (*c.*AD363-420).[27] Certainly, by possibly as early as the late sixth century, the ascetic concept of the desert had firmly embedded itself

---

[27] Horn, Marshall, and Rourke (1990), 76.

within the early Irish religious mind-set.[28] For example, the Irish text, *Antiphonarium Benchorense*, written between AD680 and AD691, makes nineteen references to Egypt.[29] It has even been claimed that 'one of the outstanding characteristics of Irish monasticism was the desire to imitate as closely as possible the monastic pattern of the first desert monks of Egypt'.[30] Although such a claim is perhaps somewhat over-enthusiastic there is again no doubt that we can see resonating through the layout of religious settlement in Egypt, Gaul, and Ireland a generic and biblically inspired understanding of the desert as a paradigm of holy space.

That Irish monasticism sought to trace its roots back through the semi-eremitic Gallic monasticism of St Martin of Tours (d.AD397) to Anthony and Pachomius and the *laura* of the first desert monks of Egypt might indicate that the morphology of early historic Irish religious settlement owed a debt to the eremitic tenor of its Egyptian and Gallic antecedents. Although the efforts of Charles Thomas to establish parallels between the supposedly rectilinear enclosure of Iona and some of the other larger eastern sites such as Clonmacnoise and Glendalough and the Egyptian and Syrian monastic fortresses of the sixth century have now been discredited[31] the Middle Eastern and Gallic roots of Irish monasticism are beyond reproach. Indeed, in terms of the physical prefiguring of Irish religious settlement patterns, we have already alluded to the possibility that the layout of early medieval Irish religious settlement had its roots in a Middle Eastern milieu. What is of particular interest for us is the extent to which the topography of Irish religious settlement might have been influenced by those roots. As with Ireland detailed topographical information is scarce but we can snatch tantalising glimpses of how these early eremitic and coenobitic settlements in both Egypt and Gaul might have looked and why they eventually took the form they did.

Our key primary source is *Vita S. Antonii*; a strongly revisionist work of hagiography written by Athanasius around the time of Antony's death. The *Vita S. Antonii* serves as a prism through which

[28] Dumville (1997b), 106.

[29] Horn, Marshall, and Rourke (1990), 77.

[30] Horn, Marshall, and Rourke (1990), 76; see also Dumville (1997b), 106.

[31] Thomas (1971), 32. Thomas's suggestion that pottery finds provide evidence of a thriving commerce with in particular Syria and Palestine in the fifth and sixth centuries as monasticism reached these shores is more credible (Thomas (1971), 23). However, following the discrediting of Tintagel, a key site in this context, as a possible early medieval monastic settlement this evidence is also not as strong as once supposed.

we get our first refracted glimpse of the early Christian anchorite. The emergence of Antony in AD305 from his self-imposed exile in the Egyptian desert to provide a focus for the growing numbers flocking to the desert in search of the eremitic life was a seminal moment for the burgeoning church. No longer could the highly individualistic ascetic witness offered by Antony and his fellow anchorites be regarded as a strictly marginal activity. Even allowing for the hyperbole of Palladius's assertion that by the end of the fourth century Nitria was home to some five thousand monks[32] it would appear that the fourth century did see a virtual epidemic of eremitic vocation.[33] Equally, Athanasius's claim in the *Vita S. Antonii* that Antony turned the desert into a virtual city of monks[34] may simply reflect hagiographical exuberance but, if other sources are to be believed, the eremitic lifestyle did indeed soon became very attractive. The *Historia monachorum in Ægypto*, a Greek account of a journey undertaken at the end of the fourth century AD, made the memorable claim that 'there is no town in Egypt or the Thebaid which is not surrounded by hermitages as if by walls'.[35] It continued in a similar vein. In its account of the city of Oxyrhynchus it described the city as being so full of monasteries that 'the very walls resound with the voices of monks'.[36]

This frenetic activity inevitably forced the monk (a term first used by Athanasius in his *Vita*)[37] to seek to protect his personal and spiritual space and so rules began to be laid down partly to regulate the increasingly communal nature of monastic life. Over the centuries these regulations grew increasingly complex and detailed but not until relatively late on in their development did they begin to take any explicit account of architecture or of planning considerations. This does not necessarily imply that the topography of the monastery was unimportant to those who composed the monastic rules. Nor does the absence of explicit reference to layout in a monastic rule or other documentation necessarily indicate that the layout of these sites was unplanned. Nevertheless, despite the prevalence of these early eremitic communities, we have little detail of

[32] Palladius, *Historia Lausiaca*, 7, 2.

[33] Braunfels (1972), 13.

[34] Athanasius, *Vita S. Antonii*, 14.

[35] *Historia monachorum in Ægypto*, Prologue, 10. See Dunn (2000), 14.

[36] *Historia monachorum in Ægypto*, 5, 1.

[37] Chitty (1966), 5.

how they might have looked for neither Antony in his surviving correspondence nor Athanasius in his *Vita* make mention of organisational or spatial structure. It may have been that it was simply assumed that the potential audience for these monastic rules would know what a monastery might look like without the need for detailed explanation.

We can, however, find evidence of the presence of some key topographical elements which prefigure those encountered within the Irish experience. For example, although we can be fairly certain that for Athanasius the term 'monk' refers to the solitary and not to the coenobitic[38] it is clear from very early on that Egyptian eremiticism was never a truly solitary affair.[39] Even Antony appears to have received visitors and offered supervision to other hermits.[40] So from very early on the focal-point of these embryonic communities (known as *laurae*)[41] was the dwelling place of a famous anchorite[42] around whom communities of the hermit monks began to settle. Early sources tell us that the dwellings of these earliest hermits were cells made from mud bricks which appear to have varied both in size and purpose, those of the most notable recluses even boasting their own enclosed compound while novice monks might find themselves living in a cave.[43] Palladius's early fifth century *Historia Lausiaca* tell us that Amoun built two cells upon the mount at Nitria[44] and Macarius built himself four cells in different locations in the desert.[45] A church would also appear to have been a very early feature of these settlements followed shortly after by a common eating-place and by the mid-fifth century the hermits at Kellia had even constructed a *kasr* or tower of refuge.[46] Kellia also provides our earliest known example of a walled monastic dwelling. The layout of these communities will, of course, have developed over time from very simple beginnings to the more elaborate settlements. At Nitria the scale and complexity of the living arrangements

[38] Chitty (1966), 5.

[39] Dunn (2000), 13; Horn (1973), 15.

[40] Athanasius, *Vita S. Antonii*, 15.

[41] The *laura* was a Syro-Palestinian anchorite and coenobitic hybrid which initially merged independently of Egyptian monasticism. It was made up of a row or cluster of single cells around a communal centre (Chitty (1966), 15).

[42] Walters (1974), 7.

[43] Walters (1974), 9; Dunn (2000), 13-15.

[44] Palladius, *Historia Lausiaca*, 8, 5.

[45] Palladius, *Historia Lausiaca*, 18, 10.

[46] Walters (1974), 7.

as described by Palladius is so striking that the passage is quoted in full below.[47]

Many of the features to be found in a Middle Eastern setting such as cells, churches, and enclosing structures, mirror those to be found in an early Irish context; often serving in both settings as diagnostic markers indicating the presence of religious settlement. Equally the widespread and large-scale embracing of the monastic way of life prefigures what we understand to have been the Irish experience. To find a more exact parallel with Ireland we need perhaps to explore the more explicitly coenobitic communities which were emerging alongside these anchoritic and semi-anchoritic experiments. The founding of the first monastery in c.AD320 at Tabernisi in the Egyptian Thebaid is attributed to Pachomius[48] and one might expect that in this new endeavour we would detect tangible evidence of a more communal and structured lifestyle which in turn was reflected in the settlement layout. Eventually eleven monasteries following the Pachomian rule were founded in the Thebaid, two of them for women,[49] and we do have some indication of what these monasteries might have looked like. The original divine planning guidelines issued by the angel to Pachomius were explicit in their detail, describing an enclosure, cells,

---

[47] Palladius, *Historia Lausiaca*, 7, 1.
On the mountain live some 5000 men with different modes of life, each living in accordance with his own powers and wishes, so that it is allowed to live alone, or with another, or with a number of others. There are seven bakeries in the mountain, which serve the needs both of these men and also of the anchorites of the great desert, 600 in all. . . . In this mountain of Nitria there is a great church. . . . . . Next to the church is a guesthouse, where they receive the stranger who has arrived, until he goes away of his own accord, without limit of time, even if he remains two or three years. . . . . . . In this mountain there also live doctors and confectioners. And they use wine and wine is on sale. All these men work with their hands at linen manufacture, so that all are self-supporting. And indeed at the ninth hour it is possible to stand and hear how the strains of psalmody rise from each habitation so that one believes that one is high above the world in Paradise. They occupy the church only on Saturday and Sunday. There are eight priests who serve the church, in which, so long as the senior priest lives, no one else celebrates, or preaches, or gives decisions, but they all just sit quietly by his side.

[48] Braunfels (1972), 14.

[49] Like Antony, Pachomius was not treading on virgin ground. Religiously inspired withdrawal was not unique to Christian monasticism but was rather in all probability a continuation of the Jewish ascetic tradition represented by groups such as the Essenes and *Therapeutae* and of the communal traditions of early Christian groups seeking to imitate the lifestyle of the early apostles (Dunn (2000), 1–2). Indeed among the pioneers of communal asceticism in Egypt were the heterodox Manichaeans who had developed their own monasteries from as early as the AD320's but Pachomius can lay claim to have been the first to establish orthodox communal life.

and a communal refectory;[50] all features to be later found within the Irish religious community.

However, perhaps reflecting Pachomius's military background, it has alternatively been suggested that the plan of the monastery may rather have resembled a military encampment and the extant literary evidence would suggest that the monks lived in large barrack style buildings holding between twenty and forty monks which were then subdivided into communal areas for eating and praying and separate cells for each monk.[51] Eventually, due to the pressure of numbers, up to three monks would have shared a cell.[52] This would suggest a development from ordered clusters of cells to rows of contiguous cells.[53] Interestingly, at this stage in monastic development there would have been no need for any internal segregation of monks from lay brothers or lay workers akin to the Irish *manaig* as the community would only have contained monks.[54] The *Vita prima S. Pachomii*, however, also mentions a number of by now familiar features such as an enclosing wall, a gate-house, a guest-house, a refectory, an assembly hall for worship (not actually referred to as a church), a hospital and various other ancillary buildings.[55] Whatever the morphology of the layout we do find here in these Pachomian monasteries a serious attempt being made to lead the *vita communis*. This entailed a much more structured lifestyle including an embryonic liturgical life[56] and a developing monastic settlement with an enclosure and a number of key buildings. The purpose of the enclosure would appear to have been similar to that within an Irish context, mainly apotropaic rather than defensive.[57]

This clear attempt to impose coenobitic order upon eremitic chaos provides evidence of an emerging causal link between the spiritual aspirations of the founder and the planning of the monastery. Yet the picture remains frustratingly opaque. The extant remains of the fifth

[50] Palladius, *Historia Lausiaca,* 32, 2.

[51] For a description of a Pachomian monastery see Chitty (1966), 22 and Dunn (2000), 30.

[52] Palladius, *Historia Lausiaca,* 32, 2.

[53] Horn (1973), 16, fig. 5.

[54] Horn (1973), 18.

[55] Anon., *Vita prima S. Pachomii,* 28, 40, 42, 70, 81, 88, 131, 136, 144, 147. See Chitty (1966), 22.

[56] Palladius, *Historia Lausiaca,* 32, 6.
And he ordered them during the whole day to make twelve prayers, and twelve at the lamp lighting, and twelve at the night vigils, and three at the ninth hour.

[57] Horn (1973), 15–16.

century foundation of St Antony's Monastery south of Cairo, near the Red Sea, are a case in point. Although the surviving buildings are no earlier than the eleventh century there is still no evidence of any discernible structured spatial relationship or that they are subject to any form of *schema*.[58] It would appear that Middle Eastern monasticism knew a 'mixed economy' in which the spirit of the *laura* continued to co-exist alongside a more structured coenobitic form.[59] To some extent this mirrors the Irish experience where a markedly eremitic lifestyle in the remote west was complimented by a more settled communal existence in the more prosperous east although Irish religious settlement has been traditionally viewed as being predominantly eremitic in character. In material terms the archaeological remains of the *laura* are elusive and it has been suggested that the communal ties were so loose in this type of setting that they needed 'no conscious architectural expression'.[60] We can, nevertheless, discern in the apparently haphazard topography of the *laura* a prefiguring of Irish settlement patterns and certainly some have compared Irish monastic settlements such as that on Skellig Michael to those located within the desert of the Middle East.[61]

Yet, in contrast to the Irish context, the failure of the extant literary evidence in an Egyptian or Syrian milieu to explicitly address issues of physical structure and spatial organisation, and the absence of an expressed sense of monastic space as sacred, prevent us from ascribing with any confidence a particular theological motivation to these early pioneers of religious settlement. The Temple may well have been a defining motif but we have no means of confirming that possibility. Indeed, the history and morphology of several key sites would suggest that the primary dynamic behind the development of the native Syrian monasteries, was the demands imposed by the pilgrimage trade rather than any theological driver.[62] Further, despite the undoubted

[58] Dimier (1964), 21.

[59] Horn (1973), 18.

[60] Horn (1973), 15.

[61] Horn, Marshall, and Rourke (1990), 76–77.

[62] At Qal'at Sim'ân in northern Syria, Simeon Stylites's idiosyncratic ascetic witness lived out on the top of a pillar became the focus for a large monastic foundation built during his lifetime and although the purpose of individual rooms is unclear it would appear that the communal life of the monks was subsidiary to servicing Simeon's needs and the needs of the pilgrims who flocked to see him. At nearby Dêr Sim'ân the monastery was again clearly designed to service the pilgrimage trade with hostels and other large rooms set aside for pilgrims. At id-Dêr in southern Syria neither the shape nor the size of the rooms betray their purpose and as at Qal'at Sim'ân there is no secluded monastic precinct for the monks (Braunfels (1972), 16–18).

influence that eastern monasticism was to have on the development of western monasticism, not least through the dissemination of Basil's monastic 'rules', this did not apparently extend to architecture. The archaeology would suggest that although the layout of the western monastic movement was to develop initially in as seemingly erratic a manner as that in the east, with the initial settlements also often centred upon the cult of a particular holy man, it was to eventually diverge significantly from that of its eastern counterpart toward a much more rigid structure and form; the decisive difference being the emergence in the west of the religious orders, a phenomenon unknown in the East.[63] With the coming of these religious orders we encounter changing architectural styles and a uniformity, both of lifestyle and of organisation which eventually extended to monastic planning.

To return to our initial query, what is of primary concern to us in the present discussion is the extent to which outside influences initially impacted upon the religious topography of early historic Ireland. The discussion above has established that Irish ecclesiology sought to trace its roots back to Egypt and Syria. There was, however, also an important ecclesiological relationship between Ireland and Gaul. Further, it is clear, despite the fact that ascetic experimentation in the west predates both the development of Egyptian monasticism and the dissemination in the West of eastern writings such as the *Vita S. Antonii*,[64] that Egyptian monasticism exercised a formative influence not only upon Irish ecclesiology but also upon the development of Gallic monasticism.[65] We are therefore inevitably also interested in those initial 'erratic' western experimentations in the ascetic life which we encounter in Gaul and how they too might have related to, and impacted upon, the Irish experience.

---

[63] Braunfels (1972), 9.

[64] Dunn (2000), 59.

Justin Martyr makes reference to Christians living together in chastity and the first formal ascetic community was formed by Bishop Eusebius at Vercelli in the mid fourth century.[64] In *c.*AD397 Augustine wrote the first western monastic rule. The authorship of the rule has been much discussed although it is now generally accepted that to ascribe it to Augustine is safe. Augustine's monastic rule was the first to introduce the concept of the Hours and came to be adopted by several religious orders including the Augustinian canons in the eleventh century, the Premonstratensians in the twelfth, the Dominicans in the thirteenth and the Austin friars. However the Augustinian Rule provides something of a planning *cul de sac* for the Rule has nothing explicitly to say about layout and there is no evidence for an Augustinian *schema* encapsulating a specifically Augustinian monastic architecture.

[65] Dumville (1997b), 86–87.

4.B.2. Gaul

There is no need here to rehearse in detail the debate surrounding the possible relationship between the various early manifestations of Christianity as encountered in Ireland, Gaul, and the Middle East. It is sufficient for our purposes to note that the debt of Gallic monasticism, like that of its Irish counterpart, to the desert spirituality of Egyptian monasticism and of the wider Middle East is clear. This debt was acknowledged explicitly in a Gallic context by the early fourth century text, *De laude eremi*, written by Eucherius of Lyons (d. *c.*AD450).[66] Certainly, by the beginning of the fifth century several eastern monastic texts, including Athanasius's *Vita S. Antonii*, Jerome's *Vita Sancti Pauli eremitae* and his translation of the Pachomian *koinonia*, Rufinus's translation of Basil's *Longer* and *Shorter Rules* (*Basilii Regula a Rufino latine versa*), and the *Historia monachorum in Ægypto*, were circulating in the West.[67] Further, a number of significant Gallic monastic settlements had been established including Lérins and Marseilles.[68] Indeed, *Vita patrum Iurensium*, written *c.*AD520 by an anonymous monk of Abbot Eugendus's monastery at Condat,[69] firmly places the 'Lérins Fathers' alongside 'eastern' monastic authors such Basil, Pachomius and Cassian in the monastic roll of honour.[70]

In ecclesiological terms the monastery of Honoratus at Lérins, dating from between AD400 and 410, was something of a 'mixed economy'.[71] This reflected both the influence of the Palestinian *laura*, with many of the monks adopting the rule of Macarius and living in hermitages scattered throughout the archipelago,[72] and a more communal

[66] Eucherius of Lyons, *De laude eremi*, 41–42.
Interestingly, Eucherius argued that although God is more easily found in the desert (*De laude eremi*, 4) the desert experience could be found and experienced *in full* in somewhere like Lérins and not just in the actual desert itself (*De laude eremi*, 41–42).

[67] Lawrence (2001), 10–11.

[68] Lawrence (2001), 14.

[69] 'Introduction' to Vivian, Vivian, and Russell (1999), 47–51.

[70] Anon., *Vita patrum Iurensium*, 174.

[71] There is an ongoing and lively debate as to the exact nature of the community at Lérins. The monastic and/or eremitic character of the settlement is clear but the notion that episcopal authority was therefore absent has been challenged in recent years by a number of scholars. As Sharpe rightly highlights much of Lérins's ecclesiastical reputation during the fifth century rested upon its capacity for producing bishops of note (Sharpe (2002), 99).

[72] O'Loughlin (2000b).

ideal focused upon a central coenobium under the control of an abbot.[73] At Marseilles the twin monasteries founded by Cassian *c.*AD410 also followed a more coenobitic regime.[74] The earliest description we have of a Gallic monastery is that founded at Marmoutier by Martin of Tours some time after AD372. Boasting no architectural innovation and resembling a village or a settlement rather than a monastery, it was described unhappily by one commentator as a 'monastic kraal'.[75] By contrast, Sulpicius Severus, Martin's biographer writing after the year AD400, was keen to portray the monastery at Marmoutiers as a loosely organised hermit group resonant of the East although the suggested parallel may be literary rather than actual.[76]

What is interesting about the description of the settlement at Marmoutiers is the reference to a cell made from wood and the fleeting description of the eremitic lifestyle of the monks.[77] Eugendus's monastery at Condat is described in very similar terms within *Vita patrum Iurensium* although clearly it was the coenobitic monasticism of Pachomius and Basil as mediated through Cassian rather than the anchorite and semi-anchorite legacy of the Egyptian desert which helped shape this particular community.[78] Again we have a reference to wooden structures and a possible evolution in layout in that the individual cells appear to have been connected rather than dispersed as at

[73] Lawrence (2001), 14.

An attempt by the Abbot in AD677 to introduce the Benedictine rule throughout the settlement resulted in his murder by the monks who rebelled against the imposition of such a structured lifestyle (Braunfels (1972), 20–21).

[74] Lawrence (2001), 14.

[75] Braunfels (1972), 20.

[76] James (1981), 36.

[77] Sulpicius Severus, *Vita S. Martini*, 10, 3–7.

For a time, therefore, he used a little cell adjoining the church; then when he could no longer bear the disturbance caused by those who flocked to see him, he built himself a cell some two miles outside the city. The place was so remote and secluded that it was equal to the solitude of the desert. For on one side it was bounded by the sheer rock of a high mountain, while on the level side, it was enclosed by a gentle bend in the river Loire. It could be approached by only one path and that a very narrow one. Martin lived in a small cell made of wood and a number of the brothers lived in a similar manner, but most of them had made shelters for themselves by hollowing out the rock of the mountain which overlooked the place. . . . No one there possessed anything of his own, everything was shared. They were not allowed to buy or sell anything (as is the practice with most monks). No craft was practised there, apart from that of the scribes; the young were set to this task while the older ones spent their time in prayer. It was rare for anyone to leave his own cell except when they gathered at the place of prayer.

[78] 'Introduction' to Vivian, Vivian, and Russell (1999), 41.

Marmoutiers.[79] The presence of an enclosing feature at Condat might also be inferred[80] and there is explicit reference to an oratory at the monastery.[81] We shall return to the subject of building materials later; what is of interest here is the depiction of the monks' lifestyle and the somewhat tangential references to the layout of the monasteries. However, beyond this we cannot go with any confidence. Our knowledge of monastic life in Gaul is very limited and archaeologically the Merovingian period represents something of a 'Dark Age'. In literary terms we leap from the *Vita S. Martini* and the wooden huts of Marmoutiers and Condat to the elaborate design of the eighth century description of the seventh century monastery at Jumièges (founded *c.*AD654–655) but the nature of the architectural leap is harder to assess. One might suspect that the sixth century hagiographies painted a suitably bleak picture of monastic life to fit the model of a group of ascetics centred around a saintly hermit but certainly by the seventh and eighth centuries the literary evidence would suggest that monasteries were being founded by lay aristocrats, who partly in response to the growing pilgrimage trade, were creating architecture on a much grander scale.[82] These aristocratic foundations ensured for their founders an extension of aristocratic power by ecclesiastical means. Families might set up monasteries on their own land but they also began to use land newly acquired from the king for this purpose. Fontanella, Jumièges and Solignac were all set up in this manner.[83]

The purple prose employed to describe the monastery at Jumièges in the anonymous *Vita Filiberti Abbatis* should make the approaching scholar somewhat cautious but we do have here our most detailed description of a Merovingian monastery and for that reason this is a seminal text for us.[84] It describes a very large enclosed site; the word

[79] Anon., *Vita patrum Iurensium*, 162.
See James (1981), 36.
[80] Anon., *Vita patrum Iurensium*, 126 and 153.
[81] Anon., *Vita patrum Iurensium*, 130 and 135.
[82] James (1981), 38.
[83] Dunn (2000), 162–163
[84] Anon., *Vita Filiberti Abbatis*, 7.
Jumièges poses some very pertinent questions for us. The key question revolves around its position on the continuum of monastic development. What were its antecedents and to what does it point? Looking to the past Jumièges may well represent the coming together of both Irish and Gallo-Roman architectural styles in the one monastery but, looking forward; it has also been seen as a possible bridge between the more explicitly eremitic layout of the early Merovingian monasteries and the highly stylized form represented by the Benedictine St. Gallen *Plan* to which we will turn our attention later.

claustra here surely indicating an enclosure rather than a cloister, possibly built on a pre-existing Roman or Saxon site.[85] It also lists a number of key buildings including a cross-shaped church, the founder's cell, a buttery, and a dormitory. We can see here a significant development in monastic planning both in scale and complexity. Philbert was a reformer who augmented the Columbanian rule with significant features of the Benedictine[86] and so the presence of an enclosure at this site might well indicate an initial Irish influence. However, although the impact of Irish influence on the development of Merovingian monasticism is often readily accepted one does need to be wary. Martin of Tours's settlement at Marmoutiers and Eugendus's monastery at Condat reflect the likelihood that Merovingian monasticism was influenced by Egyptian monasticism from an early stage. Equally, while the enclosing of inhabited space may be viewed as a defining characteristic of both Irish religious and secular settlement there is no evidence that it was exclusive to an Irish context. Nevertheless, we know that the Irish monk Columbanus practised enclosure within his own Frankish monasteries[87] not least because he was chastised by the Gaulish king for violating local custom by refusing entry to ordinary Christians into the interior of the monastery at Luxeuil.[88] There is also literary evidence of the presence of an enclosure at Clermont[89] and of a circular *vallum* at sites such as Solignac, near Limoges,[90] although again the presence of a circular enclosure may not be solely indicative of an Irish influence.[91] Nevertheless the size of the enclosing wall or *vallum* or *septa* in these examples strongly suggests that as in Egypt and as in Ireland the purpose of these boundaries was to symbolise monastic renunciation of the outside world and to mark out the sacred space rather than to fulfil a need for defence.

The severe asceticism and remoteness of the early Egyptian eremitic settlements resonate strongly with the Irish situation. It is tempting to argue that this provides evidence of the diffusionist influence of the former upon the latter. Certainly Françoise Henry's

---

[85] Horn (1973), 34–35; James (1981), 38–39.
For a contra- interpretation of *claustra* as cloister see Braunfels (1972), 28.
[86] Braunfels (1972), 28.
[87] Columbanus, *Regulae coenobialis*, 8; *Paenitentiale*, 26.
[88] Jonas, *Vita S. Columbani*, 33.
[89] Gregory of Tours, *Historiae Francorum*, 9, 40.
[90] Dado of Rouen, *Vita S. Eligii*, 16.
See also James (1982), 386.
[91] Blair (2005), 198; James (1982), 386.

description of the island-based semi-eremitic ecclesiastical settlements off the west coast of Ireland as 'eremitic monasteries'[92] provides an image reminiscent of those remote semi-eremitic *laura* that so influenced Honoratus's settlement on Lérins in the early fifth century.[93] Yet not all Irish religious settlement could be described as eremitic. Further, it is possible that the form of Irish monasticism which emerged was a product of circumstantial evolution rather than of outside influences; that the harshness of the Egyptian desert and the harshness of life in early medieval Ireland simply produced architecturally and structurally similar responses to the problems caused by an ascetic existence. However, the influence of Middle Eastern monasticism upon both the church in Gaul and the church in Ireland is well established and it is clear that while the influence might have been indirect it was no less real.

How this inter-relationship then impacted upon the morphology of religious settlement is perhaps more difficult to estimate but one can discern a basic topographical *schema* emerging from the desert, and the earliest experiments in the ascetic life, and transferring itself into the Gallic and Irish settings. This *schema* consisted of individual or small group cells usually within some form of enclosing structure. These cells were situated around communal areas for prayer and eating with the holy man or saint residing at the very heart of the community. The extent to which this *schema* was influenced by any biblical model is impossible to judge in a non-Irish context simply because of a lack of evidence, as we have already observed, but there is no doubt that much of what defined Irish coenobiticism, like its Gallic counterpart, had its roots in the Egyptian and Syrian deserts.

4.c. *An Eremitic Paradigm?*

At this point it is important not to be complacent about the appositeness of the Temple model for the early Irish religious landscape. It is certainly clear from the extant archaeology that what was being created on the Irish landscape was not a dry-stone facsimile of the Temple of Jerusalem. Indeed, our earlier comparison of the dimensions

[92] Henry (1957), 146.
[93] O'Loughlin (2000b).

of both the Tabernacle and the Temple with the dimensions of Insular Irish settlement strongly suggests that if scale and form are of importance here then the Tabernacle potentially speaks much more directly to the Irish context. So if the Temple was indeed fulfilling a paradigmatic role then what was being 'reproduced' was not simply physical form but rather a concept of how holy space might be organised. Thus while we have argued that the enclosure and tripartite zoning of holy space mirrors the layout of the Temple of Jerusalem as described in scripture we must also acknowledge the apparent physical incongruity of a Temple paradigm within an Irish context.

This should cause us to consider the possibility that other biblical paradigms may be influencing the creation of the sacred geography. An obvious candidate would be the Tabernacle of Moses with its similarly arranged enclosure and tripartite zoning pattern. We have already explored in some detail the nature of the relationship between the biblical depictions of the Tabernacle and the Temple[94] but the Tabernacle remains a relatively unexplored but potentially rich seam for our discussion of Irish religious settlement patterns given the significant eremitic strain within the early medieval Irish religious consciousness. The Moysian Tabernacle was a product of the wilderness experience of the Israelites and the ethos of what might be termed the 'spirituality of Exodus' had a profound affect upon early Christianity even before the emergence of the monastic movement.[95] The importance of ocean and desert imagery for Christian mysticism has already been well-rehearsed,[96] including within an Irish context,[97] and its impact upon the built landscape of the early Irish church should not be underestimated. On the contrary, the preponderance of small, and indeed very small, isolated religious settlements, many based around the western seaboard of Ireland, only serve to reinforce the eremitic and often remote nature of the early Irish church, with its strong Egyptian and Gallic monastic antecedents. Thus the extent to which a 'Tabernacle' model might provide significant insight into the topography and form of Irish ecclesial layout is of interest.

[94] See Chapter 3.
[95] McGinn (1994), 157.
[96] McGinn (19940, 157 n. 2.
[97] O'Loughlin (1997c).

This brings us to the key issue of the relationship between the Temple and the Tabernacle. We have already established the nature of their *scriptural* relationship where they clearly refer to two distinct structures, albeit structures which boast a similar spatial organisation and a strongly interconnected history. However, in the lexicon of early Irish exegesis this distinction has become blurred. In Hiberno-Latin texts it would appear that *tabernaculum* could in fact refer to either a church building or to the gathered body of believers in much the same way as the word 'church' does in English[98] and thus the Old Irish word *tabernacul* would appear to have referred to a consecrated building similar to a *tempul*. So for example in the tenth century text *Saltair na Rann* the *tabernacul* is identified as the place where prayer is offered daily.[99] To complicate matters further, throughout the *Hibernensis* the compiler(s) treat the words *templum* and *tabernaculum* as synonyms so that we actually find the two words being used in the same sentence to refer to the same structure.[100] It would have to be conceded that in our present discussion the two words have also on occasion been used almost interchangeably not least because, to a large degree, much of the conversation about the topography of the Temple of Solomon or of Ezekiel could also apply quite happily to the Tabernacle of Moses, and we have noted that there are both New Testament and patristic examples of where one or the other has been used to make a generic point about both. However, a rediscovery of the distinctiveness of the two structures might help elucidate our present discussion. Bede, in his *De Tabernaculo* and *De Templo*, marked out a clear physical and allegorical distinction between the Tabernacle and the Temple whereby the former was seen as a temporary and portable structure, representing the 'toil and exile of the present church', to serve on route to the Promised Land whilst the Temple, a permanent stone structure, represented the 'rest and happiness of the future church' in the heavenly Jerusalem.[101] If indeed the biblical description of the theology and form of the Tabernacle serves as a type of the 'toil and exile' of the

[98] Swift (1998), 107.

[99] *The Saltair na Rann*, 1.4206, 2.4402.
See Swift (1998), 107.

[100] *Hibernensis*, 63, 2a.
De dedicatione novi edificii.
In dedicatione tabernaculi magna solemnitas cum Iudeis fuit. Ita in dedicatione templi in Hierusalem, ita et in reedificatione ejus.

[101] Bede, *De Templo*, 1, 1.2.
See also O'Reilly (1995), xxix–xxx.

church of Bede then could such a distinction point to a more specific scriptural paradigm for the church of Adomnán? Instead of looking to the Temple as an exemplar for the topography of early medieval Irish religious settlement should we rather turn our attention to the possibilities offered by the Tabernacle?

Of course, at a superficial level the Tabernacle of the Wilderness experience might seem a more apposite biblical exemplar in the context of the wild rural setting of early medieval Ireland, not least for the numerous eremitic-style sites dotted across the landscape especially on the western seaboard, rather than the 'urban' grandeur of the Jerusalem Temple. If the 'spirituality of Exodus' was indeed such an important element within the religious mindset of the early Irish church might not the Tabernacle of the Exodus event seem a more appropriate paradigm than the Temple? This might be especially apposite for such a spiritually restless church, so given to clerical *peregrinatio* and missionary endeavour. It might be argued that it was the *stabilitas* of the 'Roman' church which more properly reflected the rootedness of the Temple complex.[102] Yet any attempt to be more specific or to develop this line of thinking further presents a number of difficulties. First, in material terms the Tabernacle presents the same challenges as the Temple. While at a superficial level the form and architecture of the Tabernacle might look more accessible to the predominantly rural character of early medieval Irish culture it is as alien to an Irish context as that of the Temple. Secondly, the close textual relationship between the description of the Tabernacle and that of the Temple means that it is impossible to reference particular landscape characteristics back to one exemplar as against the other with any confidence. This leads us to our third and most substantial point, already noted, which is that the

---

[102] Clerical wandering was such a problem for the early Irish church that prominent clerics began to protest against its undisciplined practice. Columbanus, in his letter to Pope Gregory the Great written *c*.AD600, laments the tendency for monks to go off without their abbot's permission. . . .

In the third part of my inquiry, please tell me now, if it is not troublesome, what is to be done about those monks who, for the sake of God, and inflamed by the desire for a more perfect life, impugn their vows, leave the places of their first profession, and against their abbots' will, impelled by monastic fervour, either relapse or flee to the deserts (Columbanus, *Epistula* 1, 7).

The monastic reformers of the eighth and ninth centuries advocated a more settled and disciplined life. The ninth century monastic rule named after the sixth century saint Ailbe of Emly urged 'the non-desertion of thy monastery' ('The Rule of Ailbe', 106) and Maelruain of Tallaght, a leader of the *céli Dé*, discouraged pilgrimage abroad and tried to limit any movement beyond the shores of Ireland (*The Monastery of Tallaght*, 17).

For further literary evidence of the practice of *peregrinatio* see Hughes (1960), 147.

Tabernacle as described in scripture is itself but a reflection of an exemplar, the Temple. Finally, even if a Tabernacle paradigm for early Irish religious layout could be established with some certainty it would not effectively advance our argument for we are still left trying to explain the very particular building form that we encounter within an Irish context.

4.D. *The Creation of a Religious Landscape*

4.D.I. 'Made in Ireland': The Impact of the Vernacular Form upon the Layout of Religious Settlement

There is no doubt that the 'sacralisation' of the Irish landscape; the creation of what Newman, in his work on the pre-Christian site at Tara, has called a 'ritual landscape', was not a uniquely Christian phenomenon. Within a pre-Christian context the religious significance of the landscape was indicated not only by the creation of myths whereby the landscape is interpreted but also by the presence of monuments and the built environment.[103] This pagan landscape with its sacred wells and trees and henges and monoliths was then clearly systematically Christianised in Ireland in a way unknown elsewhere in Europe.[104]

It is also self-evident that in any setting the vernacular architecture and the preference for local building materials and techniques will impact upon any newly emerging manmade landscape.[105] By the time Christianity arrived in Ireland it would appear that there already existed a unique built environment in a readily identifiable vernacular style which inevitably provided an architectural framework for the creation of the Christian landscape. This vernacular style was centred upon a circular or sub-circular ideal exemplified by the cashel or ráth.[106] It was this circular motif which served as a prototype for

---

[103] Newman (2005), 364.

[104] Doherty (2005), 6–9.

[105] Clark (2007), 86.

[106] The terms *cashel* and *ráth* need to be employed with some caution as their usage implies the existence of a typological distinction which is far from proven. However, it is generally accepted that a *cashel* is a stone-walled ring-fort as opposed to a *ráth* which rather denotes an earthen ring-fort.

See Edwards (1990), 12.

Christian building forms[107] in much the same way as the Benedictine *Plan of St Gall* developed from a Roman villa culture.[108] Indeed, if the hagiography is to be believed, the granting of land and settlements, including *ráths*, to a saint by a local significant landowner appears to have been fairly common practice.[109] We have already seen that such grants may have occurred with a number of sites including possibly High Island[110] although we have also acknowledged that reliable dating evidence to support the putative pre-Christian origin of such sites remains frustratingly elusive.[111]

Nevertheless, the adoption of the ubiquitous circular enclosure form as an aspect of Christian settlement in early medieval Ireland might suggest that the enclosure and zoning we encounter in a Christian context had secular and possibly even pre-Christian antecedents.[112] Multivallation was certainly common both for cashels and ráths. Trivallation in particular is evident at a number of such sites; striking examples of which are the cashel at Cathair Chomáin in the Burren in Co. Clare,[113] and the ráth at Garranes in Co. Cork.[114] However here again dating is an issue with both structures initially dated well into the first millennium AD and the early Christian period although more recent work on Cathair Chomáin suggests at least the possibility of a pre-Christian context for the site.[115] We have also already noted in an earlier chapter the potential significance for our discussion of the presumed pre-Christian site of Dún Aonghasa on the Aran Islands. Here we have not only a fine example of tripartite enclosure in a secular context we also now have some dating evidence that

---

[107] Blair (2005), 197–198.

[108] Marshall and Rourke (2000), 45.

[109] We are told that the original site for Armagh was a pre-Christian *ráth* given under some duress by King Daire to Patrick (Anon., *Vita tripartita*, 228; Muirchú, *Vita S. Patricii*, 108–110; see also Thomas (1971), 34). A generous gift is also thought to have been the origin of the site at Cashel, Co. Tipperary, given by King Muírchertach O'Brian to the church in AD1101 (Marshall and Rourke (2000), 176).

[110] Marshall and Rourke (2000), 175–176.

[111] Edwards lucidly makes the point that the potential dating parameters for ringforts stretch from the Late Bronze Age, through the Iron Age, to the early historic period (Edwards (1990), 17).

[112] It is thought that there may have been as many as thirty to forty thousand ringforts scattered all across Ireland (Alcock (1971), 255).

[113] Hencken (1938); Alcock (1971), plate 7.

[114] Ó Ríordáin (1942).

[115] Alcock (1971), 256; Cotter (1994), 24–25.

might indicate pre-Christian occupation activity.[116] Firmer evidence of the pre-Christian origins of the trivallate circular enclosure is provided by the iconic *Ráith na Seanadh* (the 'Rath of the Synods') at the hill-fort site at Tara, Co Meath; a site which has recently been interpreted as a ritual complex dating in its earliest phases from the Iron Age but also providing occupation remains right up to the 2nd century AD and the Roman period.[117] It has also recently been established using modern dendrochronological techniques that a large tripartite mound was built, also for ritual purposes, during the early first century BC (*c.* 95-94BC) upon the remains of a Late Bronze Age settlement at Emain Macha, now Navan Fort in Co. Armagh.[118]

All of this resonates of course both with the trivallate enclosure form found at sites such as the early Christian settlement at Nendrum (which may also have had pre-Christian origins) and with the formulaic depiction of enclosure and zoning encountered within early Irish Christian texts.[119] However, this does not of itself provide substantive evidence that the enclosure and internal zoning of sacred space which we encounter in a Christian context within early medieval Ireland had its genesis within pre-Christian and/or secular praxis. The fact that enclosure and sub-division occurs in both a secular/pre-Christian setting and a Christian setting does not establish a direct causal link between the two. Further, there is no attempt here to argue that enclosure and zoning are exclusively Christian activities or to deny that pre-Christian peoples also situated their most sacred or important buildings at the epicentre of their settlements just as Christians did. What *is* being argued however is that the motivation for this praxis within the early medieval Christian context was theological rather than simply cultural or defensive.

What we see in a Christian context in terms of enclosure and zoning is almost always qualitatively and structurally different from what we encounter in these massive, probably Iron Age, forts. Certainly the rigidity and extent of the tripartite layout at Nendrum is not normative for early Christian sites whose internal zoning is more varied in

---

[116] Cotter (1994), 27–28.

[117] Ó Ríordáin (1982), 25–26; Edwards (1990), 17; Newman (1997).

[118] Baillie (1986); Waterman (1997); Lynn (2003). See Doherty (2005), 13–14.

[119] The 1966 *Archaeological Survey of Northern Ireland* plan of the Nendrum site highlights clearly both the tripartite division and the scale of the settlement (Edwards (1990), 108 fig. 50).

pattern, usually much less regular in form, and often on a much more humble scale. What is more, if it is indeed the case that a number of these stone cashels were given as gifts by wealthy lay owners to those seeking to found Christian settlements this praxis should not be surprising or viewed as irregular; as we have acknowledged it is known to have occurred elsewhere. Such a practice does not negate the principal contention that the philosophical inspiration for early medieval religious enclosure and zoning was scriptural in origin. Whether a settlement site was marked out and divided up using stone, earth, wood, or totemic symbols such as crosses, or a combination of all four, the key impulse in a Christian context remains the apotropaic demarcation of holy space rather than the physical repulsion of mortal enemies.

Despite the reservations outlined above it is evident that the circular footprint was the dominant motif of the archaeology of the early Irish built environment. The circle was not only a sacred symbol and shape for Irish pre-Christian and secular culture; this motif carried on into the Christian era where it also became a signature of Irish religious settlement through the prevalence of the curvilinear enclosure.[120] Our survey of the extant archaeology of Irish religious settlement clearly shows that even newly created enclosing features adhered to a circular or sub-circular form. The account in *Vita tripartita* of the measuring out of the new Christian settlement at Armagh,[121] centred upon the *ráth* given by King Daire to Patrick,[122] has been interpreted as an attempt not only to affirm the Patrician antecedents of the foundation at Armagh but to place a saintly seal of approval upon the circle as the ideal form for religious settlement.[123] Despite the obvious fact that the giving of a cashel or a ráth as a Christian settlement site rather predetermined the circular shape of the enclosure the religious significance of the curvilinear layout would appear to be further indicated by the story of the foundation of the settlement of Killarney, recounted earlier.[124] We also know that when Cuthbert came to construct his hermitage upon Farne Island he enclosed his dwelling and oratory within a sub-circular enclosure.[125]

[120] Thomas (1971), 52–53.
[121] Anon., *Vita tripartita*, 236.
[122] See above n. 108.
[123] Thomas (1971), 39–40.
[124] Anon., *Vita S. Aidi*, 25.
[125] Bede, *Vita S. Cuthberti*, 17.

The predominance of the circle did not, however, mean that it was the only shape in which buildings could be constructed. Sacred buildings such as oratories and churches were usually rectilinear in shape and there is significant extant material evidence for this. Literary evidence is provided by a number of texts including the *Senchus Mór*, a body of largely pre-Christian law, revised and widely adopted in AD439.[126] In a discussion of the fine to be exacted for destroying a church it is made clear that such buildings were rectangular in plan.[127] The genesis of this rectilinear form is far from clear although Patrick has been credited by some for the innovation.[128] This claim is based on two texts, one from Tírechán's *Collecteana* and one from the *Vita tripartita*, both of which, while providing possible textual evidence that rectilinear churches were known in Patrick's day, do not explicitly ascribe their invention to the saint.[129] A more likely explanation is that the development of a rectilinear plan may well have reflected the emerging influence of Roman liturgical practice. Clearly if one accepts the 'form follows function' argument then the shape and spatial arrangements of oratories and churches may well have been dictated by liturgical need.[130] It has been suggested that the liturgy contained within the Stowe Missal[131] reflects an ecclesial culture in which only the celebrant(s) at Mass was/were to be located within the oratory. The remainder of the congregation, which it has been suggested might be

[126] Horn (1973), 25.

[127] Ms. H.3.17, Library of Trinity College Dublin, quoted in Petrie (1845), 359–360.
If it be an oratory of fifteen feet, or less than that, that is, fifteen feet in its length and ten in its breadth, it is a three-year old heifer that is paid for every foot of it across, or for every foot and a half in length; . . . . .
See Horn (1973), 28.

[128] Horn (1973), 29.

[129] Tírechán, *Collectanea*, 44, 1.
And behold, Patrick proceeded to the land which is called Foirrgea of the Sons of Amolngid to divide it between the sons of Amolngid, and he made there a square earthen church of clay, because no timber was near.
Anon., *Vita tripartita*, 110.
And Patrick afterward went into the land of Connaicne in Cul Tolaith, and established four-cornered churches in that place.

[130] Clark (2007), 84.

[131] The Stowe Missal (also known as the Lorrha Missal) is a mid-eighth century sacramentary written in Latin and Irish, and is of Irish provenance. It was in use at the monastery of Lorrha from AD1050 onwards but is believed to have been a product of the Culdees at Tallaght in Dublin. It is the oldest surviving copy of a complete western liturgy. It derives its name Stowe from the period when it formed part of the Duke of Buckingham's library at Stowe (see O'Loughlin (2000a), 129–131).

considerable in number, would be left standing outside, graded, cate-gorised into groups, and situated at various distances from the often very small oratory which had not been designed to incorporate the whole of the worshipping community.[132] If this *schema* is accurate then perhaps this might explain the presence of numerous very small orato-ries and churches on so many ecclesiastical sites. This scenario has certainly been employed to help explain the presence of terracing on sites such as Killabuonia where it is envisaged that the various cate-gories of 'monastic' resident from manaig to penitents and slaves might have been grouped during the Mass according to status.[133] Intriguing though this explanation is it is perhaps equally likely that the congregations were much smaller than just suggested and that all the participants fitted, albeit snugly, within the building.[134] Or per-haps the liturgy of the Stowe Missal was created specifically to accom-modate the limited space available within the oratory or church on the majority of ecclesiastical sites. Nevertheless, it is certainly not unrea-sonable to suppose that liturgical need did inevitably exert some influ-ence upon the development of religious architecture.

Whatever their architectural origins the internal measurements of many of these early small rectilinear churches apparently adhered to a pattern, the short single-cell oblong, the proportion of length to width being 1.5 to 1.[135] This can be seen on the ground at a number of sites, including the oratories at Gallarus and Church Island, and has been regarded as an indication of an early dating.[136] Again the key evidence for such planning consistency comes from Ms. H.3.17, this time detail-ing the payment of craftsmen who build churches.[137] Here mention is made of a *duirtheach* (an 'oakhouse') and a *daimhliag* (a stone house), both seemingly built to a length-width ratio of 1.5 to 1, namely 15 feet by 10 feet. However, the significance of this ratio as an indicator of

---

[132] Hunwicke (2002), 1, 8.

[133] Hunwicke (2002), 5–6.

[134] O'Loughlin (2000a), 132–133.

[135] Leask (1955), 49.

[136] Leask (1955), 49–51; O'Kelly (1958), 119–120.

[137] MS. H.3.17, Library of Trinity College, Dublin, quoted in Petrie (1845), 364–366.

If it be a *duirtheach* of fifteen feet, or less than that, that is, fifteen feet in its length and ten in its breadth, it is a three-year old heifer that is paid for every foot of it across, or for every foot and a half in length. . . . . The *daimhlaig*: if its covering be of shin-gles, it is of equal price with the *duirtheach*, which is proportioned to it . . .

See Radford (1977), 1–2.

antiquity needs to be treated with some caution. It may only apply to selected small western sites[138] and planning ratio alone cannot be taken as an absolute indicator of antiquity. Further, subsequent doubts as to the early dating of Gallarus itself must undermine the validity of this building style as a chronological marker.[139] What remains of significance is the observation that sacred buildings were typologically rectilinear in form in contrast to the normative beehive or circular cell form for the living quarters of the monks.[140]

Any suggestion however that the vernacular form, whether circular or rectilinear, might have impacted upon the spatial organisation of enclosure is unconvincing. The advent of the rectilinear oratory or church was undoubtedly an architectural innovation in an Irish context and it certainly contributed to the distinctive appearance of early Irish religious settlement but it did not impact upon its location within the enclosure or the overall topography of the enclosed space. Indeed, although we can see from the extant archaeology of a number of sites that good access from the living quarters to the place of worship was important, a fact indicated by the presence of paving leading to the oratory from the cell or cells even on the smallest of sites,[141] there is no evidence that even this natural desire for easy and protected lines of circulation from cell to oratory significantly altered the spatial relationships within the enclosure or negated the normative layout pattern centred upon a 'sacred core'.

4.D.2. 'Made in Ireland': The Impact of Native Building Materials and Techniques upon the Religious Landscape

Of course we may detect the impact of vernacular architecture and design upon the morphology of religious settlement not just in the structural footprint of the buildings. Native influences will also impact upon the building material from which it is constructed. This

---

[138] Marshall (1989), 92.

[139] Harbison (1970), 58; Edwards (1990), 117, 124.

[140] Leask (1955), 8.
It is possible that the *Betha Ciaráin Saighre* (II) suggests the building of a circular oratory from wood (*Betha Ciaráin Saighre* (II), 1, 2) but this would have been atypical.

[141] We have already noted the presence of paving on several very small sites including Reask (Cuppage (1986), 338–339; Fanning (1981), 78–79, 150, 158), Church Island (O'Kelly (1958), 75–76, see also plate XVII), Illaunloughan (Marshall and Walsh (2005), 128), and the hermitage on the South Peak of Skellig Michael (Horn, Marshall and Rourke (1990), 40).

material will in turn dictate the form to a greater or lesser extent. The simplicity of the single cell plan of most churches and the abundance of wood in Ireland generally has led to the conclusion that most Irish churches, like secular buildings of the period, were built in wood and that mortared stone churches are a later post-tenth century development to be found mainly on important sites.[142] Obviously the lack of archaeological evidence for the majority of these sites would make any attempts at reconstruction of these wooden structures extremely tentative but traces of wooden remains may suggest that a wooden oratory preceded the stone building at Reask,[143] Church Island,[144] and at a number of other sites[145] including that at Inishcaltra,[146] on White Island on Lough Erne in Co. Fermanagh,[147] at Derry in Co. Down,[148] and at St. Vogue's at Carnsore Point in Co. Wexford.[149] Outside of Ireland remains of a wooden chapel pre-dating its stone replacement have been found on Ardwall Isle off the southwestern coast of Scotland.[150]

This Irish preference for building in wood, at least in the seventh and eighth centuries, and perhaps right up until the eleventh and twelfth centuries, is well documented.[151] Cogitosus's mid seventh century *Vita S. Brigidae* describes in some detail the internal layout and decoration of the great, presumably wooden, church at Kildare built to replace the original.[152] The *Vita Sancte Samthanne virginis* relates how Samthann of Clonbroney (d.AD739) went to great lengths to build and to renovate her church in wood.[153] Bede refers to the building of a church in wood on Lindisfarne by St Finan as being constructed '*more Scottorum*' and Adomnán's *Vita S. Columbae* tells how St Columba went to considerable trouble to secure wood for construction on Iona.[154] Tírechán attests that

---

[142] Leask (1955), 5, 49; Radford (1977), 4–5; Hamlin (1984), 119.

[143] Fanning (1981), 86.

[144] O'Kelly (1958), 58–59.

[145] See Edwards (1990), 122–123; Hamlin (1985), 285.

[146] Harbison (1982), 628–629.

[147] Lowry-Corry, Wilson, and Waterman (1959), 65–66.

[148] Waterman (1967).

[149] O'Kelly (1975), 20–22.

[150] Thomas (1967), 138–140.

[151] Hamlin (1985), 283.

[152] Cogitosus, *Vita S. Brigidae*, 32.
See Radford (1977), 5–6; Hamlin (1985), 283.

[153] *Vita Sancte Samthanne virginis*, 6, 14, 15, and 16.

[154] *HE*, 3, 25; *VC*, 2, 45.

St. Patrick resorted to building an earthen church of clay only because he could find no wood nearby.[155] The hagiography would also seem to support the contention that wooden churches continued to be built until relatively late and certainly after the advent of stone churches. Tírechán's late seventh century reference to a stone church at *Dom Liacc* (Duleek),[156] also mentioned in the *Annals of Ulster s.a.* 724 when the death of Aldchú of *Doim Liagg* (Duleek) is recorded,[157] and in the *Annals of the Four Masters s.a.* 749 when the death of Cearban of *Daimh Liag* (Duleek) is recorded,[158] is surely not proof of a widespread building practice, as Marshall appears to suggest, but rather an indication of the rarity of a stone church in this period.[159] The next reference to a stone church is not found until an annalistic entry in AD789 when the *Annals of Ulster* record the killing of a man in the doorway of a stone church.[160] Indeed wood appears to be still being used as late as the beginning of the fifth century when a commentary on Brehon law, taken from the Book of Ballymote (*c.*1400), clearly differentiates between a stone church (*damliac*) and a wooden oratory (*dairthech*).[161] The use of the two words in the same document would appear to indicate a differentiation in building material rather than any disparity in size, function or importance.[162] Further textual evidence of the persistence of wood as a building material long after the advent of stone-built churches is found in the *Vita S. Malachi*, recalling the life of a twelfth century Bishop of Down and Archbishop of Armagh, which describes the building of a wooden church at Bangor in Co. Down as an 'Irish work'.[163]

The relationship between wooden and stone churches is exiguous not least with regard to the chronology of the evolution from wood to stone. Much of the debate concerning the advent of stone churches has revolved around the possible dating of the striking Gallarus oratory and similar structures in Co. Kerry. These boat-shaped oratories

[155] Tírechán, *Collectanea*, 44, 1.
[156] Tírechán, *Collectanea*, 27, 3.
[157] *Annals of Ulster, s.a.* 725.1.
[158] *Annals of the Four Masters, s.a.* 749.2.
[159] Marshall (1989), 94; Hamlin (1985), 284.
[160] *Annals of Ulster, s.a.* 789.8.
[161] *The Ancient Laws of Ireland*, 5, 93, quoted in Petrie (1845), 346–347. See Radford (1977), 2.
[162] Radford (1977), 2.
[163] Bernard of Clairvaux, *Vita S. Malachi*, 2, 8.

occur on both the Dingle Peninsula and Iveragh Peninsulas although some possible sites remain uncertain. Definite examples can be found most notably on Church Island and Great Skellig, and at Temple-cashel, Kildreelig, Killabuonia, Ballymorereagh, Ballywiheen, Gallarus, Illauntannig and Kilmalkedar with several other possible examples including those on Inishtooskert and Inishvickillane and that at Killelton.[164] An initial early dating for Gallarus was suggested by Petrie who rather incredibly thought that the oratory might actually pre-date the Patrician mission. Despite some half-hearted scholarly challenges to this early dating, it initially received universal acceptance although the date was brought forward somewhat to the fifth to seventh centuries.[165] Leask's contention that stone churches existed at an earlier date in the west than elsewhere in Ireland led him to give Gallarus a tentative dating of *c.* AD750.[166] This date was then used as a chronological marker for the Gallarus-style oratories on Church Island[167] and Ardwall Isle.[168] However, it is now thought that Gallarus might be as late as the twelfth century[169] and that corbelled stone oratories are unlikely to have been commonplace as early as the eighth century.[170] This dating is important because it helps us place the Gallarus-style oratory into a chronological and developmental context with other building types and thus it would appear that the early prevailing view that the Gallarus oratory and other similar structures represented a transition point on an architectural continuum from the beehive hut to the stone church with upright walls is no longer tenable.[171] Further, the suggestion that they were simply a local variant of the Irish stone-roofed church[172] now seems improbable and it is much more likely that they represented what has been described, perhaps rather disparagingly but accurately, as an 'architectural cul-de-sac'.[173] The origins of the Gallarus-style building lie firmly within the *clochán* tradition and represent the coming together of the curvilinear exterior

[164] O' Sullivan and Sheehan (1996), 247; Cuppage (1986), 362.
[165] Stokes (1878), 39.
[166] Leask (1955), 21.
[167] O'Kelly (1958), 128.
[168] Thomas (1967), 171.
[169] Harbison (1970), 58.
[170] Hamlin (1985), 284.
[171] Petrie (1845), 132f.
[172] Leask (1955), 27; Harbison (1970), 45–47.
[173] O'Keefe (1998), 114.

of the beehive hut with the rectilinear form dictated by Christian liturgical need.

So while it is evident that the earliest Irish churches were built of wood to be replaced later by stone constructions the chronology of this process is unclear[174] and it is impossible to be certain when the stone construction of churches might have become common practice throughout Ireland.[175] There is no evidence in Ireland for a large-scale replacement of wood by stone as in Northumbria after the adoption of the Roman Easter.[176] The suggestion that the paucity of wood on the western island sites and the preponderance of stone there have encouraged the early use of stone as a building material at a date prior to its widespread use on the mainland could mean that stone churches on the western sites were possibly contemporary with wooden structures elsewhere in Ireland.[177] This would potentially provide us on the islands with a relatively early example of Irish monastic construction but the existence of prior wooden buildings on western sites such as Church Island and Reask suggests that wood was available for construction. Indeed we know that wood still existed on a significant scale in the area around Tralee and Brandon Bays up to *c.*AD1600.[178] What is certain is that wood continued to be used as a building material in churches throughout Ireland long after stone had been widely adopted.[179]

It is also clear that the use of wood as a main building material necessarily affected how both wooden and eventually stone buildings were designed and constructed.[180] We have already noted that the simple single cell plan of most religious buildings was one of the factors which suggested that the earliest churches and oratories were constructed

[174] Cuppage (1986), 362.

[175] The documentation of stone churches within the *Annals* begins around the end of the eighth century which might suggest that stone churches were beginning to emerge around AD800 (O'Keefe (1998), 114).

[176] Hamlin (1985), 284.

Like Ireland there was no tradition of stone construction in England and Anglo-Saxon churches were initially built of wood (Foot (2006), 111–112). Further, paralleling once again the Irish experience, it would appear that wooden buildings continued to be built throughout the Anglo-Saxon period and certainly long after the introduction there of stone buildings following the seventh century conversion (Foot (2006), 79, 115).

[177] Leask (1955), 17; for a *contra* view see O'Keefe (1998), 112.

[178] McCracken (1959), 271ff.

[179] Radford (1977), 5; Edwards (1990), 122–123.

[180] Leask (1955), 17.

of wood.[181] At the other end of the developmental spectrum we can see the presence of wooden construction features on buildings built of stone. An outstanding example of this phenomenon are the *antae* on the strongly skeuomorphic church on St Macdara's Island off the Galway coast.[182] A further indicator of the transfer of wooden building characteristics into stone is the presence of finials on several stone constructions such as Muiredach's Cross and the West Cross at Monasterboice, and the Durrow High Cross.[183] Most strikingly of all, the depiction of the 'Temple Scene' in the potentially late eighth century Book of Kells appears to show the Temple in Jerusalem in the form of an ornate wooden church complete with carved gable finials.[184] So it would appear that wooden buildings not only influenced the style of stone buildings but also provided a template for their stone successors. It has even been suggested that the distinctive round beehive style may have derived from a circular wooden prototype.[185]

However, early Irish Christian architecture should not be regarded as unsophisticated. Corbelling is a structural method of great antiquity and complexity dating in an Irish context from as far back as the Bronze Age. Further, it was not exclusively a native Irish activity; examples of corbelling can be found as far afield as France, Spain, southern Italy and Greece and as far back as Mycenaean Greece.[186] Nor was it a static building form. This early Irish Christian architecture was susceptible to change and development. On the site at Skellig Michael we can see clear evidence of an evolution in the shape and form of the traditional beehive hut from a round to a more obviously rectilinear plan[187] and excavation evidence from other sites has also suggested a transition from a round to a rectangular plan for domestic construction during the eighth and ninth centuries.[188] There is also no doubt that this vernacular building form impacted significantly upon many of the elements of early Irish religious settlement. However while the

---

[181] Radford (1977), 4–5.

[182] Leask (1955), 45–46.
It has been counter-argued that *antae* cannot be viewed as indicative of timber architecture (O'Keefe (1998), 118–119).

[183] Leask (1955), 46–47.

[184] Thomas (1971), 77; Edwards (1990), 122, 155.

[185] Leask (1955), 17.

[186] Leask (1955), 17–18.

[187] de Paor (1955), 185.

[188] Lynn (1978), 29–45.

footprint of settlement clearly reflects the circular and rectilinear dichotomy of the secular and the holy within the built environment little influence was exerted upon the internal spatial organisation. So while vernacular building styles and materials may have affected significantly the external appearance of settlement it does not appear to have dictated the spatial organisation.

4.E. *Conclusion*

The key driver in the creation of the topography of early historic Irish religious settlement was scriptural precedent. It is my contention that the builders of these early Irish religious foundations brought to the task a received and scripturally fed, and therefore also universal, understanding of how holy space might be ordered based upon the biblical description of the topography of the Temple in Jerusalem. This would explain how a 'canon of planning' was expressed in material form across a wide range of site types and geographical location. It would also address the parallels we detect when comparisons are made with the layout of Middle Eastern, Gallic and Anglo-Saxon religious settlement. However, although the influence of the Temple as a spatial paradigm is clearly reflected within both the vernacular Irish canonical and hagiographical literature dealing with the layout of holy space the nature of its impact upon the physicality of settlement is more complex. What was being copied on the ground was not the form of the Temple but rather an ideal of how sacred space should be ordered which the Temple enshrined. This explains why we do not see any attempt to reproduce the Temple within an Irish context. What we do encounter is the embodiment of an understanding of holy space reflecting that within the Temple complex with its tripartite zoning of the enclosed space centred upon the holiest of holies and with the Ark of the Covenant at its heart. The diffraction of this Temple paradigm through the medium of a highly distinctive vernacular architectural form then created a unique sacred topography. In an Irish context this *schema* is centred upon a what I have labelled a 'sacred core', typically made up of at least one, usually more, of the following elements; an oratory, cross-slab or free-standing cross, and a saint's or founder's shrine. This 'sacred core' appears to exert a centrifugal force upon the remaining elements of settlement, such as the guesthouse and ancillary buildings, pushing these outwards in order of decreasing sanctity towards or occasionally beyond an enclosing feature. This enclosing feature in turn serves an apotropaic rather than defensive function, warding off evil, protecting the holy, and separating profane and sacred ground.

The same understanding of holy space lies behind the increasingly sophisticated subdivision of the enclosed space. This subdivision created internal zones and barriers which were designed both to delineate clearly between areas of varying sanctity and to restrict unauthorised access from one zone to another. So even on the smallest and most remote of sites such as Reask, Gallarus, and High Island we find the internal space being divided and the 'sacred core' cordoned off from the rest of the settlement, mirroring the more developed internal zoning evident on larger sites such as Clonmacnoise, Glendalough, and Iona. A similar understanding of holy space underlies the development of the ubiquitous Irish single cell church into a two-cell nave and chancel church. Here, once again, we see the physical expression of a conscious decision to segregate the holiest part of the church from the rest of the building. This was achieved in a number of different ways. Single cell churches were added to in order to create a two-cell building, such as St Mary's Church at Glendalough or the church at Cloone in Kilkenny. Single cell churches were sometimes subdivided to create a nave and chancel as at Clonmacnoise Cathedral. We also find the creation of new two-cell churches, such as Trinity Church and St Ciarán's Church at Glendalough; all developments which Leask dates to the tenth century.[189]

What we see within an early Irish context in the extant archaeology, what we encounter in the hagiography and in the canons, is the result of the exposure of the Irish Christian culture to two essentially conflicting pressures. On the one hand there is the biblical conception of holy space which dictated the layout of Tabernacle and Temple and which has shaped the topography of Judaeo-Christian religious settlement ever since. On the other hand in early Ireland this scriptural topographical *schema* encountered the architectural legacy of the pre-Christian past. This encounter occurred wherever monasticism took root. The topographical template for the layout of religious settlement in Ireland was the Bible, interpreted in an exegetical tradition that we are coming to understand in terms of its historical evolution. This reading of Scripture, governed by the influence of vernacular building and the specific geography of Irish monastic life, produced the striking religious landscape of early Ireland.

---

[189] Leask (1955), 76.

EPILOGUE

At the outset of this book I expressed the hope that we might extend the parameters within which the phenomena of enclosure and zoning of holy space in early medieval Ireland have been discussed. The academic discourse has been dominated by archaeological interpretation and this has tended to encourage a focus on material causes of enclosure. My intent has been to shift the focus from the physical processes of enclosure towards a more theologically informed approach.

This is not to distance theology from archaeology; the two rightly are used together to understand the material and literary record. It is the widespread and consistent material evidence for enclosure which draws our attention to its praxis. The recurring pattern of internal zoning suggests the existence of a ritual and theology of enclosure. Once this regularity of layout is placed alongside the literary depiction of holy space found within a number of key early medieval Irish texts, including in particular the *Collectio canonum Hibernensis*, the likelihood of a connection becomes clear. What we read depicted in the pages of much of the canonical and hagiographical material we can also see embodied in the physicality of settlement. A key task before us is to ascertain the nature of this relationship in terms of 'cause and effect'.

An examination of the physical and literary evidence in detail opens up the possibility that the interaction of the two is not simply one-way, either cause *or* effect but rather cause *and* effect; 'inspiration' and 'justification'. Certainly, the understanding of the importance of boundaries which we see reflected, especially in the text of the *Hibernensis*, we see also manifested in the archaeology of sites dating from a similar dating horizon. However, the extent to which the *Hibernensis* in particular, and other texts in general, might have served as some form of 'building guide' to those who were seeking to establish a religious settlement remains unresolved. We have, of course, argued that Scripture remains the primary source of inspiration but the possibility that some of these texts played a similar role remains open. What is evident is that the textual evidence is able to provide a theological hermeneutic for the decoding of the praxis and physical reality of enclosure. This is apparent when one reads works such as Adomnán's *De locis sanctis* or his *Vita S. Columbae*, both of which provided not only an explicitly theological framework for interpreting the religious landscape but also reflect some of the more prosaic and secular concerns that were facing his community. Above all it is the text of the *Hibernensis*, especially Book 44 which indicates a scriptural and liturgical framework within which the Irish monastic conception of the importance of boundaries and enclosed space was formed.

Although the historiography to date has relatively little significant theological comment to make about the motivation behind enclosure it is evident from the textual and material witness referred to above that the praxis of enclosure and zoning reflected a scripturally based understanding of the nature of holy space. The evidence, particularly that contained within the literature of Iona, further explicitly indicated that this biblical paradigm was the topography of the Jerusalem Temple. This biblical paradigm I chose to refer to as a scriptural 'canon of planning'.

Interestingly, when we set the Irish experience within a broader context and make comparisons with the patterns of religious settlement found in near neighbours such as Anglo-Saxon England and Gaul, and in more distant lands such as Egypt and Syria, it becomes obvious that Irish topography conforms to some form of widespread planning *schema* which transcended national or cultural boundaries. We have been clear from the start that whatever 'canon of planning' lay behind the layout of Irish religious settlement it was not idiosyncratic or a vernacular oddity despite a traditional scholarly approach to Irish ecclesiology that suggested the contrary and so this finding was of interest. In architectural terms the layout of Irish religious settlement appears to mirror, in a number of key elements, monasteries in England, Gaul, and Egypt. The comparative dearth of *physical* evidence in an Anglo-Saxon and Gaulish setting and the accompanying paucity of *textual* evidence in a Middle Eastern context seriously limit comparison. On the limited evidence, however, it can begin to be shown how the topography of Egyptian and Syro-Palestinian monastic settlement prefigured that to be found in Gaul and Ireland and that this shared inheritance reflected a generic conception of the ordering of holy space. Indeed, arguing back from the explicit scriptural attestation found within an Irish perspective we might seek to use the Irish evidence to postulate a similar paradigm for Gaul and beyond. However, outside the Irish context we lack the same degree of explicit evidence for the Temple as the predominant model for monastic enclosure. I am thus wary of postulating a universal determinative influence without being able to show how it was applied in practice.

What was being created and then guarded was a piece of heaven here on earth, a divine *locus*, a 'thin place', a peripheral place, where the nature of the enclosed space was ontologically different from the profane space outside of the enclosure. Once inside the Temple complex or within the monastic enclosure the space was regarded as being 'qualitatively different'.[1] We have already noted that in the Bible space was often rendered holy or 'qualitatively different' by divine appearances or by the occurrence of miracles. What sanctified the set-aside space we encounter within the Bible, the Temple in particular, and within Irish religious settlement in general was essentially divine intervention mediated through human activity; the actions of the super-holy, men and women such as Abraham, Moses, David, Patrick, Columba, and Brigid. The Jerusalem Temple was built at the location of the threshing floor of Ornan the Jebusite[2] on Mount Moriah, itself the site of two especially holy events, the offering of Isaac by his father Abraham[3] and the appearance of the Lord to David as he offered sacrifice.[4] In our discussion of the changing role of the Temple in the New Testament period we have also noted that notions of holiness were increasingly focused upon individuals rather than place and certainly in an Irish Christian context the belief that it was personal piety which might make a place holy, along with the strong influence of the cult of saints, meant that the presence of the founder's tomb or slab-shrine at the heart of the settlement site was what made it holy ground. Though on a more extensive scale, the same principle is at work in

[1] Eliade (1959), 26.
[2] 1 Chronicles 21:18–28.
[3] Genesis 22.
[4] 2 Chronicles 3:1.

Adomnán's *Vita S. Columbae*. Here we see the terrain of the island of Iona being sanctified simply by Columba's presence upon it.

In order to control and protect this 'holy' space both 'hard' physical boundaries, such as ditches, walls, and gates, and 'soft' boundaries, created by special rules and regulations, were employed. These served first of all to filter access to the enclosed or 'holy' space according to religious caste, personal piety, and even gender. They also then controlled and restricted movement *within* the enclosed area. In both the Israelite and Irish settings the conception of holy space was predicated, as we already outlined, upon a layout *schema* which placed its most holy objects at the centre within what has been referred to in this book as a 'sacred core'. In an Irish context this 'sacred core' consisted of some combination of a cross-slab or free-standing cross, an oratory, and a founder's or saint's tomb at the heart of a settlement. In a scriptural context this 'sacred core' was represented by the 'holiest of holies' containing the Ark of the Covenant at the epicentre of the Temple complex. In both settings the 'sacred core' was surrounded by layers or zones of decreasing sanctity, like the layers of an onion.

This layering or zoning inevitably created areas of varying importance. So, for example, one would expect to find within an Irish enclosure areas set apart for the more mundane routines of everyday life such as cooking and cleaning as well as for ritual or cultic purposes. The zones to be regarded as most special or 'holy' were those directly concerned with the cultic life of the community while those of lesser importance were those which fulfilled a supporting or peripheral role. This sliding scale of sanctity was reflected not only in the physical environment and positioning of the area in question but by the degree of access allowed to a particular zone. In an Irish context it is likely that only the monks were allowed to access the inner core of the settlement in much the same way as the holier areas of the Temple was accessible only to the priests while the outer parts of the enclosure, like the Temple vestibule, were open to a much wider group of people. In both the Temple and the Irish enclosure the presence of zoning opened up access to the hallowed ground to many whilst at the same time ensuring that the 'sacred core', which in effect bestowed sanctity upon the whole enclosure, was protected from spoliation and open to only the few. Spatial location within the enclosure was another indicator of the importance of a particular zone or area with the *locus* of the ritual activity providing the physical core of the settlement and the supporting or ancillary activities such as crop cultivation and craft working exiled to the perimeter.

Crucial to my hypothesis concerning a shared vision of religious space is how a 'canon of planning' may have been transmitted. The evidence for the sharing of intellectual property between the European mainland and Ireland confirms the exposure of Irish clerics to both the Vulgate and a wide range of other classical and patristic texts. The idea of the existence of some form of written or pictorial plan is a chimera supported neither by the surviving literary evidence nor the nature of the sites themselves. There was a 'received' understanding of holy space which was biblically based and universally available and known to those who built religious settlements. The extant archaeology reflects a built environment which was a far cry from the scale and opulence of the Temple complex of early first millennium Jerusalem.

In terms of the impact of a biblical model upon the form of settlement found within early medieval Ireland, it is clear that whatever the nature of the relationship between the layout of the Temple and early Irish settlement patterns it was not one of mirror image. This was to be expected given the extant archaeology of the Irish vernacular building form. Instead, what we encounter is the result of the distillation of a scriptural planning ideal through the medium of a native architectural culture in which wood and then dry-stone are the materials of choice, or more often of necessity, and where the scale and detail of building structure are less advanced than those represented by the Temple complex in Jerusalem. Added to this was the need on occasion to adapt the shape and lie of the enclosure to take account of the topography of the chosen terrain and one can begin to see how vernacular Irish religious settlement took on the form it did. The material product of this synthesis needs to be decoded and set in its theological and scriptural context. It is nonetheless clear that both the cell and oratory settlements of Ireland and the Temple complex of Jerusalem bear witness to the same understanding of holy space.

BIBLIOGRAPHY

PRIMARY TEXTS

Adomnán, *Vita Sancti Columbae*, (eds. and trans.) A. O. and M. O. Anderson, *Adomnán's Life of Columba* (London, 1961; 2nd edn Oxford, 1991); (trans.) R. Sharpe, *Adomnán of Iona, Life of Columba* (Harmondsworth, 1995).

— *De locis sanctis*, (ed.) D. Meehan, *Adamnan's De locis sanctis*, Scriptores Latini Hiberniae 3 (Dublin, 1958).

Æthelwulf, *De abbatibus*, (ed.) A. Campbell (Oxford, 1967).

The Ancient Laws of Ireland, (eds.) W. N. Hancock *et al.*, 6 Vols (Dublin, 1865–1901).

Annals of the Kingdom of Ireland by the Four Masters, (ed. and trans.) J. O'Donovan, 2 Vols (Dublin, 1848–51).

Annals of Inishfallen (MS. Rawlinson B.503), (ed. and trans.) S. MacAirt, (Dublin, 1951).

Annals of Ulster, (eds. and trans.) S. MacAirt, S. and G. MacNiocaill (Dublin, 1983).

Anon., *On Angus the Culdee*, (trans.) K. Meyer, *Selections from Ancient Irish Poetry* (London, 1911), 88.

Anon., *Vita Filiberti Abbatis*, (ed.), W. Levison, Monumenta Germaniae Historica, Scriptores Rerum Merovingicarum 5 (Hanover and Leipzig, 1910), 568–606.

Anon., *Vita patrum Iurensium*, (trans.) T. Vivian, K. Vivian, J. B. Russell, *The Life of the Jura Fathers*, Cistercian Series 178 (Kalamazoo, 1999), 95–184.

Anon., *Vita prima Sancti Pachomii*, (ed.) A. Veilleux, *The Lives, Rules and Other Writings of Saint Pachomius and His Disciples*, Cistercian Studies 45, Vol. 1 (Kalamazoo, 1980).

Anon., *Vita Sancte Samthanne virginis*, (ed.) C. Plummer, *Vitae Sanctorum Hiberniae*, Vol. 2 (Oxford, 1910), 253–261.

Anon., *Vita Sancti Aidi Episcopi Killariensis*, (ed.) W. W. Heist, *Vitae Sanctorum Hiberniae e codice olim Salmanticensi nunc Bruxellensi*, Subsidia Hagiographica 28 (Brussels, 1965), 167–181.

Anon., *Vita Sancti Barri Episcopi Corcagie*, (ed.) C. Plummer, *Vitae Sanctorum Hiberniae*, Vol. 1 (Oxford, 1910), 65–74.

Anon., *Vita Sancti Ciarani de Cluain mic Nois*, (ed.) C. Plummer, *Vitae Sanctorum Hiberniae*, Vol. 1 (Oxford, 1910), 200–216.

Anon., *Vita Sancti Cuthberti*, (ed. and trans.) B. Colgrave, *Two Lives of Saint Cuthbert* (Cambridge, 1940), 60–138.

Anon., *Vita Sancti Fechini*, (ed.) B. Jennings, *Acta sanctorum Hiberniae of John Colgan* (Louvain, 1645; repr. Dublin, 1948), 133–139.

Anon., *Vita prior Sancti Fintani seu Munnu Abbatis de Tech Munnu*, (ed.) W. W. Heist, *Vitae sanctorum Hiberniae e codice olim Salmanticensi nunc Bruxellensi*, Subsidia Hagiographica 28 (Brussels, 1965), 198–209.

Anon., *Vita tripartita Sancti Patricii,* (ed. and trans.) W. Stokes, *The Tripartite Life of Patrick and Other Documents Relating to the Saint,* 2 Vols (London, 1887).

Antiphonarium Benchorense, (ed.) F. E. Warren, *Antiphonary of Bangor: An Early Irish Manuscript in the Ambrosian Library at Milan,* 2 Vols, Henry Bradshaw Society 4 and 10 (London, 1893–1895).

Asser, *De rebus gestis Ælfredi,* (ed.) W. H. Stevenson, *Asser's Life of King Alfred* (Oxford, 1950); (trans.) S. Keynes and M. Lapidge, *Alfred the Great* (Harmondsworth, 1983).

Athanasius, *Vita Sancti Antonii,* (trans.) R. C. Gregg, *Athanasius: The Life of Antony and the Letter to Marcellinus,* Classics of Western Spirituality (New York, 1980).

Augustine, *De civitate Dei,* (trans.) M. Dods, *The City of God,* in P. Schaff (ed.), A Select Library of the Nicene and Post-Nicene Fathers, First Series, Vol. 2 (New York, 1886; repr. Edinburgh, 1993), 1–511; also (trans.) D. Knowles, *Augustine, City of God* (Harmondsworth, 1972).

— *De doctrina Christiana,* (trans.) J. F. Shaw, On Christian Doctrine, in P. Schaff (ed.), A Select Library of the Nicene and Post-Nicene Fathers, First Series, Vol. 2 (New York, 1886; repr. Edinburgh, 1993), 519–597.

— *De utilitate credendi,* (trans.) C. L. Cornish, *On the Profit of Believing,* in P. Schaff (ed.), A Select Library of the Nicene and Post-Nicene Fathers, First Series, Vol. 3 (New York, 1890; repr. Edinburgh, 1993), 347–366.

— *De consensu evangelistarum,* (ed.) F. Weihrich, Corpus Scriptorum Ecclesiasticorum Latinorum 43 (Vienna, 1904); (trans.) S. D. F Salmond, *The Harmony of the Gospels,* in P. Schaff (ed.), A Select Library of the Nicene and Post-Nicene Fathers, First Series, Vol. 6 (New York, 1887; repr. Edinburgh, 1996), 77–236.

Bechbretha: An Old Irish Law-tract on Bee-keeping, (eds.) T. Charles-Edwards and F. Kelly, Early Irish Law Series 1 (Dublin, 1983).

Bede, *De locis sanctis,* (trans.) W. T. Foley, *On the Holy Places,* in W. T. Foley, and A. G. Holder (trans.), *Bede: A Biblical Miscellany,* Translated Texts for Historians 28 (Liverpool, 1999), 5–25.

— *De Tabernaculo,* (trans.) A. G. Holder, *Bede: On the Tabernacle,* Translated Texts for Historians 18 (Liverpool, 1994).

— *De Templo,* (trans.) S. Connolly, with an introduction by J. O'Reilly, *Bede: On the Temple,* Translated Texts for Historians 21 (Liverpool, 1995).

— *Epistola ad Ecgbertum Episcopum,* (trans.) D. H. Farmer, *Letter to Egbert,* in L. Sherley-Price (trans.); R. E. Latham (rev.), *Bede's Ecclesiastical*

History of the English People, with Bede's Letter to Egbert and Cuthbert's Letter on the Death of Bede (Harmondsworth, 1990), 337–351.

— *Historia ecclesiastica*, (eds.) B. Colgrave and R. A. B. Mynors, *Bede's Ecclesiastical History* (Oxford, 1969).

— *In Ezram et Neemiam*, (trans.) S. DeGregorio, *Bede: On Ezra and Nehemiah*, Translated Texts for Historians 47 (Liverpool, 2006).

— *In Regum Librum XXX quaestiones*, (trans.) W. T. Foley, *Thirty Questions on the Book of Kings*, in W. T. Foley, and A. G. Holder (trans.), *Bede: A Biblical Miscellany*, Translated Texts for Historians 28 (Liverpool, 1999), 89–138.

— *Vita Sancti Cuthberti*, (ed. and trans.) B. Colgrave, *Two Lives of Saint Cuthbert* (Cambridge, 1940), 142–306.

Benedict, *Regula monachorum*, (trans.) Abbot Parry OSB, *The Rule of St Benedict* (Leominster, 1990).

Bernard of Clairvaux, *Vita Sancti Malachi*, (trans.) R. T. Meyer, *The Life and Death of St Malachy the Irishman*, Cistercian Fathers 10 (Kalamazoo, 1978).

Betha Bhairre Ó Chorcaigh, (ed. and trans.) C. Plummer, *Bethada Náem nÉrenn, Lives of the Irish Saints*, 2 Vols (Oxford, 1922), 1:11–22, 2:11–21.

Betha Ciaráin Saighre (II), (ed. and trans.) C. Plummer, *Bethada Náem nÉrenn, Lives of the Irish Saints*, 2 Vols (Oxford, 1922), 1:113–124, 2:109–120.

Betha Máedóc Ferna (I), (ed. and trans.) C. Plummer, *Bethada Náem nÉrenn, Lives of the Irish Saints*, 2 Vols (Oxford, 1922), 1:183–189, 2:177–183.

Betha Máedóc Ferna (II), (ed. and trans.) C. Plummer, *Bethada Náem nÉrenn, Lives of the Irish Saints*, 2 Vols (Oxford, 1922), 1:190–290, 2:184–281.

Betha Mochuda, (ed. and trans.) C. Plummer, *Bethada Náem nÉrenn, Lives of the Irish Saints*, 2 Vols (Oxford, 1922), 1:291–299, 2:282–290.

Betha Molaga, (ed.) J. G. O'Keeffe, in J. Fraser, P. Grosjean and J. G. O'Keeffe (eds.), *Irish Texts*, Vol. 3 (London, 1931), 11–22.

Betha Shenain meic Geirginn, (ed.) W. Stokes, *Lives of the Saints from the Book of Lismore* (Oxford, 1890), 54–74; 201–221.

Chronicum Scotorum, (ed. and trans.) W. M. Hennessey, Rerum Britannicarum Medii Aevii Scriptores 46 (London, 1866).

Cogitosus, *Vita Sanctae Brigidae*, (trans.) S. Connolly and J-M. Picard, 'Cogitosus: Life of St Brigit', *Journal of the Royal Society of Antiquaries of Ireland* 117 (1987), 5–27.

Collectio canonum Hibernensis, (ed.) F. W. H. Wasserschleben, *Die irische Kanonensammlung* (Leipzig, 1885; repr. Aalen, 1966).

Columbanus, *Epistulae*, (ed.) G. S. M. Walker, *Sancti Columbani Opera*, Scriptores Latini Hiberniae 2 (Dublin, 1957), 2–58.

Columbanus, *Paenitentiale*, (ed.) G. S. M. Walker, *Sancti Columbani Opera*, Scriptores Latini Hiberniae 2 (Dublin, 1957), 168–180.

Columbanus, *Regulae coenobialis*, (ed.) G. S. M. Walker, *Sancti Columbani Opera*, Scriptores Latini Hiberniae 2 (Dublin, 1957), 142–168.

Corpus Iuris Hibernici, (ed.) D. A. Binchy, 6 Vols (Dublin, 1978).

Cummian, *De controversia Paschali*, (eds.) D. Ó Cróinín and M. Walsh, *Cummian's Letter 'De controversia Paschali'*, Pontifical Institute of Medieval Studies 86 (Toronto, 1998).

Dado of Rouen, *Vita Sancti Eligii*, (trans.) J. A. McNamara, *Dado of Rouen, Life of St Eligius of Noyon*, in T. Head (ed.), *Medieval Hagiography: An Anthology* (New York, 1999), 137–168.

Eddius Stephanus, *Vita Sancti Wilfridi*, (trans.) J. F. Webb, *Eddius Stephanus: Life of Wilfrid*, in D. H. Farmer and J. F. Webb (trans.), *The Age of Bede* (Harmondsworth, 1965; rev. edn 1983), 105–184.

Eucherius of Lyons, *De laude eremi*, (trans.) C. Cummings; rev. J. B. Russell, *In Praise of the Desert*, in T. Vivian, K. Vivian, J. B. Russell (trans.), *The Life of the Jura Fathers*, Cistercian Series 178 (Kalamazoo, 1999), 197–215.

Eusebius, *Historia Ecclesiastica*, (trans.) H. J. Lawlor and J. E. L. Oulton, *The Ecclesiastical History*, 2 Vols. (London, 1927); also (trans.) A. C. McGiffert, *Eusebius, Church History*, in P. Schaff and H. Wace (eds.), A Select Library of the Nicene and Post-Nicene Fathers, Second Series, Vol. 1 (New York, 1890; repr. Edinburgh, 1991), 73–403.

Felix, *Vita Sancti Guthlaci*, (ed.) B. Colgrave, *Life of Saint Guthlac* (Cambridge, 1956).

Giraldus Cambrensis, *Topographia Hiberniae*, (trans.) J. J. O'Meara, *Gerald of Wales; The History and Topography of Ireland* (Harmondsworth, 1951, rev. edn 1982).

Gregory of Tours, *Historiae Francorum*, (trans.) L. Thorpe, *Gregory of Tours, The History of the Franks* (London, 1974).

Gregory the Great, *Homiliae in Ezechielem*, (ed.) J-P. Migne, *Sanctus Gregorius I Magnus, Homiliarum in Ezechielem prophetam libri duo*, Patrologia Latina 76 (Paris, 1857); (trans.) T. Gray, *The Homilies of Gregory the Great on the Book of the Prophet Ezekiel* (California, 1990).

Historia monachorum in Ægypto, (trans.) N. Russell and B. Ward, *The Lives of the Desert Fathers: The Historia monachorum in Ægypto*, Cistercian Studies 34 (Oxford and Kalamazoo, 1981).

Isidore, *Etymologiae*, (ed.) W. M. Lindsay, *Isidore Hispalensis episcopi etymologiarum sive originum*, 2 Vols (Oxford, 1911).

Jerome, *Commentarii in Ezechielem*, (ed.) J-P. Migne, Patrologia Latina 25 (Paris, 1844).

John Cassian, *Collationes*, (trans.) C. Luibheid, *John Cassian: Conferences*, Classics of Western Spirituality (New York, 1985).

Jonas, *Vita Sancti Columbani*, (ed.) B. Krusch, *Ionae Vitae Sanctorum Columbani, Vedastis, Iohannis*, Monumenta Germaniae Historica, Scriptores

Rerum Merovingicarum, separatim (Hanover and Leipzig, 1905), 144–295; (ed. and trans.) D. C. Munro, *The Life of St Columban by the Monk Jonas* (Philadelphia PA, 2nd edn 1895), reprinted by E. M. Peters (ed.), *Monks, Bishops, and Pagans* (Philadelphia PA, 1975), 75–113.

Josephus, *Antiquitates Iudaicae*, (trans.) W. Whiston, *The Works of Josephus* (Peabody MA; 2nd edn 1987), 27–542.

Josephus, *De bello Iudaico*, (trans.) W. Whiston, *The Works of Josephus* (Peabody MA; 2nd edn 1987), 543–772.

The Letter of Aristeas, in R. H. Charles (ed.), *The Apocrypha and Pseudepigrapha of the Old Testament*, Vol. 2 (Oxford, 1913), 82–122.

Liber Angeli, (ed. and trans.) L. Bieler, *The Patrician Texts in the Book of Armagh*, Scriptores Latini Hiberniae 10 (Dublin, 1979), 184–190.

The Martyrology of Oengus the Culdee, (ed. and trans.) W. Stokes, Henry Bradshaw Society 29 (London, 1905).

The Martyrology of Tallaght, (eds. and trans.) R. I. Best and H. J. Lawlor, Henry Bradshaw Society 68 (London, 1931).

The Mishnah, (trans.) H. Danby (Oxford, 1933).

The Monastery of Tallaght, (eds. and trans.) E. J. Gwynn and W. J. Purton, *Proceedings of the Royal Irish Academy* 29C (1911), No. 5, 115–179.

Muirchú, *Vita Sancti Patricii*, (ed. and trans.) L. Bieler, *The Patrician Texts in the Book of Armagh*, Scriptores Latini Hiberniae 10 (Dublin, 1979), 62–122.

Navigatio Sancti Brendani, (trans.) J. J. O'Meara, *The Voyage of St Brendan* (Gerrards Cross, 1976).

Origen, *In Exodum homiliae*, (trans.) R. Heine, *Homilies on Genesis and Exodus*, Fathers of the Church 71 (Washington, 1982).

Palladius, *Historia Lausiaca*, (trans.) W. K. L. Clarke, *The Lausiac History of Palladius* (London and New York, 1918).

Patrick, *Confessio*, (trans.) T. O'Loughlin, in T. O'Loughlin, *Saint Patrick: The Man and his Works* (London, 1999), 52–89.

Ríagal Phátraic, (ed. and trans.) J. G. O'Keeffe, 'The Rule of Patrick', *Ériu* 1 (1904), 216–224.

'The Rule of Ailbe of Emly', (ed. and trans.) J. O'Neill, *Ériu* 3 (1907), 92–115.

The Saltair na Rann: A Collection of Early Middle Irish Poems, (ed.) W. Stokes (Oxford, 1883).

Sanas Cormaic: An Old Irish Glossary, (ed.) K. Meyer, in O. J. Bergin, R. I. Best, K. Meyer, and J. G. O'Keeffe (eds.), Anecdota from Irish Manuscripts 4 (Halle, 1912; repr. with Meyer's corrections added to the text, Felinfach, 1994); also in *Three Irish Glossaries* (ed.) W. Stokes (Dublin, 1862; repr. Felinfach, 2000).

Sulpicius Severus, *Vita Sancti Martini*, (trans.) C. White, *Life of St Martin by Sulpicius Severus*, in C. White (ed. and trans.), *Early Christian Lives*

(London, 1998), 129–159; also (trans.) A. Roberts, *Sulpitius Severus, Life of Saint Martin*, in P. Schaff and H. Wace (eds.), A Select Library of the Nicene and Post-Nicene Fathers, Second Series, Vol. 11 (New York, 1894; repr. Edinburgh, 1991), 3–17.

Tírechán, *Collectanea*, (ed. and trans.) L. Bieler, *The Patrician Texts in the Book of Armagh*, Scriptores Latini Hiberniae 10 (Dublin, 1979), 122–162.

War of the Gaedhil with the Gaill; or the Invasion of Ireland by the Danes and Other Norsemen, (ed.) J. H. Todd (London, 1867).

SECONDARY TEXTS

Aitchison, N. B. (1994), *Armagh and the Royal Centres in Early Medieval Ireland: Monuments, Cosmology and the Past* (Woodbridge).

Albright, W. (1959), 'Was the Age of Solomon without Monumental Art?', in M. Avi-Yonah, H. Z. Hirschberg, Y. Yadin, and H. Tadmor (eds.), *Eretz-Israel* 5, 1–9.

Alcock, L. (1971), *Arthur's Britain* (Harmondsworth).

Baillie, M. G. L. (1986), 'The Central Post from Navan Fort: The First Step towards a Better Understanding of the Early Iron Age', *Emania* 1, 20–21.

Barber, J. W. (1981), 'Excavations on Iona, 1979', *Proceedings of the Society of Antiquaries of Scotland* 111, 282–380.

Barker, M. (1991), *The Gate of Heaven: The History and Symbolism of the Temple in Jerusalem* (London).

Barker, M. (1995), *On Earth as It is in Heaven* (Edinburgh).

Binchy, D. A. (1962a), 'Patrick and his Biographers, Ancient and Modern', *Studia Hibernica* 2, 7–173.

— (1962b), 'The Passing of the Old Order' in *Proceedings of the International Congress of Celtic Studies held in Dublin, 6–10 July, 1959* (Dublin), 119–132.

— (1967), 'Review of Hughes, 1966', *Studia Hibernica* 7, 217–219.

Bitel, L. M. (1990), *Isle of the Saints: Monastic Settlement and Christian Community in Early Ireland* (New York).

Blair, J. (2005), *The Church in Anglo-Saxon Society* (Oxford).

Boland, D. (1996), 'Clonmacnoise Bridge', in I. Bennett (ed.), *Excavations 1995: Summary Accounts of Archaeological Excavations in Ireland* (Bray), 75–76.

Bourke, C., (1980) 'Early Irish Hand-Bells', *Journal of the Royal Society of Antiquaries of Ireland* 110, 52–66.

Bradley, J. (1990), 'The Role of Town Plan Analysis in the Study of the Medieval Irish Town', in T. R. Slater (ed.), *The Built Form of Western Cities* (Leicester), 39–59.

— (1991), 'Town Life in Medieval Ireland', in *Archaeology Ireland* 5, No. 3 (Autumn), 25–28.

— (1995), *Walled Towns in Ireland* (Dublin).

— (1998), 'The Monastic Town of Clonmacnoise', in H. King (ed.), *Clonmacnoise Studies, Vol.* 1: Seminar Papers 1994 (Dublin), 42–56.

Braunfels, W. (1972), *Monasteries of Western Europe, The Architecture of the Orders* (London).

Breatnach, C. (2005), 'The Significance of the Orthography of Irish Proper Names in the Codex Salmanticensis', *Ériu* 55, 85–101.

Breen, A. (1984), 'Some Seventh Century Hiberno-Latin Texts and Their Relationships', *Peritia* 3, 204–214.

Bright, W. (1960), *A History of Israel* (London).

Bullough, D. A. (1964), 'Columba, Adomnan and the Achievement of Iona', *Scottish Historical Review* 43, 111–130.

Burrow, I. (1973), 'Tintagel – Some Problems', *Scottish Archaeological Forum* 5, 88–103.

Bury, J. B. (1905), *The Life of St. Patrick and His Place in History* (London).

Campbell, E. (1987), 'A Cross-Marked Quern from Dunadd and Other Evidence for Relations between Dunadd and Iona', *Proceedings of the Society of Antiquaries of Scotland* 117, 105–117.

— (2007), *Continental and Mediterranean Imports to Atlantic Britain and Ireland, AD400–800*, Council for British Archaeology, Research Report 157 (York).

Carey, J. (1986), 'The Heavenly City in *Saltair na Rann*', *Celtica* 18, 87–104.

— (2000), *King of Mysteries: Early Irish Religious Writings* (Dublin).

Carney, J. (1963), 'Review [of Selmer's Navigatio]', *Medium Ævum* 32, 37–44; repr. in J. Wooding (ed.), *The Otherworld Voyage in Early Irish Literature – An Anthology of Criticism* (Dublin, 2000), 42–51.

Carver, M. (2004), 'An Iona of the East: The Early-Medieval Monastery at Portmahomack, Tarbat Ness', *Medieval Archaeology* 48, 1–30.

— (2008), *Portmahomack: Monastery of the Picts* (Edinburgh).

— and C. Spall (2005), 'Excavating a *Parchmenerie*: Archaeological Correlates of Making Parchment at the Pictish Monastery at Portmahomack, Easter Ross', *Proceedings of the Society of Antiquaries of Scotland* 134, 183–200.

Cassidy-Welch, M. (2001), *Monastic Spaces and Their Meanings: Thirteenth Century English Cistercian Monasteries* (Turnhout).

Champneys, A. C. (1910), *Irish Ecclesiastical Architecture* (London).

Charles-Edwards, T. (1980), 'Review Article: *The Corpus iuris Hibernici*', *Studia Hibernica* 20, 141–162.

— (1986), '*Crith Gablach* and the Law of Status', *Peritia* 5, 53–73.

— (1998), 'The Construction of the Hibernensis', *Peritia* 12, 209–237.

— (2000), *Early Christian Ireland* (Cambridge).

Chitty, D. (1966), *The Desert a City* (Oxford).

Clark, D. L. C. (2007), 'Viewing the Liturgy: a Space Syntax Study of Changing Visibility and Accessibility in the Development of the Byzantine Church in Jordan', *World Archaeology* 39 (1), 84–104.

Cohn, R.L. (1981), *The Shape of Sacred Space* (Chicago).

Cotter, C. (1994), 'Atlantic Fortifications–The Duns of the Aran Islands', *Archaeology Ireland* 8, No. 1 (Spring), 24–28.

Cramp, R. (1973), 'Anglo-Saxon Monasteries of the North', *Scottish Archaeological Forum* 5 (Edinburgh), 104–124.

— (1976), 'Monastic Sites', in D. M. Wilson (ed.), *The Archaeology of Anglo-Saxon England* (London), 201–252, 453–457.

— (1995), 'Whithorn and the Northumbrian Expansion Westwards', *Third Whithorn Lecture* (Stranraer).

Cuppage, A. (1986), *Archaeological Survey of the Dingle Peninsula* (Dublin).

Curran, M. (1981), 'Early Irish Monasticism', in M. Maher (ed.), *Irish Spirituality* (Dublin), 10–21.

Daniels, R. (1988), 'The Anglo-Saxon Monastery at Church Close, Hartlepool, Cleveland', *Archaeological Journal* 145, 158–210.

Dark, K. R. (1985), 'The Plan and Interpretation of Tintagel', *Cambridge Medieval Celtic Studies* 9, 1–18

Davies, D. (1994), 'Christianity', in J. Holm and J. Bowker (eds.), *Sacred Place* (London), 33–61.

Davies, J. R. (1998), 'The Book of Llandaff: a Twelfth-century Perspective', *Anglo-Norman Studies* 21, 31–46.

Davies, L.M. (1997), 'Isidorian Texts and the Hibernensis', *Peritia* 11, 207–249.

Davies, W. (1992), 'The Myth of the Celtic Church', in N. Edwards and A. Lane (eds.), *The Early Church in Wales and the West* (Oxford).

— (1996), "Protected Space' in Britain and Ireland in the Middle Ages', *Scotland in Dark Age Britain* (St Andrews), 1–19.

de Paor, L. (1955), 'A Survey of Sceilg Mhichíl', *Journal of The Royal Society of Antiquaries of Ireland* 85, 174–187.

— (1993), *St Patrick's World* (Dublin).

— and M. de Paor, (1958), *Early Christian Ireland* (London).

Dimier, A. (1964), *Stones Laid before the Lord*, Cistercian Studies Series 152 (Massachusetts).

Doherty, C. (1980), 'Exchange and Trade in Early Medieval Ireland', *Journal of the Royal Society of Antiquaries of Ireland* 110, 67–89.

— (1982), 'Some Aspects of Hagiography as a Source for Irish Economic History', *Peritia* 1, 3–28.

— (1985), 'The Monastic Town in Early Medieval Ireland', in H. B. Clarke and A. H. Simms (eds.), *The Comparative History of Urban Origins in Non-Roman Europe*, British Archaeological Reports, International Series 255 (Oxford), 45–75.

— (1991), 'The Cult of St Patrick and the Politics of Armagh in the Seventh Century', in J-M. Picard (ed.), *Ireland and Northern France AD 600–850*, (Dublin), 53–94.

— (2005), 'Kingship in Early Ireland', in E. Bhreathnach (ed.), *The Kingship and Landscape of Tara* (Dublin), 3–31.

Dumville, D. N. (1984), 'Some British Aspects of the Earliest Irish Christianity', in P. Ní Chatháin and M. Richter (eds.), *Ireland and Europe: The Early Church* (Stuttgart), 16–24.

— (1988), 'Two Approaches to the Dating of *Navigatio Sancti Brendani*', *Studi Medievali*, Third Series, 29 (1988), 87–102; repr. in J. Wooding (ed.), *The Otherworld Voyage in Early Irish Literature – An Anthology of Criticism* (Dublin, 2000), 120–132.

— (1993), *St. Patrick A.D. 493–1993* (Woodbridge).

— (1994), 'Ireland, Brittany and England: Transmission and Use of *Collectio canonum Hibernensis*', in C. Laurent, and H. David (eds.), *Irlande et Bretagne: vingt siècles d'Histoire* (Rennes), 85–95.

— (1997a), 'Review of McCone and Simms (1996)', *Peritia* 11, 451–468.

— (1997b), 'The Origins and Early History of Insular Monasticism', *Bulletin of the Institute of Oriental and Occidental Studies* 30 (Kansai), 85–107.

Dunn, M. (2000), *The Emergence of Monasticism* (Oxford).

Eade, J. and M. J. Sallnow (1991), 'Introduction', in J. Eade and M. J. Sallnow, (eds), *Contesting the Sacred: the Anthropology of Christian Pilgrimage* (London, 1991; repr. Urbana, 2000), 1–29.

Edwards, N. (1990), *The Archaeology of Early Medieval Ireland* (London).

— and A. Lane (1992), 'The Archaeology of the Early Church in Wales: An Introduction', in N. Edwards and A. Lane (eds.), *The Early Church in Wales and the West* (Oxford), 1–11

Eliade, M. (1959), *The Sacred and the Profane: The Nature of Religion* (San Diego).

Enright, M. (1985), *Iona, Tara, and Soissons: The Origins of the Royal Anointing Ritual*, Arbeiten für Frühmittelalterforschung 17 (Berlin).

Etchingham, C. (1991), 'The Early Irish Church: Some Observations on Pastoral Cares and Dues', *Ériu* 42, 99–118.

— (1993), 'The Implications of Paruchia', *Ériu* 44, 139–162.

— (1994), 'Bishops in the Early Irish Church: A Reassessment', *Studia Hibernica* 28, 35–62.

— (1996), 'Early Medieval Irish History', in K. McCone and K. Simms (eds.), *Progress in Medieval Irish Studies* (Maynooth), 123–153.

— (1999), *Church Organisation in Ireland AD650 to 1000* (Naas)

— (2007), 'Review of *A New History of Ireland Vol.* 1: Prehistoric and Early Ireland (ed. D. Ó Cróinín)', *English Historical Review* 122, No. 498, 1023–1025.

Fanning, T. (1981), 'Excavation of an Early Christian Cemetery and Settlement at Reask, Co. Kerry', *Proceedings of the Royal Irish Academy* 81C, 67–172.

Farr, C. (1997), *The Book of Kells, Its Function and Audience* (London).

Flanagan, D. (1984), 'The Christian Impact on Early Medieval Ireland: Place-name Evidence', in P. Ní Chatháin and M. Richter (eds.), *Ireland and Europe: The Early Church* (Stuttgart), 25–51.

Foot, S. (1990), 'What was an Anglo-Saxon Monastery?', in J. Loades (ed.), *Monastic Studies* (Bangor), 48–57.

— (2006), *Monastic Life in Anglo-Saxon England, c.*600–900 (Cambridge).

Gaskell Brown, C., and A. Harper (1984), 'Excavations on Cathedral Hill, Armagh 1968', *Ulster Journal of Archaeology* 47, 109–161.

Gittos, H. (2002), 'Creating the Sacred: Anglo-Saxon Rites for Consecrating Cemeteries', in S. Lucy and A. Reynolds (eds.), *Burial in Early Medieval England and Wales* (London), 195–208.

Goodenough, E. R. (1964), *Jewish Symbols in the Greco-Roman Period*, 13 Vols (New York, 1953–1965).

Goodman, M. (2005), 'The Temple in First Century CE Judaism', in J. Day (ed.), *Temple and Worship in Biblical Israel* (London), 459–468.

Graham, B. (1987a), 'Urban Genesis in Early Medieval Ireland', *Journal of Historical Geography* 13, 3–16.

— (1987b), 'Urbanisation in Medieval Ireland, *c.a.* AD900 to *c.a.* AD1300', *Journal of Urban History* 13, No.2, 169–196.

Gwynn, E. J. and W. J. Purton, eds. (1911), 'The Monastery of Tallaght', *Proceedings of the Royal Irish Academy* 29C, 115–179.

Hamblin, W. J. and D. R. Seely (2007), *Solomon's Temple, Myth and History* (London).

Hamlin, A. (1972), 'A Chi-Rho Carved Stone at Drumaqueran, Co. Antrim', *Ulster Journal of Archaeology* 35, 22–28.

— (1977), 'A Recently Discovered Enclosure at Inch Abbey, County Down', *Ulster Journal of Archaeology* 40, 85–88.

— (1982), 'Early Irish Stone Carving: Content and Context', in S. Pearce (ed.), *The Early Church in Western Britain and Ireland*, British Archaeological Reports, British Series 102 (Oxford), 283–296.

— (1984), 'The Study of Early Irish Churches', in P. Ní Chatháin and M. Richter (eds.), *Ireland and Europe: The Early Church* (Stuttgart), 117–126.

— (1985), 'The Archaeology of the Irish Church in the Eighth Century', *Peritia* 4, 279–299.

— (1992), 'The Early Irish Church: Problems of Identification', in N. Edwards and A. Lane (eds.), *The Early Church in Wales and the West* (Oxford), 138–144.

Haran, M. (1978), *Temples and Temple Service in Ancient Israel: An Inquiry into the Character of Cult Phenomena and the Historical Setting of the Priestly School* (Oxford).

Harbison, P. (1970), 'How Old is Gallarus Oratory?', *Medieval Archaeology* 14, 34–59.

— (1976), *The Archaeology of Ireland* (London).

— (1982), 'Early Irish Churches', in H. Lowe (ed.), *Die Iren und Europa im früheren Mittelalter* (Stuttgart), 624–629.

— (1987), 'The Date of the Crucifixion Slabs from Duvillaun More and Inishkea North, Co. Mayo', in E. Rynne (ed.), *Figures from the Past* (Dun Laoghaire), 73–91.

— (1992), *National and Historic Monuments of Ireland* (Dublin).

Hencken, H. (1938), 'Cahercommaun; a Stone Fort in Co. Clare', *Journal of the Royal Society of Antiquaries of Ireland*, Special Volume.

Henry, F. (1940), *Irish Art in the Early Christian Period* (London).

— (1947), 'The Antiquities of Caher Island (Co. Mayo)', *Journal of the Royal Society of Antiquaries of Ireland*, 77, 23–38.

— (1957), 'Early Monasteries, Beehive Huts, and Dry-stone Houses in the Neighbourhood of Cahirciveen and Waterville (Co. Kerry), *Proceedings of the Royal Irish Academy* 58C, 45–166.

— (1964), *Irish High Crosses* (Dublin).

— (1965), *Irish Art in the Christian Period (to* 800 A.D.) (London).

Herbert, M. (1988), *Iona, Kells and Derry* (Oxford).

Herity, M. (1977), 'The High Island Hermitage', *Irish University Review* 7, 52–69; repr. in Herity (1995), *Studies in the Layout, Buildings and Art in Stone of Early Irish Monasteries* (London), 1–18.

— (1983), 'The Buildings and Layout of Early Irish Monasteries before the Year 1000', *Monastic Studies* 14, 247–84; repr. in Herity (1995), *Studies in the Layout, Buildings and Art in Stone of Early Irish Monasteries* (London), 19–56.

— (1984), 'The Layout of Irish Early Christian Monasteries', in M. Richter and P. Ní Chatháin (eds.), *Ireland and Europe: The Early Church* (Stuttgart), 105–16; repr. in Herity (1995), *Studies in the Layout, Buildings and Art in Stone of Early Irish Monasteries* (London), 57–65.

— (1985), 'The Ornamented Tomb of the Saint at Ardoileán', in M. Ryan (ed.), *Irish and Insular Art, AD* 500–1200 (Dublin); repr. in Herity (1995), *Studies in the Layout, Buildings and Art in Stone of Early Irish Monasteries* (London), 66–71.

— (1989), 'Early Irish Hermitages in the Light of the *Lives* of Cuthbert', in Bonner, Stancliffe and Rollason (eds.), *St Cuthbert, His Cult and His community to AD* 1200 (Woodbridge), 45–64.

— (1990), 'The Hermitage on Ardoileán, County Galway', *Journal of the Royal Society of Antiquaries of Ireland* 20, 65–101; repr. in Herity (1995), *Studies in the Layout, Buildings and Art in Stone of Early Irish Monasteries* (London), 179–225.

Hill, P. (1991), 'Whithorn: The Missing Years', in R.D. Oram and G. P. Stell (eds.), *Galloway: Land and Lordship* (Edinburgh), 27–44.

— (1992), *Whithorn* 4: Excavations 1990–1991 (Whithorn).

— (1997), *Whithorn and St Ninian: The Excavation of a Monastic Town 1984–91* (Stroud).

Hillgarth, J. N. (1961), 'The East, Visigothic Spain and the Irish', *Studia Patristica* 4, 442–456.

— (1984), 'Ireland and Spain in the seventh century', *Peritia* 3, 1–16.

Horn, W. (1973), 'On the Origins of the Medieval Cloister', *Gesta* 12, No. 1/2, 13–52.

— and J. W. Marshall and G. Rourke (1990), *The Forgotten Hermitage of Skellig Michael* (Berkeley).

Hughes, K. (1960), 'The Changing Theory and Practice of Irish Pilgrimage', *The Journal of Ecclesiastical History* 11, 143–151.

— (1966), *The Church in Early Irish Society* (London).

— (1972), *Early Christian Ireland: Introduction to the Sources* (London).

— (1981), 'The Celtic Church: Is This a Valid Concept?', *Cambridge Medieval Celtic Studies* 1, 1–20.

— and A. Hamlin (1977), *The Modern Traveller to the Irish Church* (London).

Hunwicke, J. W. (2002), 'Kerry and Stowe Revisited', *Proceedings of the Royal Irish Academy* 102C, 1–19.

Hurley, V. (1982), 'The Early Church in the South-West of Ireland: Settlement and Organisation', in S. M. Pearce, (ed.), *The Early Church in Western Britain and Ireland*, British Archaeological Reports, British Series 102 (Oxford), 297–332.

Hurowitz, V. A. (2005), 'YHWH's Exalted House – Aspects of the Design and Symbolism of Solomon's Temple', in J. Day (ed.), *Temple and Worship in Biblical Israel* (London), 63–110.

Ivens, R. (1988), 'Tullynish: Around an Early Church', in A. Hamlin and C. Lynn (eds.), *Pieces of the Past* (Belfast), 55–56.

Jackson, B. (1978), 'On the Origins of *Scienter*', *The Law Quarterly Review* 94, 85–102.

James, E. (1981), 'Archaeology and the Merovingian Monastery', in H. B. Clarke and M. Brennan (eds.), *Columbanus and Merovingian Monasticism*, British Archaeological Reports, International Series 113 (Oxford), 33–55.

— (1982), 'Ireland and Western Gaul in the Merovingian Period', in D. Whitelock *et al.* (eds.), *Ireland in Early Medieval Europe: Studies in Memory of Kathleen Hughes* (Cambridge), 362–386.

Jeremias, J. (1969), *Jerusalem in the Time of Jesus* (London).

Joyce, P. (2005), 'Temple and Worship in Ezekiel', in J. Day (ed.), *Temple and Worship in Biblical Israel* (London), 145–163.

Kenney, J. F. (1929), *The Sources for the Early History of Ireland*, Vol. I, Ecclesiastical (New York).

Killanin, Lord, and M. V. Duignan (1989), *The Shell Guide to Ireland* (MacMillan).

King, H. (1992), 'Excavations at Clonmacnoise', *Archaeology Ireland* 6, No.3, 12–14.

— (1995), 'Clonmacnoise: High Crosses', in I. Bennett (ed.), *Excavations 1994: Summary Accounts of Archaeological Excavations in Ireland* (Bray), 74.

— (1996), 'New Graveyard, Clonmacnoise: Early Christian Settlement', in I. Bennett (ed.), *Excavations 1995: Summary Accounts of Archaeological Excavations in Ireland* (Bray), 76–77.

— (1997), 'New Graveyard, Clonmacnoise: Early Christian Settlement', in I. Bennett (ed.), *Excavations 1996: Summary Accounts of Archaeological Excavations in Ireland* (Bray), 92–93.

Latham, R. E., ed. (1965), *Revised Medieval Latin Word List from British and Irish Sources* (Oxford).

Lawlor, H. J. (1897), *Chapters on the Book of Mulling* (Edinburgh).

Lawlor, H. C. (1925), *The Monastery of Saint Mochaoi of Nendrum* (Belfast).

Lawrence, C.H. (2001), *Medieval Monasticism* (3rd edn Harlow).

Leask, H. G. (1929), 'Further Notes on the Church', *Journal of the Royal Society of Antiquaries of Ireland* 59, 25–28.

— (1930), 'The Church of St. Lua, or Molua, Friar's Island, Co. Tipperary, near Killaloe', *Journal of the Royal Society of Antiquaries of Ireland* 60, 130–136.

— (1955), *Irish Churches and Monastic Buildings*, 2 Vols (Dundalk).

Lionard, P. (1961), 'Early Irish Graveslabs', *Proceedings of the Royal Irish Academy* 61C, 95–169.

Loveluck, C. (2001), 'Wealth, Waste and Conspicuous Consumption: Flixborough and its Importance for Mid and Late Saxon Settlement Studies', in H. Hamerow and A. MacGregor (eds.), *Image and Power in the Archaeology of Early Medieval Britain* (Woodbridge), 78–130.

Lowe, C. (1999), *Angels, Fools and Tyrants: Britons and Anglo-Saxons in Southern Scotland* (Edinburgh).

— (2001), *Early Ecclesiastical Enclosures at Whithorn: An Archaeological Assessment* (Edinburgh).

— (2006), *Excavations at Hoddom, Dumfriesshire; An Early Ecclesiastical Site in South-West Scotland* (Edinburgh).

Lowry-Corry, D., B. C. S., Wilson, and D. M. Waterman, (1959), 'A Newly Discovered Statue at the Church on White Island, Co. Fermanagh', *Ulster Journal of Archaeology* 22, 59–66.

Lynn, C. J. (1977), 'Recent Archaeological Excavations in Armagh City: An Interim Summary', *Seanchas Ard Macha* 8, No. 2, 275–280.

— (1978), 'Early Christian Period Domestic Structures: A Change from Round to Rectangular Plans?', *Irish Archaeological Research Forum* 5, 29–45.

— (1988), 'Excavations at 46–48 Scotch Street, Armagh (1979–80)', *Ulster Journal of Archaeology* 51, 69–84.

— (1994), 'Houses in Rural Ireland A.D. 500–1000', *Ulster Journal of Archaeology* 57, 81–94.

— (2003), *Navan Fort: Archaeology and Myth* (Bray).

Macalister, R. A. S. (1896), 'The Antiquities of Ardillaun, County Galway', *Journal of the Royal Society of Antiquaries of Ireland* 26, 197–210.

MacDonald, A. (1981), 'Notes on Monastic Archaeology and the Annals of Ulster, 650–1050', in D. Ó Corráin (ed.), *Irish Antiquity* (Cork), 304–319.

— (1984), 'Aspects of the Monastery and the Monastic Life in Adomnán's *Life of Columba*', *Peritia* 3, 271–302.

— (1997), 'Adomnán's Monastery of Iona', in C. Bourke (ed.), *Studies in the Cult of Saint Columba* (Dublin), 24–44.

— (2001), 'Aspects of the Monastic Landscape in Adomnán's *Life of Columba*', in J. Carey, M. Herbert, and P. Ó Riain (eds.), *Studies in Irish Hagiography: Saints and Scholars* (Dublin), 15–30.

McCormick, F. (1993), 'Excavations on Iona in 1988', *Ulster Journal of Archaeology* 56, 78–108.

— (1997), 'Iona: the Archaeology of a Monastery', in C. Bourke (ed.), *Studies in the Cult of Saint Columba* (Dublin), 45–68.

McCracken, E. (1959), 'The Woodlands of Ireland *circa* 1600', *Irish Historical Studies* 11, 271–296.

McGinn, B. (1994), 'Ocean and Desert as Symbols of Mystical Absorption in the Christian Tradition', *The Journal of Religion* 74 (Chicago), 155–181.

McGuire, B. P. (1992), 'An Introduction to the *Exordium magnum Cisterciense*', *Cistercian Studies* 27: 4, 277–297.

Manning, C. (1994a), 'Clonmacnoise Cathedral', in H. King (ed.), *Clonmacnoise Studies, Vol. I: Seminar Papers* (Dublin), 57–86.

— (1994b), 'The Earliest Plans of Clonmacnoise', *Archaeology Ireland* 8, No. 1 (Spring), 18–20.

— (1995a), 'Clonmacnoise Cathedral-the Oldest Church in Ireland?', *Archaeology Ireland* 9, No. 4 (Winter), 30–33.

— (1995b), *Early Irish Monasteries* (Dublin).

Marshall, J. W. (1989), *The Spread of Mainland Paruchiae to the Atlantic Islands of Illauntannig, High Island and Inishmurray* (Los Angeles).

— and C. Walsh (1998), 'Illaunloughan, Co. Kerry: An Island Hermitage', in J. Sheehan and M. Monk (eds.), *Early Medieval Munster* (Cork), 102–111.

— and G. D. Rourke (2000), *High Island: An Irish Monastery in the Atlantic* (Dublin).

— and C. Walsh (2005), *Illaunloughan Island, An Early Medieval Monastery in Co. Kerry* (Dublin).

Monson, J. (2000), 'The New 'Ain Dara Temple: Closest Solomonic Parallel', *Biblical Archaeological Review* 26 (3), 20–35, 67.

Morris, C. D. (1989), *Church and Monastery in the Far North: An Archaeological Evaluation* (Jarrow).

Morris, R. (1989), *Churches in the Landscape* (London).

Murphy, D. (2003), 'Excavation of an Early Monastic Enclosure at Clonmacnoise', in H. King (ed.), *Clonmacnoise Studies, Vol. 2: Seminar Papers* (Dublin), 1–33.

Mytum, H. (1992), *The Origins of Early Christian Ireland* (London).

— (2003), 'Surface and Geophysical Survey at Clonmacnoise: Defining the Extent of Intensive Monastic Settlement', in H. King (ed.), *Clonmacnoise Studies, Vol. 2: Seminar Papers* (Dublin), 35–58.

Nees, L. (1983), 'The Colophon Drawing in the Book of Mulling', *Cambridge Medieval Celtic Studies* 5, 67–91.

Newman, C. (1997), *Tara: An Archaeological Survey*, Discovery Programme Monographs 2 (Dublin).

— (2005), 'Re-composing the Archaeological Landscape of Tara', in E. Bhreathnach (ed.), *The Kingship and Landscape of Tara* (Dublin), 361–409.

Nicholson, E. W. B. (1901), 'The Origin of the 'Hibernian' Collection of Canons', *Zeitschrift für celtische Philologie* 3, 99–103.

Norman, E. R. and J. K. S. St Joseph (1969), *The Early Development of Irish Society; The Evidence of Aerial Photography* (Cambridge).

Noth, M. (1962), *Exodus* (London).

Ó Carragáin, T. (2003), 'A Landscape Converted: Archaeology and Early Church Organisation on Iveragh and Dingle, Ireland', in M. Carver (ed.), *The Cross Goes North* (Woodbridge), 127–152.

— (2005), 'Regional Variation in Irish Pre-Romanesque Architecture', *The Antiquaries Journal* 85, 23–56.

Ó Corráin D. (1972), *Ireland before the Normans* (Dublin).

— (1981), 'The Early Irish Churches: Some Aspects of Organisation', in D. Ó Corráin (ed.) *Irish Antiquity* (Cork), 327–342.

— (1994), 'The Historical and Cultural Background of the Book of Kells', in F. O'Mahony (ed.), *Proceedings of a conference at Trinity College Dublin, 6–9 September 1992*, (Dublin), 1–32.

— and L. Breatnach and A. Breen (1984), 'The Laws of the Irish', *Peritia* 3, 382–438.

Ó Cróinín, D. (1995), *Early Medieval Ireland* (London).

O'Donovan, J. (1839), *Ordnance Survey Letters, County Galway* (Dublin), 75–87.

O'Keefe, T. (1998), 'Architectural Traditions of the Early Medieval Church in Munster', in J. Sheehan and M. Monk (eds.), *Early Medieval Munster* (Cork), 112–124.

O'Kelly, M. J. (1958), 'Church Island near Valencia, Co. Kerry', *Proceedings of the Royal Irish Academy* 59C, 57–136.

— (1973), 'Monastic Sites in the West of Ireland', *Scottish Archaeological Forum* 5, 1–16.

— (1975), *Archaeological Survey and Excavation of St Vogue's Church, Enclosure and Other Monuments at Carnmore, Co. Wexford* (Dublin).

O'Loughlin, T. (1992), 'The Exegetical Purpose of Adomnán's *De locis sanctis*', *Cambridge Medieval Celtic Studies* 24, 37–53

— (1994), 'The Library of Iona in the Late Seventh Century: The Evidence from Adomnán's *De locis sanctis*', *Ériu* 45, 33–52.

— (1995), 'Adomnán the Illustrious', *The Innes Review* 46, No. 1 Spring, 1–14.

— (1996), 'The View from Iona: Adomnán's Mental Maps', *Peritia* 10, 98–122.

— (1997a), 'Adomnán and Arculf: The Case of an Expert Witness', *The Journal of Medieval Latin*, Vol. 7, 127–146.

— (1997b), 'Adomnán's *De locis sanctis*: a Textual Emendation', *Ériu* 48, 37–40.

— (1997c), 'Living in the Ocean', in C. Bourke (ed.), *Studies in the Cult of Saint Columba* (Dublin), 11–23.

— (1998), *Teachers and Code Breakers: The Latin Genesis Tradition, 430–800* (Turnhout).

— (1999), 'Res, Tempus, Locus, Persona: Adomnán's Exegetical Method', in D. Broun and T. Clancy (eds.), *Spes Scotorum Hope of Scots* (Edinburgh), 139–158.

— (2000a), *Celtic Theology* (London).

— (2000b), 'Island Monasteries: Christian', in W. Johnston (ed.), *Encyclopaedia of Monasticism*, Vol. 1 (Chicago), 669–673.

— (2000c), 'The Plan of the New Jerusalem in the Book of Armagh', *Cambrian Medieval Celtic Studies* 39, 23–38.

O'Reilly, J. (1994), 'Exegesis and the Book of Kells: The Lucan Genealogy', in F. O'Mahony (ed.), *The Book of Kells: Proceedings of a Conference at Trinity College Dublin, 6–9 September 1992* (Aldershot), 344–397.

— (1995), 'Introduction', in S. Connolly (trans.), *Bede: On the Temple*, Translated Texts for Historians 21 (Liverpool), xvii–lv.

— (1997), 'Reading the Scriptures in the Life of Columba', in C. Bourke (ed.), *Studies in the Cult of Saint Columba* (Dublin), 80–106.

Ó Ríordáin, S. and J. G. Foy (1941), 'The Excavation of Leacanabuile Stone Fort near Cahirciveen, Co. Kerry', *Journal of Cork Historical and Archaeological Society* 46, 84–97.

Ó Ríordáin, S. (1942), 'A Large Earthen Ring-Fort at Garranes, Co. Cork', *Proceedings of the Royal Irish Academy* 47, 77–150.

— (1982), *Tara* (Dundalk).

O' Sullivan, A. and J. Sheehan (1996), *The Iveragh Peninsula: An Archaeological Survey* (Cork).

— and D. Boland (1997), 'Clonmacnoise: Early Medieval Bridge', in I. Bennett (ed.), *Excavations 1997: Summary of Archaeological Excavations in Ireland*, (Bray), 148–149.

— and D. Boland (2000), 'The Clonmacnoise Bridge: An Early Medieval River Crossing in County Offaly', *Archaeology Ireland Heritage Guide* No. 11.

O'Sullivan, D. (1989), 'The Plan of the Early Christian Monastery on Lindisfarne: A Fresh Look at the Evidence', in G. Bonner, D. Stancliffe and C. Rollason (eds.), *St Cuthbert, His Cult and His community to AD 1200* (Woodbridge), 125–142.

— (2001), 'Space, Silence and Shortage on Lindisfarne: The Archaeology of Asceticism', in H. Hamerow and A. MacGregor (eds.), *Image and Power in the Archaeology of Early Medieval Britain* (Woodbridge), 33–52.

O'Sullivan, J. (1999), 'Iona: Archaeological Investigations, 1875–1996', in D. Broun and T. Clancy (eds.), *Spes Scotorum Hope of Scots* (Edinburgh), 215–244.

— and T. Ó Carragáin (2008), *Inishmurray: Monks and Pilgrims in an Atlantic Landscape* (Cork).

Olson, L. (1989), *Early Monasteries in Cornwall* (Woodbridge).

Oram, R. (2001), *Expressions of Faith: Ulster's Church Heritage* (Newtownards).

Orschel, V. (2001), 'Mag nEó na Sacsan: An English Colony in Ireland in the Seventh and Eighth Centuries', *Peritia* 15, 81–107.

Padel, O. J. (1981), 'Tintagel – an alternative view', in C. Thomas, *A Provisional List of Imported Pottery in Post-Roman Western Britain and Ireland*, Institute of Cornish Studies, Special Report No. 7 (Redruth), 28–29.

— (1985), *Cornish Place-name Elements*, English Place-name Society, Vol. 56–57 (Nottingham).

Peers, C. R. and C. A. R. Radford, (1943), 'The Saxon Monastery at Whitby', *Archaeologia* 89, 27–88.

Petrie, G. (1845), *The Ecclesiastical Architecture of Ireland* (Dublin).

Petts, D. (2002), 'Cemeteries and Boundaries in Western Britain', in S. Lucy and A. Reynolds (eds.), *Burial in Early Medieval England and Wales* (London), 24–46.

Picard, J-M. (1982), 'The Purpose of Adomnán's *Vita Columbae*', *Peritia* 1, 160–177.

Porter, J. R. (2001), *The Lost Bible: Forgotten Scripture Revealed* (Chicago).

Preston-Jones, A. (1992), 'Decoding Cornish Churchyards', in N. Edwards and A. Lane (eds.), *The Early Church in Wales and the West* (Oxbow), 104–124.

Price, L. (1982), *The Plan of St. Gall in Brief* (California).

Pryce, H. (1992), 'Pastoral Care in Early Medieval Wales', in J. Blair and R. Sharpe (eds.), *Pastoral Care before the Parish* (Leicester), 41–62.

Radford, C. A. R. (1935), 'Tintagel; The Castle and The Celtic Monastery-Interim Report', *The Antiquaries Journal* 15, 401–419.

— (1954), 'Trial Excavations at Jarrow', *Archaeological Journal* III, 205–209.

— (1973a), 'Summary and Discussion', *Scottish Archaeological Forum* 5, 136–140.

— (1973b), 'Tintagel Castle and Celtic Monastery', *Archaeological Journal* 130, 248–250.

— (1977), 'The Earliest Irish Churches', *Ulster Journal of Archaeology* 40, 1–11.

Rahtz, P. (1973), 'Monasteries as Settlements', *Scottish Archaeological Forum* 5, 125–135.

— (1976), 'The Building Plan of the Anglo-Saxon Monastery of Whitby Abbey', in D. M. Wilson (ed.), *The Archaeology of Anglo-Saxon England* (Cambridge), 459–462.

Reece, R. (1973), 'Recent Work on Iona', *Scottish Archaeological Forum* 5, 36–46.

— (1981), *Excavations in Iona 1964 to 1974*, Institute of Archaeology, Occasional Publication 5 (London).

Reeves, W. (1857), *The Life of St Columba, Founder of Hy* (Dublin).

RCAHMS (1982), *Iona* (Edinburgh).

Richter, M. (1999), *Ireland and her Neighbours in the Seventh Century* (Dublin).

Rosenwein, B. H. (1999), *Negotiating Space: Power, Restraint and Privileges of Immunity in Early Medieval Europe* (Manchester).

Rowland, C. (2007), 'The Temple in the New Testament', in J. Day (ed.), *Temple and Worship in Biblical Israel* (London), 469–483.

Ryan, J. (1931), *Irish Monasticism* (Dublin).

Sharpe, R. (1984), 'Some Problems Concerning the Organisation of the Church in Early Medieval Ireland', *Peritia* 3, 230–270.

— (1991), *Medieval Irish Saints' Lives* (Oxford).

— (1992), 'Churches and Communities in Early Medieval Ireland: Towards a Pastoral Model', in J. Blair and R. Sharpe (eds.), *Pastoral Care before the Parish* (Leicester), 81–109.

— (1995), *Adomnán of Iona, Life of Columba* (Harmondsworth).

— (2002), 'Martyrs and Local Saints in Late Antique Britain', in A. Thacker and R. Sharpe (eds.), *Local Saints and Local Churches in the Early Medieval West* (Oxford), 75–154.

Sheehan, J. (1982), 'The Early Historic Church-sites of North Clare', *North Munster Antiquarian Journal* 24, 29–47.

Sheehy, M. P. (1982), 'The *Collectio canonum Hibernensis*–a Celtic Phenomenon', in H. Lowe (ed.), *Die Iren und Europa im früheren Mittelalter* (Stuttgart), 525–35.

— (1987), 'The Bible and the Collectio canonum Hibernensis', in P. Ní Chatháin and M. Richter (eds.), *Irland und die Christenheit: bibelstudien und mission* (Stuttgart), 277–283.

Sheldrake, P. (1995), *Living Between Worlds: Place and Journey in Celtic Spirituality* (London).

— (2001), *Spaces for the Sacred* (London).

Simpson, D. P., ed. (1968), *Cassell's Latin Dictionary* (5th edn London).

Smith, C. (1756), *The Ancient and Present State of the County of Kerry* (Dublin; repr. Cork, 1969).

Smith, J. Z. (1987), *To Take Place: Towards Theory in Ritual* (Chicago).

Smyth, M. (1986), 'The Physical World in Seventh-Century Hiberno-Latin Texts', *Peritia* 5, 201–234.

— (1996), *Understanding the Universe in Seventh-Century Ireland* (Woodbridge).

Stalmans, N. (2003), *Saints d'Irlande; analyse critique des sources hagiographiques, VIIe-IXe siècles* (Rennes).

Stokes, M. (1878), *Early Christian Architecture in Ireland* (London).

Stronach, S. (2005), 'The Anglian Monastery and Medieval Priory of Coldingham: *Urbs Coludi* Revisited', *Proceedings of the Society of Antiquaries of Scotland* 135, 395–422.

Sullivan, R. E. (1998), What was Carolingian Monasticism?', in A. C. Murray (ed.), *After Rome's Fall: Narrators and Sources of Early Medieval History* (Toronto, Buffalo and London), 251–287.

Swan, D. L. (1978), 'The Hill of Tara, Co. Meath', *Journal of the Royal Society of Antiquaries of Ireland* 108, 51–66.

— (1983), 'Enclosed Ecclesiastical Sites and their Relevance to Settlement Patterns of the First Millennium', in T. Reeves-Smyth and F. Hammond (eds.), *Landscape Archaeology in Ireland*, British Archaeological Reports, British Series 116 (Oxford), 269–294.

— (1985), 'Monastic Proto-towns in Early Medieval Ireland', in H. B. Clarke and A. H. Simms (eds.), *The Comparative History of Urban Origins in Non-Roman Europe*, British Archaeological Reports, International Series 255 (Oxford), 77–102.

Swift, C. (1998), 'Forts and Fields: A Study of 'Monastic Towns' in Seventh and Eighth Century Ireland', *The Journal of Irish Archaeology* 9, 105–125.

Thom, C. (2006), *Early Irish Monasticism* (London).

Thomas, C. (1957), 'Excavations on Iona (1956 and 1957)', *The Coracle* 31, 10–14.

— (1964), 'Ardwall Island, Gatehouse-of-Fleet', *Discovery and Excavation, Scotland,* 34–35.

— (1966), 'Ardwall Isle: The Excavation of an Early Christian Site of Irish Type (1964-1965)', *Transactions of the Dumfriesshire and Galloway Natural History and Archaeological Society* 43, 84–116.

— (1967), 'An Early Christian Cemetery and Chapel on Ardwall Isle, Kirkcudbright', *Medieval Archaeology* 11, 127–188.

— (1971), *The Early Christian Archaeology of North Britain* (London).

— (1978), 'Hermits on Islands or Priests in a Landscape?', *Cornish Studies* 6, 28–44.

— (1981), *A Provisional List of Imported Pottery in Post-Roman Western Britain and Ireland*, Institute of Cornish Studies, Special Report No. 7 (Redruth).

— (1985), *Exploration of a Drowned Landscape – Archaeology and History of the Isles of Scilly* (London).

— (1986), *Celtic Britain* (London).

— (1988), 'The Archaeology of Tintagel Parish Churchyard', *Cornish Studies* 16, 79–92.

— (1993), *Tintagel: Arthur and Archaeology* (London).

— (1995), 'Cellular Meanings, Monastic Beginnings', *Emania* 13, 51–67.

Thompson, D., ed. (1995), *The Concise Oxford English Dictionary*, (9ᵗʰ edition Oxford).

Todd, J. H. (1864), *St Patrick, Apostle of Ireland* (Dublin).

Turner, S. (2003), 'Making a Christian Landscape: Early Medieval Cornwall', in M. Carver (ed.), *The Cross Goes North* (Woodbridge), 171–194.

Valante, M. (1998), 'Reassessing the Irish "Monastic Town"', *Irish Historical Studies* 31, 1–18.

Wakeman, W. F. (1863), 'An Uninhabited Island', *Hibernian Magazine* 4 (July to December 1863), 213–224.

— (1885–1886), 'Inis Muiredaich, Now Inismurray, and its Antiquities', *Journal of the Royal Society of Antiquaries of Ireland* 17, 175–332.

— (1893), *Survey of the Antiquarian Remains on the Island of Inismurray*, Journal of the Royal Society of Antiquaries of Ireland, Special Vol. 1892, (London/Edinburgh).

Walsh, P. (1983), 'The Monastic Settlement on Rathlin O'Birne Island, County Donegal', *Journal of the Royal Society of Antiquaries of Ireland* 113, 53–66.

Walters, C. C. (1974), *Monastic Archaeology in Egypt* (Warminster).

Ware, J. (1658), *De Hibernia et antiquitatibus eius disquitiones* (London).

Waterman, D. M. (1967), 'The Early Christian Churches and Cemetery at Derry, Co. Down', *Ulster Journal of Archaeology* 30, 53–75.

— (1997), *Excavations at Navan Fort 1961–71. Completed and Edited by C. J. Lynn. Northern Ireland Archaeological Monographs 3 (Belfast).

Wooding, J. (2000), *The Otherworld Voyage in Early Irish Literature – An Anthology of Criticism* (Dublin)

Yadin, Y. (1985) *The Temple Scroll* (London).

Zimmer, H. (1902), *The Celtic Church in Britain and Ireland* (London).

INDEX